Writing Perl Modules for CPAN

SAM TREGAR

Writing Perl Modules for CPAN
Copyright ©2002 by Sam Tregar

ISBN (pbk): 1-59059-018-X

Printed and bound in the United States of America 12345678910

Trademarked names may appear in this book. Rather than use a trademark symbol with every occurrence of a trademarked name, we use the names only in an editorial fashion and to the benefit of the trademark owner, with no intention of infringement of the trademark.

Technical Reviewers: Jesse Erlbaum and Neil Watkiss

Editorial Directors: Dan Appleman, Gary Cornell, Jason Gilmore, Simon Hayes, Karen Watterson, John Zukowski

Managing Editor and Production Editor: Grace Wong

Project Managers: Erin Mulligan, Alexa Stuart

Copy Editor: Ami Knox

Proofreader: Brendan Sanchez

Compositor: Susan Glinert

Indexer: Valerie Perry

Cover Designer: Kurt Krames

Manufacturing Manager: Tom Debolski

Marketing Manager: Stephanie Rodriguez

Distributed to the book trade in the United States by Springer-Verlag New York, Inc., 175 Fifth Avenue, New York, NY, 10010 and outside the United States by Springer-Verlag GmbH & Co. KG, Tiergartenstr. 17, 69112 Heidelberg, Germany.

In the United States, phone 1-800-SPRINGER, email orders@springer-ny.com, or visit http://www.springer-ny.com.

Outside the United States, fax +49 6221 345229, email orders@springer.de, or visit http://www.springer.de.

For information on translations, please contact Apress directly at 2560 Ninth Street, Suite 219, Berkeley, CA 94710. Phone 510-549-5930, fax: 510-549-5939, email info@apress.com, or visit http://www.apress.com.

The source code for this book is available to readers at http://www.apress.com in the Downloads section. You will need to answer questions pertaining to this book in order to successfully download the code.

In memory of Luke and to Kristen who introduced us

Contents at a Glance

Contents

About the Author

SAM TREGAR has been working as a Perl programmer for four years. He is currently employed by About.com in the PIRT group, where he develops content management systems. Sam holds a bachelor of arts degree in computer science from New York University.

Sam started programming on an Apple *IIc* in BASIC when he was 10 years old. Over the years his love of technical manuals led him through C, C++, Lisp, TCL/Tk, Ada, Java, and ultimately to Perl. In Perl he found a language with flexibility and power to match his ambitious designs. Sam is the author of a number of popular Perl modules on CPAN including HTML::Template, HTML::Pager, Inline::Guile, and Devel::Profiler. The great enjoyment he derives from contributing to CPAN motivated him to write this book, his first.

Aside from programming, Sam enjoys reading, playing Go, developing black-and-white photographs, thinking about sailing, and maintaining the small private zoo curated by his wife that contains three cats, two mice, two rats, one snake, and one rabbit.

Sam lives with his wife Kristen in Croton-on-Hudson, New York. You can reach him by e-mail at sam@tregar.com or by visiting his home page at http://sam.tregar.com.

About the Technical Reviewers

JESSE ERLBAUM has been developing software professionally since 1994. He has developed custom software for a variety of clients including Time, Inc., the WPP Group, the Asia Society, and the United Nations. While in elementary school, Jesse was introduced to computer programming. It became his passion instantly, and by the time he was in middle school, he wrote and presented a "learning" program to his class to satisfy a science assignment. In 1989, he started his own bulletin board system (BBS), "The Belfry(!)," which quickly attracted a cult of regulars who enjoyed its vibrant and creative environment.

Jesse's enthusiasm for the World Wide Web was the natural result of the intersection of his two principal interests at the time, online communities and programming. Over the next few years, as the state of the art grew to embrace more interactive capabilities, he focused his efforts on building the systems and standards from which his clients increasingly benefited. In 1997, he established a library of reusable, object-oriented Perl libraries called "Dynexus," which was the foundation upon which he developed Web-based, database-connected systems.

It was during this period that Jesse met Sam Tregar. For two years Sam and Jesse worked together on a variety of custom software systems. In 1999, Jesse encouraged Sam to release HTML::Template (originally Dynexus::HTML::Template) to CPAN. In July 2000 Sam returned the favor, encouraging Jesse to release CGI::Application (originally Dynexus::OOCGI::Standard). CGI::Application is a framework for building Web-based applications. This framework has been adopted by a wide array of organizations around the world as the basis for their Web-development efforts.

Jesse is the CEO and founder of The Erlbaum Group, a software engineering and consulting firm in New York City. He can be reached by e-mail at jesse@erlbaum.net.

NEIL WATKISS is a Perl developer at ActiveState. He has a degree in computer engineering, and fell in love with Perl while maintaining a community Linux server in university. While at ActiveState, Neil met Brian Ingerson and was recruited to help work on the award-winning Inline module. Now the author of several Inline modules, Neil continues to delve into the Perl internals on a regular basis. He has worked on ActiveState's regular expression debugger, a Perl milter plug-in for Sendmail, and an automated Perl package build system for ActiveState's PPM (Perl Package Manager) repository.

Acknowledgments

FIRST AND FOREMOST I would like to thank my wife, Kristen, for patience and forbearance above and beyond reasonable limits. I would also like to thank our horse, Rhiannon, for giving her something to do while I worked. My parents, Jack and Rosemary, supported me in numerous ways throughout the writing of the book. In particular I would like to thank my father for the prescient advice he often gave me, "Write if you get work." All the members of my and Kristen's family gave me encouragement, for which I am grateful.

I must thank Jesse Erlbaum, who served as the chief technical editor for this book. However, his contributions to my life began years ago. When I came to work for Jesse at Vanguard Media in 1999, I knew plenty about coding but very little about being a programmer. Jesse took me under his wing and taught me how to be a professional, how to value quality in my work, and how to demand it from others. Under his direction I published my first CPAN module—HTML::Template—which is based on his work. Jesse's friendship, humor, and advice have been indispensable to me; that he helped me complete this book is but the latest in a long series of kindnesses.

Neil Watkiss joined our team as a technical editor during the crucial final weeks. Under extreme pressure he delivered admirably. Without his help the book might never have been completed.

The people I worked with at Apress did a great job on the book and kept me motivated throughout the project. Jason, Grace, Alexa, Ami, Erin, Stephanie, Doris, Susan, Kari—thanks!

My friends put up with my haggard face on many occasions during the writing of this book. They even managed to seem interested when I would describe it at length and in mind-numbing detail. Chris, Sean, Catherine, Mia, Fritz, Nat, Jarett, Carson, Danielle, Fran, Agneta—thank you all. I plan to become human again soon and look forward to seeing you all more often.

My coworkers at About.com were often helpful and always patient when I couldn't keep the stress from showing. Len, Peter, Rudy, Matt, Adam, Lou, Rachel, Nathan, Tim—thank you.

I would like to thank Larry Wall for giving us both Perl and the Perl community. Without his work, I'm certain the programming world would be a much less interesting place. I must also thank Jarkko Hietaniemi and Andreas J. Köenig for giving the Perl community CPAN and also for patiently answering my questions about its history. I'd also like to thank the many developers who contribute to CPAN and maintain Perl. In particular, the following people answered my questions and provided me with invaluable insight into the minds behind Perl: Elaine Ashton,

Damian Conway, Jochen Wiedmann, Raphael Manfredi, Steffen Beyer, James G. Smith, Ken Williams, Mark-Jason Dominus, Michael G. Schwern, Simon Cozens, Barrie Slaymaker, Graham Barr, Lincoln D. Stein, Matt Sergeant, Sean M. Burke, T.J. Mather, and Rich Bowen.

I must thank Brian Ingerson for assisting me in the early development of the book. Scott Guelich, author of *CGI Programming with Perl,* also deserves special mention—his early encouragement was crucial to getting the project off the ground. Finally, I would like to thank Leon Brocard for allowing me to use his CPAN network illustration, a version of which appears in Chapter 1.

Introduction

As Larry Wall, creator of Perl, puts it, "Perl makes easy jobs easy and hard jobs possible." This is a large part of what makes Perl such a great language—most jobs really are easy in Perl. But that still leaves the hard ones—database access, GUI development, Web clients, and so on. While they are undeniably possible in pure Perl, they are also certainly not easy. Until you discover CPAN, that is. After that, all these jobs and more become a simple matter of choosing the right module. *CPAN makes hard jobs easy*. The first chapter of this book will show you how to get the most out of CPAN.

Although you can get a lot done just by using CPAN modules, you can go further by creating your own reusable Perl modules. Chapter 2 will teach you how to create Perl modules from the ground up. No prior module programming experience is required. Chapter 3 will improve your skills with a detailed discussion of module design and implementation.

Once you're a full-fledged Perl module programmer, you'll naturally want to share your work. Chapter 4 will show you how to package your modules in module distributions. The next step, registering as a module author on CPAN and uploading your modules, is covered in Chapter 5. Chapter 6 is all about what happens after you upload—maintaining your modules as they grow and change over time. Of course, some modules are better than others. Chapter 7 examines a collection of CPAN's most successful modules to discover the secrets of their success.

The final four chapters offer advanced training in the art of module building. Chapters 8, 9, and 10 teach the mysterious art of building Perl modules in C, using both XS and Inline::C. Chapter 11 shows you how to package whole CGI applications as Perl modules using CGI::Application.

What You Need to Know

To get the most out of this book, you need to know the Perl language. You don't need to be a Perl guru, but you should be comfortable with basic syntax. If you can write small programs in Perl, then you're ready to get the most out of this book. If you're not a Perl programmer, there's still a good deal of information about CPAN and open-source development in this book that you can use. Chapters 1, 6, and 7 were written to be accessible to nonprogrammers. If those chapters pique your interest, consider reading a good introduction to the Perl language and come back for the rest when you're ready to write your first module.

System Requirements

This book assumes you have a computer at your disposal with Perl installed. If not, then you can still read the book, but you won't be able to try the examples. Many of the examples assume you're working on a UNIX system, Perl's "home court." Where possible, I've noted differences under Microsoft Windows, but if you're using anything more exotic, you may need to make minor adjustments to get the examples to work.

Perl Version

This book was written using Perl version 5.6.1. If you're using a newer version, you may find that the examples given need small adjustments. If you're using an older version, you should consider upgrading to get the most out of this book (and Perl).

CHAPTER 1

CPAN

THE COMPREHENSIVE PERL ARCHIVE NETWORK (CPAN) is an Internet resource containing a wide variety of Perl materials—modules, scripts, documentation, and Perl itself—that are open source and free for all to download and use. CPAN has more Perl modules available than any other resource, including modules for almost every conceivable task from database access to GUI development and everything in between. The primary gateway to CPAN is http://www.cpan.org.

No other programming community has a resource like CPAN. CPAN enables the Perl community to pool its strength and develop powerful solutions to difficult problems. Once a module is available on CPAN, everyone can use it and improve it. Only the most unusual Perl project needs to start from scratch.

CPAN is more than just a repository—it's a community. The modules on CPAN are released under open-source licenses, and many are under active development. Modules on CPAN often have mailing lists dedicated to their development with hundreds of subscribers.

As the name implies, CPAN is a network. CPAN servers around the world provide access to the collection. See the "Network Topology" section later in this chapter for details.

Why Contribute to CPAN?

CPAN thrives on the time and energy of volunteer programmers. You may be surprised that so many talented programmers are willing to work for free. Some CPAN programmers aren't actually donating their time—they're being paid to work on CPAN modules! This is certainly the minority, so let's look at some other reasons to join the CPAN community.

The Programmer's Incentive

For the lone programmer, contributing to CPAN is an excellent way to show the world your programming savvy. A programmer's resume is only an introduction; a smart employer wants proof. This can be hard to provide if all your work has been on closed-source projects. Open-source software is easy to evaluate—if you're good, employers will know it immediately. There's nothing quite like walking into an interview and having the programmer across the table suddenly realize he's been using your code for the past two months.

As software reaches higher levels of maturity and complexity, it is less and less realistic for a programmers to "go it alone." Today, conscientious and talented programmers first look to CPAN to provide a shortcut in their development process—and the *best* programmers contribute their work to CPAN, so that others may benefit. Tomorrow, it may even be considered a lack of professionalism to *not* start your software development efforts with a search through the CPAN repository.

By writing code for CPAN, you'll come into contact with other highly talented Perl programmers. This has been a great help to me personally—the many bug reports and suggestions I've received over the years have helped me improve my skills. With Perl, there's *always* more than one way to do it, and the more of them you master, the better.

The Business Incentive

Just as contributing to CPAN enhances a programmer's resume, so can a business benefit by association with popular Perl modules. Contributing your modules to CPAN can have the effect of establishing a standard around your practices. This makes answering the perennial question "Why aren't you using *[Java, C++, ASP, PHP]*?" much easier.

Some of the world's best programmers are open-source programmers. By actively supporting CPAN, you improve your hiring ability in the competitive market for Perl experts.

The Idealist's Incentive

For the idealist, contributing to CPAN is a good way to help save the world. CPAN is open to everyone—multinational corporations and tiny nonprofits eat at the same table. When you donate your work to CPAN, you ensure that your work will be available to anyone who needs it. Furthermore, by putting your work under a free software[1] license you can help convince others to do the same; when they make changes to your code, they'll have to release them as free software.[2]

---

1. See http://www.fsf.org for more information about free software.
2. With some notable exceptions—see the "Choosing a License" section of Chapter 4 for more details.

CPAN History

The idea for CPAN, a single comprehensive archive of all things Perl, was first introduced in 1993 by Jared Rhine on the perl-packrats mailing list.[3] The concept derived from the Comprehensive TeX Archive Network (CTAN). At this point a number of large Perl archives were maintained on various FTP sites around the world. It was widely agreed that there would be many advantages to collecting all the available Perl materials in one hierarchy; however, the discussion died without producing a working version.

In early 1995 Jarkko Hietaniemi resurrected the idea and began the monumental task of gathering and organizing the entire output of the Perl community into a single tree. Six months later he produced a working "private showing." This CPAN was essentially a sorted, classified version of the contents of every Perl archive on the Internet.

However, a critical piece was missing—a way for Perl authors to upload their work and have it automatically included in CPAN. Andreas Köenig came to the rescue by creating the **P**erl **A**uthor **U**pload **SE**rver (PAUSE). PAUSE automatically builds the authors and modules-by directories that form the bulk of content on CPAN (86.5 percent at present).

With PAUSE in place, CPAN was nearly complete. After two months of testing and fixing with the help the perl-packrats, Jarkko released CPAN to the world as the Self-Appointed Master Librarian. The master server was set up at FUNet, where Jarkko worked as a systems administrator, which is where it remains today. From then on CPAN played a central role in the growth of the Perl community.

Network Topology

CPAN is composed of servers spread across the globe (over 200 as I write). Every server provides access to the same data. Figure 1-1 shows a map of CPAN servers. You can explore the CPAN network interactively at http://mirror.cpan.org.

---

3. he perl-packrats list, active from 1993 to 1996, was formed to discuss archiving Perl. Mailing list archives can be found at http://history.perl.org/packratsarch/.

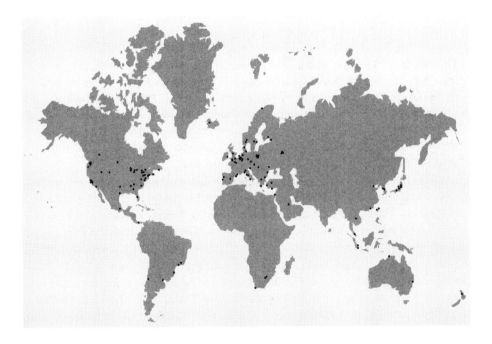

Figure 1-1. World map from http://mirrors.cpan.org *showing CPAN server locations*

CPAN is modeled on a hub-and-spokes topology, shown in Figure 1-2. At the center of the CPAN network is the main CPAN server, ftp.funet.fi, in Finland. Most of the CPAN servers mirror this main server directly. To *mirror* is to maintain a synchronized copy of the files between two machines. CPAN servers use either FTP or rsync to automatically mirror files.

Modules enter CPAN through a system called PAUSE, short for the Perl Author Upload SErver. I'll provide more details about PAUSE in Chapter 4.

Since CPAN is a network, you can choose a mirror close to you that may offer faster download times than http://www.cpan.org. At http://mirror.cpan.org you'll find a search facility that enables you to search for mirrors by country.[4]

---

4. Of course, the fastest way to access CPAN is by running your own mirror. See
   http://www.cpan.org/misc/cpan-faq.html#How_mirror_CPAN for details.

CPAN Network Topology

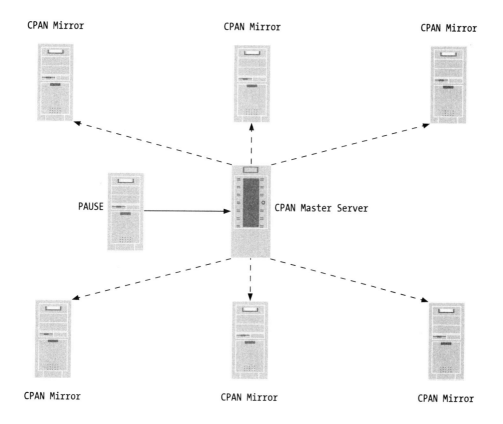

Figure 1-2. The CPAN Network Topology

Browsing CPAN

If this is your first time visiting CPAN, the first thing you should do is have a look around. On the entry screen (Figure 1-3) you'll find links to each section of the CPAN collection—modules, scripts, binaries, the Perl source, and other items. Also available are links to documentation about CPAN; if you still have questions after finishing this chapter, then you should give them a look.

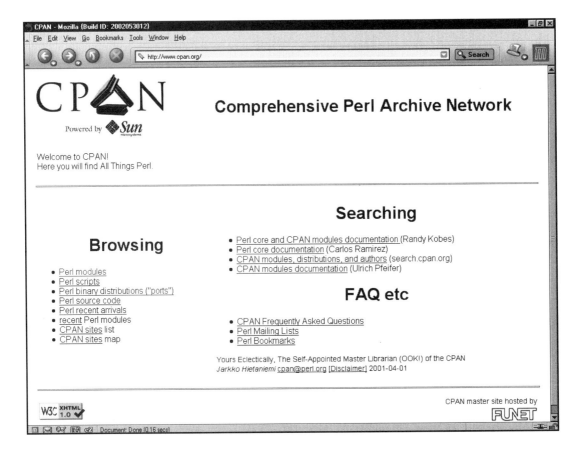

Figure 1-3. Entry screen for http://www.cpan.org

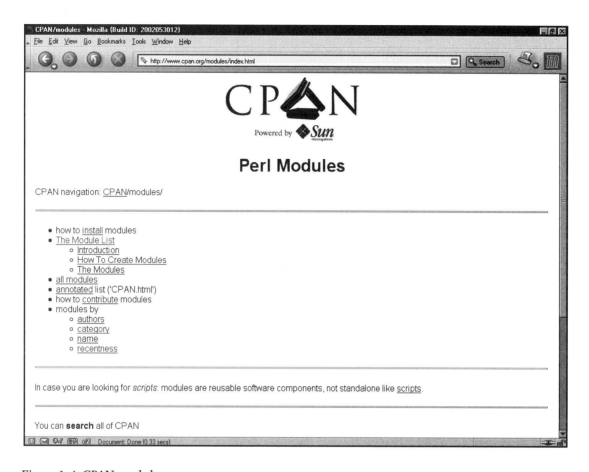

Figure 1-4. CPAN modules menu

I suggest you begin by entering the modules section of CPAN. This is by far the most useful area of the site and also the subject of this book. It's good to know where to find Perl, but you probably already know a thing or two about that if you're thinking about writing CPAN modules. Figure 1-4 shows the CPAN modules menu, where you'll find a number of different ways to navigate through the module collection.

The Module List

The Module List is a semi-manually maintained list of most of the Perl modules on CPAN. A section of the Module List is shown in Figure 1-5.

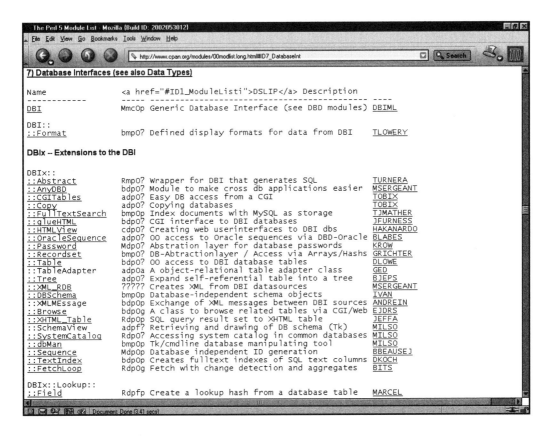

Figure 1-5. The start of Database Interfaces section in the Module List

In many ways, its function has been superseded by the newer search interfaces detailed later in this chapter, but it does have some unique features that can be helpful. First, it organizes the modules into categories by function. These categories are listed here:

Module List Categories

Perl Core Modules, Perl Language Extensions, and Documentation Tools

Development Support

Operating System Interfaces, Hardware Drivers

Networking, Device Control, and Interprocess Communication

Data Types and Data Type Utilities

Database Interfaces

User Interfaces

Interfaces to or Emulations of Other Programming Languages

File Names, File Systems, and File Locking

String Processing, Language Text Processing, Parsing, and Searching

Option, Argument, Parameter, and Configuration File Processing

Internationalization and Locale

Authentication, Security, and Encryption

World Wide Web, HTML, HTTP, CGI, MIME, and so on

Server and Daemon Utilities

Archiving, Compression, and Conversion

Images, Pixmap, and Bitmap Manipulation

Mail and Usenet News

Control Flow Utilities

File Handle, Directory Handle, and Input/Output Stream Utilities

Microsoft Windows Modules

Miscellaneous Modules

Interface Modules to Commercial Software

Bundles

Secondly, each listing contains a DSLIP code that can give you some information about the status of the module. *DSLIP* stands for Development Stage, Support Level, Language Used, Interface Style, and Public License. For example, a DSLIP code of *bmpOp* specifies that the module is in beta testing (*b*), is supported by a mailing-list (*m*), is written in pure Perl (*p*), has an object-oriented interface (*O*) and is licensed under the same license as Perl (*p*). Table 1-1 lists the various DSLIP codes.

Table 1-1. Module List DSLIP codes

D–Development Stage	
I	Idea
c	Under construction
a	Alpha testing
b	Beta testing
R	Released
M	Mature
S	Standard, comes with Perl 5
S–Support Levels	
m	Mailing list
d	Developer
u	Usenet newsgroup comp.lang.perl.modules
n	None
L–Language Used	
p	Perl-only
c	C and Perl
h	Hybrid, written in Perl with optional C code
+	C++ and Perl
o	Perl and another language other than C or C++
I–Interface Style	
f	Plain functions
O	Object oriented
h	Hybrid, object, and function interfaces available
r	Unblessed references or ties
n	None

Table 1-1. Module List DSLIP codes (Continued)

P-Public License

p	Standard Perl license (Artistic and GPL hybrid)
g	GPL (GNU General Public License)
l	LGPL (GNU Lesser General Public License)
b	The BSD License
a	Artistic license
o	Other (but distribution allowed without restrictions)

The biggest problem with the Module List is that it is incomplete, although this situation may be improved in the future.

Alternative Browsing Methods

An alternative to browsing the Module List is the "modules by" listings. You can browse modules grouped by author, by category, by name, and by recentness. The advantage to this method is that it deals directly with the directory structure of CPAN and as a result all available modules are accessible.

By Author

Upon entering the Modules By Author view, you see a directory listing with what appears to be a directory for every author on CPAN. This is misleading—the list you're seeing is a relic of the past. When CPAN started every author received an entry in this directory, but there's a limit to how many subdirectories a single directory can efficiently contain. These days there are far too many authors on CPAN to house them all in one directory, so CPAN switched to a multilevel hierarchy for storing author directories, which is used today.

To see the real list, open the file 00whois.html. There you'll find three pieces of information for each author—his or her CPAN ID, his or her full name, and his or her e-mail address. A CPAN ID is a unique identifier for CPAN authors—I'll show you how to apply for one in Chapter 5. If you click an author's CPAN ID,[5] you'll be taken to that author's CPAN directory, which contains all the modules he or she has uploaded to CPAN. Some authors have registered Web sites for themselves, and you can click their full names to visit these.

---

5. Some CPAN authors do not have CPAN directories. Their IDs will not be links.

By Category

The By Category view brings you to a directory hierarchy based on the categories in the Module List, listed earlier in this chapter. Inside each category you have an interface similar to the Module By Name interface described next.

By Name

Navigating CPAN modules by name allows you to traverse the module names directly, where each :: is translated into a path separator. This can be helpful when you know part of the name for the module you're looking for and need to see a list of possibilities. If you know the exact name of a module, then the search interface described later in this chapter is a faster alternative.

By Recentness

The By Recentness view shows you the most recent 150 uploads to CPAN. The format is a bit nicer than the Recent Arrivals list available on the opening screen, but it's not as nice as the format provided by http://search.cpan.org.

Searching CPAN

CPAN also sports a variety of search engines. Currently, the most useful is http://search.cpan.org (see Figure 1-6 for the entry screen). Not only does this search engine provide search capabilities, it also serves HTML versions of module documentation and gives access to a pleasantly formatted list of recently updated modules. This enables you to evaluate a group of modules without the trouble of installing them.

To use the search engine, just type a word in the search box and click the Search button. You can also enter a regular expression or choose a specific part of CPAN if you need to narrow your search. When you find a module that sounds interesting, just click the name, and you'll be brought to a details screen where you can view the module documentation.

The search interface also includes interfaces that mimic features offered by http://www.cpan.org. You can browse by category and see a list of recently uploaded files with an arguably prettier interface. You should try both interfaces and choose the one you like the best.

Figure 1-6. http://search.cpan.org *entry screen*

Installing CPAN Modules

So, you've found the module you've been searching for. Now you'll need to install it. And, like many things in Perl, TMTOWTDI.[6] The sections that follow discuss the two main installation methods: the easy way and the hard way.

The Easy Way

I'll start with the easy way—if you encounter problems, you should consult the "The Hard Way" section later in this chapter.

---

6. There's more than one way to do it.

Recent versions of Perl come with a module called CPAN,[7] which as you might have guessed is used to access the contents of CPAN. The CPAN module makes installing CPAN modules incredibly easy. It downloads modules from CPAN and automatically follows their dependencies, saving you a lot of work (which you'll learn all about in the upcoming section, "The Hard Way").

To get started with the CPAN module, enter the following command:

```
# perl -MCPAN -e shell
```

If you're using a UNIX system and want to install modules system-wide, you'll have to run this command as the *root* user. It is possible to use the CPAN module as a normal user, but you won't be able to install modules into the system.

The first time you run this command the CPAN module will ask you a series of questions:

```
# perl -MCPAN -e shell

CPAN is the world-wide archive of perl resources. It consists of about
100 sites that all replicate the same contents all around the globe.
Many countries have at least one CPAN site already. The resources
found on CPAN are easily accessible with the CPAN.pm module. If you
want to use CPAN.pm, you have to configure it properly.

If you do not want to enter a dialog now, you can answer 'no' to this
question and I'll try to autoconfigure. (Note: you can revisit this
dialog anytime later by typing 'o conf init' at the cpan prompt.)

Are you ready for manual configuration? [yes]
```

Each question has a default answer in square brackets. In most cases the default will be correct and you can just press Enter to continue. One important question to look for is this one, about following prerequisites:

```
The CPAN module can detect when a module that which you are trying to
build depends on prerequisites. If this happens, it can build the
prerequisites for you automatically ('follow'), ask you for
confirmation ('ask'), or just ignore them ('ignore'). Please set your
policy to one of the three values.

Policy on building prerequisites (follow, ask or ignore)? [ask]
```

---

7. Written and maintained by Andreas Köenig

The default, ask, is the most conservative setting, but you should consider answering follow since this will greatly ease the task of installing modules with lots of dependencies.

The CPAN modules uses various external programs, and you'll be asked to confirm their location:

```
Where is your gzip program? [/bin/gzip]
```

If you don't want the CPAN module to use a particular external program type a space and press Enter. This can be useful if you know a program is broken on your system or won't be able to perform its task.

Towards the end of the questions, the CPAN module will present you with a choice of which mirrors to use. First, you'll identify your continent:

```
(1) Africa
(2) Asia
(3) Central America
(4) Europe
(5) North America
(6) Oceania
(7) South America
Select your continent (or several nearby continents) []
```

then country:

```
(1) Canada
(2) Mexico
(3) United States
Select your country (or several nearby countries) []
```

and finally you'll select several mirrors from a list:

```
(1) ftp://archive.progeny.com/CPAN/
(2) ftp://carroll.cac.psu.edu/pub/CPAN/
(3) ftp://cpan.cse.msu.edu/
...
Select as many URLs as you like,
put them on one line, separated by blanks []
```

Make sure you pick more than one since many mirrors have limits on the number of people that can use them at one time. Also, not all mirrors are equally up-to-date. To make the best possible picks, you should visit http://mirror.cpan.org, where you can view a profile of each mirror including how up-to-date they are.

The very first thing you should do after configuring the CPAN module is install the newest version of the CPAN module and reload it. You can do that with these commands:

```
cpan> install CPAN
cpan> reload CPAN
```

This will save you the trouble of bumping into bugs in the CPAN module that have been fixed since the version that comes with Perl came out. In particular, older versions of the CPAN module had a nasty habit of trying to upgrade Perl without asking permission. The examples in this book are based on version 1.59_54 of the CPAN module, but using the newest version is always a good idea.

TIP   If you're having trouble connecting to CPAN using the CPAN module, you might need to manually install the Net::FTP module. See the section that follows on installing modules the hard way for details on how to do this.

After that, your next stop should be the CPAN bundle. The CPAN bundle contains a number of modules that make the CPAN module much easier to use and more robust. To install the bundle, use this command:

```
cpan> install Bundle::CPAN
```

NOTE   See the "Bundles" section later in this chapter to find out how Bundles work.

Now you're ready to install modules. For example, to install the CGI::Application module,[8] you would enter the following command:

```
cpan> install CGI::Application
```

And the CPAN module will handle downloading the module, running module tests, and installing it. If CGI::Application requires other modules, then the CPAN module will download and install those too.

---

8.   Described in Chapter 11

The CPAN module is versatile tool with myriad options and capabilities. While in the CPAN shell, you can get a description of the available commands using the help command. Also, to learn more about the module itself, you can access the CPAN documentation, using the perldoc utility:

```
$ perldoc CPAN
```

The Hard Way

The CPAN module may not be right for you. You may be behind a firewall or you might prefer more control over the module installation process. Also, some CPAN modules, usually older ones, aren't written to work with the CPAN module. If this is the case, then you'll need to install modules the hard way. Put on your opaque sunglasses and grab your towel.

Location

First, find the module you want to download on the CPAN server near you. An easy way to do this is by using the CPAN Search facilities described earlier. The file you're looking for will end in either .tar.gz or .zip. CPAN modules have version numbers, and there will usually be a list of versions to choose from. You'll generally want to choose the highest version number available. Download the module file and put it in a working directory on your local machine.

Decompression

These files are compressed, so the first thing you'll need to do is uncompress them to get at their contents. Under UNIX systems this is usually done with the tar and gzip utilities:

```
$ gzip -dc ModuleNameHere.tar.gz | tar xvf -
```

Under Windows you can use tools such as WinZip, available at http://www.winzip.com, or install a Windows port of the GNU utilities such as CygWin, which includes tar and gzip. CygWin is available at http://cygwin.com.

Build

Now that you've unpacked the module, you need to build it. Enter the directory created by unpacking the compressed module file. It's usually named the same as the compressed file but with the .tar.gz or .zip ending removed.

If the module has no installation instructions, look for a file called Makefile.PL. If it exists, enter the following commands:

```
$ perl Makefile.PL
$ make
```

These commands will fail if you're missing a *prerequisite module*. A prerequisite module is a module that is needed by the module you're installing. If the module has unsatisfied prerequisites, you'll need to find the required module or modules and install them before returning to installing this module.

These commands may also fail if you're using a Microsoft Windows system, because few Windows systems have the make utility installed. You may need to install the CygWin toolkit I mentioned in the "Decompression" section, which offers the GNU make utility as an optional component. Alternately, you may have a program called nmake[9] or dmake, which can function as make.

Regrettably, there are some modules on CPAN that don't use the standard module packaging system. Sometimes these modules will include an INSTALL file containing installation instructions, or installation instructions will be contained in the README file.

Test

Many CPAN modules come with tests to verify that the module is working properly on your system. The standard way to run module tests is with this command:

```
$ make test
```

---

9. You can download nmake from
    http://download.microsoft.com/download/vc15/Patch/1.52/W95/EN-US/Nmake15.exe.

Install

Finally, you will need to install the module to be able to use the module in your programs. To do so, enter the following command:

```
# make install
```

You will need to be *root* to perform this step on UNIX systems.

ActivePerl PPM

If you are using Perl on a Microsoft Windows system, there's a pretty good chance you are using ActiveState's[10] ActivePerl distribution. ActivePerl is also available for Linux and Solaris. If you're using ActivePerl, then you have a utility called PPM that can potentially make module installation even easier than using the CPAN module. Specifically, PPM will install binary distributions from the PPM repository at ActiveState (and elsewhere). This makes installing C-based modules possible on machines without C compilers. It also alleviates the need to install make, nmake, or dmake as previously described.

The downside is that the ActiveState PPM repository isn't CPAN. It contains many of the most popular CPAN modules, but many are missing. Even worse, the modules that are present are often out-of-date compared to the CPAN versions.

Using PPM is a lot like using the CPAN module's shell. To get started, use this command in your system's shell:

```
ppm
```

Now you'll be presented with a PPM prompt. The most common command is install, which allows you to install modules. This command will install a (probably out-of-date) version of my HTML::Template module:

```
install HTML::Template
```

To learn more about PPM, you can use the online help facility in the PPM shell with the help command.

---

10. See http://www.activestate.com.

Bundles

A bundle is a module that allows you to install a list of modules automatically using the CPAN module. A bundle is simply a module in the Bundle:: namespace containing a list of modules to download; it doesn't contain other modules. A bundle can also specify the versions of the modules to be downloaded, so that it can serve as a "known-good" module set.

To use a bundle, simple install it with the CPAN module. For example, to install Bundle::CPAN, enter the following:

```
# perl -MCPAN -e shell
cpan> install Bundle::CPAN
```

There are bundles available for many popular module groups: Bundle::LWP, Bundle::DBI, and Bundle::Apache, for example. To get a list of all bundles on CPAN, use the bundle search command b in the CPAN shell:

```
cpan> b /Bundle::/
Bundle          Bundle::ABH         (A/AB/ABH/Bundle-ABH-1.05.tar.gz)
Bundle          Bundle::ABH::Apache (A/AB/ABH/Bundle-ABH-1.05.tar.gz)
...
```

CPAN's Future

Writing about CPAN is a risky proposition, as it is under constant development. Use this chapter as a starting point and be prepared to find things a bit different than I've described them.

Summary

This chapter has introduced you to the wonderful world of CPAN. If I've done my job, by now you're interested in joining the CPAN community. The next chapter will introduce the science of building modules in Perl.

### CHAPTER 2

Perl Module Basics

SPAGHETTI CODE—if you don't know what it means, you're probably writing it. Spaghetti code gets its name from the numerous and thoroughly knotted paths your program takes through its source code. In the classic case, every subroutine in the program will call every other subroutine at least once (if there are subroutines—goto is *marinara* for spaghetti code). Nothing is commented, or if it is, then the comments are misleading. Executable code is mixed in with subroutine declarations at random. Basically, it's your worst nightmare.

What makes spaghetti code so bad is that even a small change in one part of the program can have dire consequences in an unrelated area. Fixing bugs becomes a dangerous activity—find one, and two more spring from the mist. Code like this invariably gets rewritten rather than enhanced, at tremendous expense.

To combat spaghetti code, you need *modular programming*. Modular programming is the practice of breaking a large program into smaller pieces called *modules*. Each module offers its service through a well-documented *interface*. The internals of the module are considered private, or *encapsulated*.

The beauty of modular programming is that the internals of the module can change without affecting code that uses the module. Fixing bugs is usually just a matter of finding the offending code and making sure that the fix doesn't affect the interface. Furthermore, modular programming makes your job easier; you only need to worry about the implementation of a single module at a time, rather than an entire complex program.

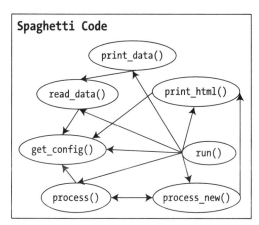

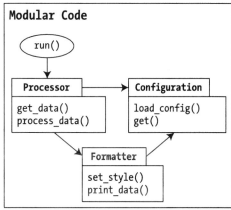

This chapter will explain Perl's support for modular programming and delve into modular programming's funny-looking cousin, *object-oriented programming*. You may want to skip this chapter if you have experience programming modules in Perl.

Using Modules

Using modules in Perl is extremely easy. Simply place a use statement at the top of your program specifying the name of the module. For example, here's a program that lists all the files over 1 megabyte in size below the current directory, using the File::Find module that comes with Perl:

```
#!/usr/bin/perl
use File::Find;
find(sub { print "$_\n" if -s $_ > 1_024_000; }, ".");
```

The File::Find module provides the find() function that traverses directories. For every file it finds, it calls the subroutine you pass as the first argument. The name of the current file is made available in the $_ variable. In the preceding example the subroutine examines the size of the file using -s and prints its name if the size is over a megabyte.

You could, of course, write this program without using File::Find. However, it would certainly be much longer than the two lines required to do the job with File::Find. File::Find, like many modules, makes your life easier by providing you with functionality that you can use without having to write it yourself. Like most modules, File::Find provides documentation in POD format (covered in detail in Chapter 3). You can read this documentation using perldoc:[1]

```
$ perldoc File::Find
```

File::Find provides its functionality through the find() function. This function is *exported*. Exporting means that the module provides access to a symbol,[2] in this case the find() subroutine, in the namespace where the module is used. I'll cover exporting in more depth later in this chapter.

---

1. UNIX users may also be able to use man to read module documentation. This is generally faster than using perldoc.

2. "Symbol" is a fancy word for named things in Perl. Variables, subroutines, and file-handles are all "symbols."

You can use modules without exporting symbols by using require instead of use:

```
#!/usr/bin/perl
require File::Find;
File::Find::find(sub { print "$File::Find::name\n" if -s > 1_024_000; }, '.');
```

As a result, the reference to find must be prefixed with a full package name and written as File::Find::find.

Another difference between the two is that use happens during *compile time*, whereas require happens at runtime. Perl runs a program in two phases—first, the program and all modules used by the program are compiled into an internal byte-code format. This is known as *compile time*. Next, the byte-code is executed and the program actually runs. Perl programs can actually go back and forth between runtime and compile time using two mechanisms: BEGIN and eval.

A BEGIN block is a way of getting a bit of runtime during compile time. When Perl encounters a BEGIN block, it executes the code found inside the BEGIN block as soon as it has been compiled, before any code that comes later in the program. For example, this line will print even if there's a compilation error later in the script:

```
BEGIN { print "Hello!  I'm running in the middle of compiling.\n" }
```

An eval with a string argument is a way of getting a bit of compile time during runtime. For example, this code will be compiled and run after the program is in runtime, which allows the code to be built during runtime:

```
eval "print 'Hello!  I'm compiling in the middle of running.\n";
```

Since use is just a way of doing a require operation and an import operation at compile time, use can be defined in terms of require using BEGIN:

```
BEGIN { require File::Find; import File::Find; }
```

And require can be defined in terms of use with eval:

```
eval "use File::Find ();";
```

The pair of parenthesis after File::Find tells use not to import any symbols, which emulates how require works.

This comprises practically all of the universally applicable directions that can be given about using modules. In practice, you'll have to at least skim the documentation for each module you want to use in order to find out how it's meant to be used. As you'll see in the following text, there are many, many ways to do it!

Packages

Perl supports modular programming through *packages*. Packages provide a separate namespace for variables and subroutines declared inside. This means that two packages can have subroutines and variables with the same names without inadvertently stepping on each other's toes. You declare a package with a package statement:

```
package CGI::SimplerThanThou;
```

After that, any subroutines or global variables you declare will be in the package. For example, this code creates a subroutine param() in the CGI::SimplerThanThou package:

```
package CGI::SimplerThanThou;
sub param {
    return ('fake', 'params');
}
```

Now if you want to call this subroutine from some other package, you'll need to prefix it with the package name:

```
my @params = CGI::SimplerThanThou::param();
```

Variables can also be created in a package. Here's an example that creates a hash called %params in the CGI::SimplerThanThou package:

```
package CGI::SimplerThanThou;
%params = ( ten => 10 );
```

To refer to this variable from another package, you again use the package prefix:

```
print "Ten: $CGI::SimplerThanThou::params{ten}\n";
```

Packages may not seem immediately useful, but they form the basis for modular programming in Perl by providing *encapsulation*. Since each package forms a separate namespace for variables and subroutines, a package is free to implement its functionality without concern for the rest of the program. For example, let's say I'd like to override Perl's logarithmic function, log(),[3] inside my package Acme::PotatoPeeler:

```
package Acme::PotatoPeeler;
sub log {
    print STDERR "PotatoPeeler Says: $_[0]\n";
}
```

If packages didn't provide encapsulation, I would have just overridden the logarithm function for the entire program, and the stock simulation algorithms in Acme::StockPicker wouldn't work so well! Of course, if that's what you *really* want, you can do that too. I'll explain how to use packages to "redefine the world" later.

Symbol Tables

Packages work through the magic of *symbol tables*. Each package has a hash associated with it called a symbol table. For every symbol in the package, there is a key in the hash. The value stored in the hash is a typeglob[4] containing the value for the symbol.

Why doesn't the hash directly store the value of the variable? Perl supports, for better or worse, variables of different types with the same name—you can have a scalar named $foo, an array named @foo, and a hash named %foo in the same package. The typeglob provides the level of indirection necessary to make this work.

Most compilers for other languages use symbol tables to keep track of variables declared in a program. Perl is unique in that it exposes its symbol tables to the programmer for examination and even manipulation at runtime. You can refer to a symbol table hash by using the package name plus a trailing package specifier, :: (double colon). Here's an example that prints out a sorted list of symbols for the File::Find package:

```
use File::Find;
print "$_\n" for sort keys %File::Find::;
```

---

3. Didn't know you could do that? I'll explain in more depth later in the "Exporting" section.
4. There isn't room here to dip into the arcane world of typeglobs. Suffice it to say that, outside of some useful idioms that I'll cover later, you can use them to do some really odd things that are probably best left undone.

The list includes all the subroutines and variables defined in the package. It also includes the symbol tables for any packages that begin with File::Find. For example, if you were to also use the fictitious package File::Find::Faster, then the preceding code would list "Faster::" for File::Find::Faster's symbol table.

All nonlexical[5] symbols are stored in a symbol table—even global variables. What is normally referred to as a global variable in Perl is actually just a variable in the default package called "main::". You can access the main package's symbol table through two names—%main:: and %::. So, in actuality, Perl has no global variables— just package variables in the default package.

Aside from this default package, no automatic prefix is assumed. This means that all package names must be spelled out fully and are not based on the current package. For example, this code:

```
package Poets::Appolinaire;
@Books = qw(Alcools Calligrams);
```

is not equivalent to:

```
package Poets;
@Appolinaire::Books = qw(Alcools Calligrams);
```

In order to reference @Poets::Appolinaire::Books from within the Poets package, the full package name is required:

```
package Poets;
@Poets::Appolinaire::Books = qw(Alcools Calligrams);
```

This is a good reason to keep your package names reasonably short—you'll have to type the full name whenever you need to refer to the package.

 CAUTION Modules with similar names do not necessarily have any relationship. For example, the CGI and CGI::Thin modules have nothing in common. CGI::Thin is not necessarily a subclass of CGI, as those with object-oriented experience might think. The most you can say with confidence is that they both have something to do with CGI.

---

5. Lexical symbols are those created with the my operator.

Modules

Modular programming requires two facilities in a programming language—
encapsulation and *interfaces*. Packages provide encapsulation by furnishing
separate namespaces for subroutines and variables. Modules are Perl's facility for
providing packages with interfaces. In actuality, Perl's support for interfaces are a
set of conventions around the use of packages and module filenaming. There is no
module keyword[6] and no extra syntax to learn.

You tell Perl your module's name in two ways—first, by naming the module file.
The filename corresponds to the module name by replacing the :: marks with file-
system separators and appending a .pm extension to the end. For example, here are
some module names and their associated filenames on UNIX and Windows systems:

*Table 2-1. Examples of Module Names Converted to Filenames on UNIX and
Windows systems*

Module Name	UNIX Filename	Windows Filename
CGI	CGI.pm	CGI.pm
HTML::Template	HTML/Template.pm	HTML\Template.pm
Scalar::List::Utils	Scalar/List/Utils.pm	Scalar\List\Utils.pm

Secondly, at the top of your module file you declare the name in a package line:

```
package Hello;
sub greet {
   my $name = shift;
   print "Hello, $name!\n";
}
1;
```

TIP   Perl modules must end by with a true statement. This tells Perl
that your module compiled successfully. Leaving off the true statement
will result in a compilation error.

---

6.   At least not yet! Early Perl 6 designs include mention of a new keyword for modules and
classes separate from normal packages.

If you place the preceding code in a file called `Hello.pm`, then you can use the module in a script placed in the same directory as `Hello.pm`:

```
#!/usr/bin/perl
use lib '.';
use Hello;
Hello::greet("World");
```

This produces the following output:

```
Hello, World!
```

Most of the code example should look familiar, but the `use lib` line might be new. I'll explain that in the next section.

Module Names

A module's name is its introduction. If you choose good names for your modules, you'll rarely have to answer the question "What does it do?" For example, programmers rarely ask me what HTML::Template does, but HTML::Pager draws inquiries on every mention.

Perl modules must have unique names. Having two modules with the same name will cause difficulties. This is similar to machines on the Internet—if there were two Web sites called `http://www.cpan.org`, how would a browser know where to send you?[7]

An easy solution to the problem of finding a unique name is to use a multipart name. Module names can be composed of parts delimited by double-colons— (`::`). Most modules have names with two parts and some have three—Inline::C, Scalar::List::Utils, Parse::RecDescent, CGI::Application. Following this practice is a good idea—it keeps your module names short enough to easily remember. If you do use a long name, then you should be careful to choose a name within a hierarchy that will make it easy for others to find.

Many organizations use a common prefix for all their internal modules. For example, Vanguard Media (`http://www.vm.com`) creates their internal modules under the name "Dynexus"—Dynexus::Template::File, Dynexus::Class::Base, and so on. This keeps the internal modules names from conflicting with names of externally produced modules. If you are creating private modules, you should consider a similar naming convention.

---

7. Ok, bad example—round-robin DNS works using this technique, but you get my point.

This is similar to the system used by Java where class names are preceded by the reversed domain name of their creators. For example, Java classes written by Sun have names beginning with "com.sun". The intent is the same—that module names never accidentally conflict, but the Perl system is considerably simpler and results in shorter names. Of course, if you'd like to create a module called Com::Acme::AutomaticDogCatcher module, you can.

How Perl Finds Modules

Let's take a brief detour into Perl mechanics. You need to know how Perl finds modules before you can start writing your own. When Perl encounters a use statement during compilation, it turns the module name into a filename as described earlier in this chapter. For example, Scalar::List::Utils becomes Scalar/List/Utils.pm. Next, Perl uses the global array @INC[8] to find a list of candidate directories to look for Scalar/List/Utils.pm. When Perl finds a module file, it is immediately compiled. You can find out what your Perl's default @INC is with this command:

```
perl -e 'print join("\n", @INC) . "\n";'
```

One way to use modules is to put your modules into one of the listed directories—usually one with site_perl in the name. This is what happens when you install a module from CPAN. Another way to use modules is to modify @INC before Perl starts looking for modules to include a different directory where you store your modules. An easy way to do that is through the use lib statement shown earlier. A use lib statement prepends a directory onto @INC at compile time.

For example, if you have a private modules directory in your home directory[9] called modules, you could start your programs with the following:

```
use lib '/home/sam/modules';
```

You can see the effect of this command on @INC by printing out after a use lib:

```
use lib '/home/sam/modules';
print join("\n", @INC) . "\n";
```

---

8. The name @INC refers to its use as an "include" path, although using a module is rarely referred to as "including" the module.

9. This is a UNIX-specific example since Windows (and other single-user operating systems) don't provide a "home directory." However, use lib works just as well on Windows as it does on UNIX, so the techniques should be easily adaptable.

Of course, this code will only work if your home directory is called "/home/sam". You can use the following to pull the home directory out of the environment:

```
use lib "$ENV{HOME}/modules";
```

But this won't work:

```
$home_dir = $ENV{HOME};
use lib "$home_dir/modules";
```

If you do something like this you'll receive the following error:

```
Empty compile time value given to use lib
```

The problem is that Perl processes use statements at compile time but the variable assignment to $home_dir happens at runtime. Perl needs to know where to look for modules at compile time so that it can find the modules to compile— runtime is much too late. One way to solve this problem is to ask Perl for a little runtime before compile time is over with BEGIN:

```
BEGIN {  $home_dir = $ENV{HOME}; }
use lib $home_dir;
```

Of course, you can also modify @INC directly, which also needs to be in a BEGIN block to be useful:

```
BEGIN { unshift(@INC, "/home/sam/modules"); }
```

The preceding line is equivalent to use lib "/home/sam/modules". In general use lib is the preferred method of adding a custom library path to your programs.

Once Perl has loaded a module, it creates an entry in the global hash %INC. The keys of this hash are module filenames (that is, File/Find.pm), and the values are the full path to the files loaded for the module (that is, /usr/local/lib/perl5/5.6.1/File/Find.pm). You can use this hash to get a list of loaded modules and where they were loaded from:

```
print map { "$_ => $INC{$_}\n" } keys %INC;
```

This can be very useful as a debugging aid when you're not sure Perl is picking up the right version of a module. Perl uses %INC to avoid loading a module file more than once.

Functional Modules

The most obvious way to build a module is to place subroutines in the module and document them as the module's *interface*. For example, here's a module that provides a logging facility for a fictional application called BOA:

```perl
package BOA::Logger;

$LOG_LEVEL = 1; # default log level is 1

# open log file
sub open_log {
   my $filename = shift;
   open(LOG_FILE, ">>$filename") or die "Unable to open $filename : $!";
   print LOG_FILE "BOA log started: " . localtime(time) . "\n";
}

# set logging level
sub log_level { $LOG_LEVEL = shift; }

# write a log message if level is set high enough
sub write_log {
   my ($level, $message) = @_;
   print LOG_FILE "$message\n" if $level <= $LOG_LEVEL;
}

1;
```

CAUTION   A real logging module would use flock() to prevent file corruption, but that would make these examples twice as long! The code in this chapter is kept as simple as possible—real production code would need significant enhancement.

The concept for the module is simple—BOA::Logger will provide logging at varying levels of detail known as *log levels*. The module's *interface* consists of three subroutines—open_log(), log_level(), and write_log(). The application must call open_log() before the first call to write_log(). When a piece of code calls write_log(), it provides two arguments, $level and $message itself. If $level is less than or equal to the currently set log level, the message is printed to the log. The log level defaults to 1 and the application can change the value using the log_level() subroutine.

Notice how the package variable $LOG_LEVEL is used to maintain *state* between calls to log_level() and write_log(). By state I mean that the module contains variables that store the value of past operations between calls to the interface. Thus the *state* of the module changes over time as the interface is used.

Here's a possible usage of the module, which would go in a separate script file:

```
# use the module
use BOA::Logger;

# open the log file
BOA::Logger::open_log("logs/boa.log");

# set the log level higher
BOA::Logger::log_level(10);

# write a log entry at level 5
BOA::Logger::write_log(5, "Hello log reader.");

# write a log entry at level 15 - this won't be printed to the log
BOA::Logger::write_log(15, "Debugging data here.");
```

Exporting

BOA::Logger is useful enough, but it could be improved. For one thing, the module takes too much typing. To solve this problem, you can use the *Exporter*. The Exporter enables you to *export* symbols from your module into the package of the calling module. Exporting makes an entry in the calling package's symbol table that points to the called package. To export the three subroutines in BOA::Logger, you would change the top of the module source file, BOA/Logger.pm, to read as follows:

```
package BOA::Logger;
require Exporter;
@ISA = qw(Exporter);
@EXPORT = qw(open_log log_level write_log);
```

The second line loads the Exporter module—require is commonly used here, but use also works. The third line accesses Perl's inheritance mechanism—I'll describe inheritance in more detail in the "Object-Oriented Modules" section, but for now you can just treat it as magic code that makes the Exporter work. Finally, the @EXPORT array is initialized with the list of symbols to export.

Now code that uses BOA::Logger can dispense with the package name:

```
use BOA::Logger;
open_log("logs/boa.log");
log_level(10);
write_log(5, "Hello log reader.");
write_log(15, "Debugging data here..");
```

Of course, the full package specification would still work—you can always refer to BOA::Logger::write_log().

Now, BOA is a big application. In fact, BOA stands for **big ol'** application, so many other modules will be using BOA::Logger. Most of these modules will only be calling write_log(). The only code that will call open_log() and log_level() is the startup code. Fortunately users of the module can choose what symbols they want exported—by providing a list of symbols to use:

```
use BOA::Logger qw(write_log);
```

Without this addition, a use BOA::Logger will import all exported symbols. To import nothing from a module that exports symbols by default, use an empty list:

```
use BOA::Logger ();
```

Subroutines aren't the only thing you can export. Variables can also be exported. For example, BOA::Logger could omit the log_level() subroutine and just export $LOG_LEVEL directly:

```
@EXPORT = qw(open_log $LOG_LEVEL write_log);
```

Now code that wants to set the logging level can import the $LOG_LEVEL variable and manipulate it directly:

```
use BOA::Logger qw($LOG_LEVEL write_log);
$LOG_LEVEL = 10;
write_log(10, "Log level set to 10.");
```

I'll return to the Exporter to provide more details in the next chapter.

BEGIN

Another problem with the BOA::Logger module is that other modules have to wait for open_log() to get called before they can use write_log(). This makes it difficult for modules to log their compilation and initialization. To solve this problem, the module could be changed to automatically open the log file as soon as possible—during compile time. To cause code to be run at compile time, move the code from open_log() into a BEGIN block:

```
BEGIN {
    open(LOG_FILE, ">>logs/boa.log") or die "Unable to open log : $!";
    print LOG_FILE "BOA log started: " . localtime(time) . "\n";
}
```

Now the log file is opened as soon as the BOA::Logger module is compiled. The downside here is that the location of the log file is hard-coded into BOA::Logger.

END

It is often useful to know when an application exited. BOA::Logger can provide this by registering an action to take place when the application exits. This is done with an END block—the opposite of the BEGIN block described earlier.

```
END {
    print LOG_FILE "BOA log exited: " . localtime(time) . "\n";
    close LOG_FILE or die "Unable to close log/boa.log : $!";
}
```

As an added bonus I get to feel like a good citizen by closing the LOG_FILE file handle instead of letting *global destruction* do it for me. Global destruction refers to the phase in a Perl program's life when the interpreter is shutting down and will automatically free all resources held by the program. END blocks are often used to clean up resources obtained during BEGIN blocks.

Error Reporting

BOA::Logger is a careful module—it always checks to make sure system calls like open() and close() succeed. When they don't, BOA::Logger calls die(), which will cause the program to exit if not caught by an eval.[10] This is all well and good, but unfortunately the error messages generated aren't very helpful—they make it look as though there's a problem in BOA::Logger. For example, if you call open_log() on a file that can't be opened, you'll receive the following error message:

```
Unable to open /path/to/log : No such file or directory at BOA/Logger.pm line 8.
```

---

10. This is Perl's poor-man exception handling. For a more evolved system, see the Exception module on CPAN.

When my fellow BOA developers see this message, they'll likely jump to the conclusion that there's something wrong with BOA::Logger. They'll send me angry e-mails and I'll be forced to sign them up for spam.[11] Nobody wants that, and thankfully the situation can be avoided. The Carp module, which comes with Perl, can be used to place the blame where it belongs. Here's a new version of the module header and open_log() using Carp:

```perl
package BOA::Logger;
use Carp qw(croak);

sub open_log {
   my $filename = shift;
   open(LOG_FILE, ">>$filename") or croak("Unable to open $filename : $!");
   print LOG_FILE "BOA log started: " . localtime(time) . "\n";
}
```

Now the blame is properly placed and the resulting error is

```
Unable to open /path/to/log : No such file or directory at caller.pl line 5
```

The croak() routine provides a die() replacement that assigns blame to the caller of the subroutine. The Carp module also provides a warn() replacement called carp(), as well as routines to generate full back traces. See the Carp documentation for more details; you can access it with the command perldoc Carp.

Object-Oriented Modules

As previously mentioned, BOA is a big ol' application. In fact, it's so big that just one log file will not be enough. There are several subsystems (GUI, Network, Database, and so on) that each need their own log files with independent log levels. One way to address this would be to create a new package for each log file and copy and paste the code from BOA::Logger into each one—creating BOA::Logger::GUI, BOA::Logger::Network, and so on. This approach has some obvious drawbacks— the code becomes harder to maintain since a change in once place has to be carefully replicated in each copy. Also, it would be difficult to use multiple BOA::Logger clones at the same time—they all want to export write_log(), so you'd have to forgo exporting and type the whole package name for every call.

There is an easier way. Instead of creating a new package just to hold some state information, you'll create an object-oriented module that provides an object for each log file. These objects will contain the state necessary to support a single

---

11. I recommend Oprah's book club mailing list.

log file as well as the functions needed to operate on this state data. This is the basic definition of an object: state data and functions to operate on that state wrapped up in one data structure. The benefits of object orientation are increased flexibility and improved potential for code reuse.

References: A Brief Refresher

Perl supports object-oriented programming through *references*. It's possible to do a lot of useful things with Perl without using a single reference. As a result you may be ready to learn object-oriented Perl without having ever used a single reference. I'll give you a quick refresher on the topic, but if you're left with questions, I suggest you head for a good introductory book on Perl for details.

A reference is simply a variable that *points to* another variable. By points to, I mean that you can follow the link from a reference to the variable it references. This action of following a reference is known as *dereferencing*.

Here's a simple example that prints "Hello, New World" using a reference to a scalar:

```
$message = "Hello, New World.\n";
$ref = \$message;
print $$ref;
```

This example shows two important operations on references. First, a reference is created using the \ operator:

```
$ref = \$message;
```

After this line, $ref points to $message. You can see this in action by changing $message and observing that the new value is visible through $ref:

```
$message = "Goodbye, dear friend.";
print $$ref; # prints "Goodbye, dear friend."
```

Second, the reference is dereferenced using a second $ in front of the reference:

```
print $$ref;
```

You can create a reference to other types of variables but the result is always stored in a scalar. For example, this example prints "Hello, New World" using a reference to an array:

```
@array = ("Hello,", "New", "World");
$ref = \@array;
print join(" ", @$ref) . "\n";
```

This example works similarly to the earlier example and uses an @ to deference the reference to @array. This works fine for access to the whole array, but more often you'll want to pick out a single value:

```perl
print $ref->[0] . "\n";  # prints "Hello,"
```

This syntax is known as *arrow notation*. You can use arrow notation with hashes as well. For example, here's another way to print "Hello, New World", this time using a reference to a hash:

```perl
%hash = ( message => "Hello, New World" );
$ref = \%hash;
print $ref->{message} . "\n";
```

Finally, Perl contains operators to create array and hash references without requiring an intermediate variable. These are known as *anonymous arrays* and *anonymous hashes,* respectively. For example, the preceding example could be rewritten to use an anonymous hash:

```perl
$ref = { message => "Hello, New World" };
print $ref->{message} . "\n";
```

The curly braces ({}) produce a reference to an anonymous hash. Similarly, square braces ([ ]) produce a reference to an anonymous array:

```perl
$ref = [ "Hello", "New", "World" ];
print join(" ", @$ref) . "\n";
```

References are often used to implement *call-by-reference* in subroutines. Call-by-reference means that the subroutine takes a reference as a parameter and acts on the data pointed to by the reference. For example, here's a function that takes a reference to an array of words and uppercases them:

```perl
sub upper {
   my $words = shift;
   $words->[$_] = uc($words->[$_]) for (0 .. $#$words);
}
```

Notice that this subroutine doesn't return anything—it works by modifying the array pointed to by the reference passed as the first parameter. Here's an example of how upper() would be used:

```perl
my @words = ("Hello,", "New", "World");
upper(\@words);
print join(" ", @words) . "\n";  # prints "HELLO, NEW WORLD"
```

Object Vocabulary

Object-oriented (OO) programming has a language all its own. Fortunately for us, Perl provides a simple translation from the OO lexicon to everyday Perl.[12] See Table 2-2 for a cheat sheet. Don't worry if this vocabulary isn't immediately clear, I'll provide more explanation as we go.

Table 2-2. OO Vocabulary Cheat Sheet

OO	Perl
Class	Package
Object	A reference blessed into a package
Method	A subroutine in a class
Object method	A method that expects to be called using an object
Class method	A method designed to be called using a class
Constructor	A class method that returns a new object

Using OO Modules

Before I show you the details of creating an OO module, it helps to know how to use one. Here's an example using IO::File, an OO wrapper around Perl's file operators (open, print, seek, and so on) included with Perl:

```
use IO::File;
# create a new IO::File object for writing "file.txt"
my $filehandle = IO::File->new(">file.txt");

# print to the file
$filehandle->print("This line goes into file.txt\n");

# close the file
$filehandle->close();
```

The three subroutine calls—new(), print() and close()—are examples of method calls. Method calls are the bread-and-butter of object-oriented programming, and in typical Perl fashion, there's more than one way to do it. The preceding example

---

12. Which is not the case for all those C programmers learning C++—they don't have a leg to stand on!

uses the arrow operator, ->. The left-hand side of the arrow operator must be either a package name (such as IO::File) or an object (such as $filehandle). The right-hand side is the name of a subroutine to call.

Methods automatically receives as an extra initial parameter—the variable on the left-hand side of the arrow operator. You can imagine that the call to new() is translated into the following:

```
my $filehandle = IO::File::new("IO::File", "> file.txt");
```

But you shouldn't write it that way—using method call syntax enables Perl's inheritance to work. I'll describe inheritance in more detail later.

Perl offers another method call syntax known as *indirect object syntax*. Here's the code from the example rewritten to use indirect object method calls:

```
my $filehandle = new IO::File ">file.txt";
print $filehandle "This line goes into file.txt\n";
close $filehandle;
```

In this style, the method name comes first followed by either a package name or an object. Both calling styles result in the same method invocation—the extra initial argument is supplied to the method subroutine in both cases. Choosing which one to use is largely a matter of preference, although many Perl programmers prefer the arrow notation since it is less visually ambiguous. Furthermore, Perl itself occasionally has trouble parsing indirect object syntax. For these reasons, I'll be using arrow notation in my examples from this point forward.

 CAUTION   C++ programmers take note—there is nothing special about methods named new(). It is only by convention that constructors are often named new().

A method that is called using a package name is a *class method*. A method called with an object is an *object method*. Class methods are used to provide services that are not specific to any one object; object construction is the most common example but I'll explore others in the next sections.

The Class

A *class* in Perl is nothing more than a package that happens to have subroutines meant to be used as methods. Here's an example of BOA::Logger transformed into a class.

```perl
package BOA::Logger;
use Carp qw(croak);
use IO::File;

# constructor - returns new BOA::Logger objects
sub new {
   my ($pkg, $filename) = @_;

   # initialize $self as a reference to an empty hash
   my $self = {};

   # open the log file and store IO::File object in $self->{fh}
   my $filehandle = IO::File->new(">>$filename");
   croak("Unable to open $filename : $!") unless $filehandle;

   # print startup line
   $filehandle->print("BOA log started: " . localtime(time) . "\n");

   # store the filehandle in $self
   $self->{fh} = $filehandle;

   # set default log_level of one
   $self->{level} = 1;

   # bless $self as an object in $pkg and return it
   bless($self, $pkg);
   return $self;
}

# level method - changes log level for this log object
sub level {
   my ($self, $level) = @_;
   $self->{level} = $level;
}
```

```
# write method - writes a line to the log file if log-level is high enough
sub write {
    my ($self, $level, $message) = @_;
    $self->{fh}->print($message) if $level <= $self->{level};
}


1;
```

The module begins by using two modules you've met before: Carp and IO::File. Next, the first subroutine, new(), is defined. This is the *constructor*—a class method that returns new objects. new() receives two arguments—the name of the package and the filename to open.

The object itself is just a hash underneath. Most objects in Perl are really hashes, but it's possible to create objects based on anything you can make a reference to. Hashes are used so often for their inherent flexibility. In this case, the hash contains two keys—"fh" and "level". The "fh" key contains an open IO::File object for the log file. The "level" key is set to the default log level of 1. Data elements kept in an object are known as the object's *attributes*.

So far so good, but what about that last section:

```
bless($self, $pkg);
return $self;
```

The call to bless()[13] tells Perl that $self is an object in the package named $pkg. This is how a reference becomes an object. After this point, methods can be called using the object, and they will result in subroutine calls in $pkg—BOA::Logger in this case. A call to ref($self) will return $pkg ("BOA::Logger") after blessing. Finally, since this is a constructor, the new object is returned to the caller.

Methods all share a common structure. They receive their $self object as an automatic first argument and any additional arguments after that. The two methods here, level() and write(), work with the data stored in the $self hash. The contents of the $self hash is known as *instance data*. Instance data is different for each *instance* (a fancy word for object) of this class.

---

13. There is also a single-argument form of bless that blesses into the current package. This should be avoided because it doesn't allow for inheritance. Since there's no drawback to using the two-argument form, it should be used in all cases.

Here's an example of using the module, which would be placed in a separate script file:

```
use BOA::Logger;
my $logger = BOA::Logger->new('logs/boa.log');
$logger->level(10);
$logger->write(10, "Hello world!");
```

One thing to notice is that making the module object oriented allows you to simplify the names of the subroutines in BOA::Logger. This is because object-oriented modules should never export their methods. Thus there's no need to worry about confusion with other subroutines called level() and write(). Another advantage of the object-oriented BOA::Logger is that you can have multiple loggers active at the same time with different log files and different log levels.

Accessors and Mutators

The level() method shown earlier is called a *mutator*—it is used to change, or mutate, the value of the level attribute. It is not an accessor since it doesn't allow the user to query the current value of the level attribute. An accessor for the value of level could potentially be useful—a user of the module could avoid executing costly debugging code if the log level is set too low to show the results. Here's a new level() method that functions as both an accessor and a mutator:

```
sub level {
    my ($self, $level) = @_;
    $self->{level} = $level if @_ == 2;
    return $self->{level};
}
```

Now it's possible to call the level() method with no arguments to receive the current value of the level attribute. For example, this checks the log level before calling write():

```
if ($logger->level() >= 5) {
    $logger->write(5, "Here's the full state of the system: " . dump_state());
}
```

This way you can avoid calling dump_state() if the result will never be printed.

Writing accessor-mutators for each attribute in your object enables you to perform checks on the value being set. For example, it might be useful to verify that the level value is a nonnegative integer. One way to do this is to check it with a regular expression that only matches digits:

```
sub level {
   my ($self, $level) = @_;
   if (@_ == 2) {
      croak("Argument to level() must be a non-negative integer!")
         unless $level =~ /^\d+$/;
      $self->{level} = $level;
   }
   return $self->{level};
}
```

It might seem convenient to allow users to simply access the hash keys directly:

```
$logger->{level} = 100;  # works, but not a good idea
```

The problem with this is that it breaks the *encapsulation* of your class. You are no longer free to change the implementation of BOA::Logger—you can't change the class to use an array underneath or change the keys of the hash. Also, you can't perform any checking of the value set for an attribute. As a general rule, all access to an object-oriented class should be through methods, either class methods or object methods.

Destructors

The non-OO version of BOA::Logger had a useful feature that this version lacks—it prints a message when the program exits. You can provide this by setting up a *destructor* for the class. Destructors are the opposite of constructors—they are called when an object is no longer being used.[14] They can perform cleanup actions, such as closing file handles. To create a destructor, simply define a method called DESTROY.

```
sub DESTROY {
   my $self = shift;
   $self->write($self->{level}, "BOA log exited: " . localtime(time) . "\n");
   $self->{fh}->close() or die "Unable to close log file : $!";
}
```

Class Data

By now you know that BOA is a big ol' application. As such, there are many modules that will want to write to the same log file. With the example OO implementation,

---

14. When the last variable holding a reference to the object goes out of scope, or at program exit—whichever comes first

this means that each client module will create its own BOA::Logger object. This will have a number of unpleasant side effects. First, when each BOA::Logger object is destroyed, it will write its own "BOA log exited" message. Second, each BOA::Logger object will consume a file handle. Many systems limit the number of open file handles a process can have, so it's best not to use more than necessary.

We can solve this problem using, you guessed it, *class data*. Class data is data that is stored at the class level and is not associated with any specific object. In Perl, class data is supported through package-scoped variables. It can be used to maintain state separate from each objects' own state. Common uses of class data include keeping track of the number of objects created or the number of objects still alive. In this case, you'll use a hash called %CACHE to maintain a cache of BOA::Logger objects:

```
# constructor - returns new BOA::Logger objects
sub new {
   my ($pkg, $filename) = @_;

   # lookup $filename in %BOA::Logger::CACHE - if an entry exists, return it
   return $CACHE{$filename} if $CACHE{$filename};

   # initialize $self as a reference to an empty hash
   my $self = {};

   # store in %CACHE
   $CACHE{$filename} = $self;

   # ... same as previous example ...
}
```

When new() is called, it will first check the cache to see if you've already got a BOA::Logger object for the filename. If it does, the existing object is immediately returned. If not, the new object is stored in the cache for future lookups.

This works, but it causes a subtle change in BOA::Logger's behavior. After adding the cache, DESTROY is only called at program exit, rather than when the last reference to a BOA::Logger object goes out of scope. This is because objects aren't destroyed until the last reference to them goes out of scope; %CACHE maintains a reference to every object created by new() and as a package variable it never goes out of scope. This might be acceptable behavior, but if it's not, you could fix it by using the WeakRef module.[15] WeakRef provides weaken(), which enables you to create references that don't prevent objects from being destroyed. This version will allow the BOA::Logger objects to be destroyed as soon as possible:

---

15. Written by Tuomas J. Lukka and available on CPAN

```
use WeakRef qw(weaken);

# constructor - returns new BOA::Logger objects
sub new {
   my ($pkg, $filename) = @_;

   # lookup $filename in %BOA::Logger::CACHE - if an entry exists, return it
   return $CACHE{$filename} if $CACHE{$filename};

   # initialize $self as a reference to an empty hash
   my $self = {};

   # store in %CACHE
   $CACHE{$filename} = $self;
   weaken($CACHE{$filename});

   # ... same as previous example ...
}
```

Inheritance

BOA::Logger is a simple module, but simple doesn't last. As more BOA developers start using BOA::Logger, requests for new features will certainly start piling up. Satisfying these requests by adding new features to the module might be possible, but the effect on performance might be severe. One solution would be to create a new module called BOA::Logger::Enhanced that supported some enhanced features and just copy the code in from BOA::Logger to get started. This has an unpleasant consequence: The code would be harder to maintain since bugs would need to be fixed in two places at once.

There is a better way. Object-oriented classes can be enhanced using *inheritance*. Inheritance enables one module to be based on one (or more) classes known as *parent* or *base* classes. The new derived class that inherits from the parent class is known as the *child* class. Here's an example module, called BOA::Logger::Enhanced, that inherits from BOA::Logger:

```
package BOA::Logger::Enhanced;
use BOA::Logger;
@ISA = qw(BOA::Logger);
```

By assigning "BOA::Logger" to the package variable @ISA, the module tells Perl that it is inheriting from the BOA::Logger class. This variable is pronounced "is a" and refers to the fact that a BOA::Logger::Enhanced object "is a" BOA::Logger object. Inheritance relationships are known as "is a" relationships.

To provide the advertised enhanced functionality, the class will *override* the write() method. Overriding is when a child class replaces a parent class's method. Here's a new write() method that puts a timestamp on every log line. This code would be placed in BOA/Logger/Enhanced.pm:

```
sub write {
    my ($self, $level, $message) = @_;
    $message = localtime(time) . " : " . $message;
    $self->{fh}->print($message) if $level <= $self->{level};
}
```

The method modifies the $message parameter to contain a timestamp and then prints out the line in the same way as the original BOA::Logger::write(). Here's an example using the new module:

```
use BOA::Logger::Enhanced;
my $logger = BOA::Logger::Enhanced->new("logs/boa.log");
$logger->level(10);
$logger->write(10, "The log level is at least 10!");
```

When BOA::Logger::Enhanced->new() is called, Perl first looks in the BOA::Logger::Enhanced package to see if a subroutine called new() is defined. When it finds that there is no BOA::Logger::Enhanced::new(), Perl checks to see if @ISA is defined and proceeds to check each package name listed in @ISA for the required method. When it finds BOA::Logger::new(), it calls the subroutine with two arguments, BOA::Logger::Enhanced and logs/boa.log. BOA::Logger::Enhanced gets assigned to $pkg in BOA::Logger::new() and used in the call to bless():

```
bless($self, $pkg);
```

The result is that BOA::Logger::new() returns an object in the BOA::Logger::Enhanced class without needing to know anything about BOA::Logger::Enhanced! Isn't Perl great?

 CAUTION   Don't be fooled by the similar class names—no automatic inheritance is happening between BOA::Logger and BOA::Logger::Enhanced. Inheritance must be explicitly declared through @ISA to be used.

UNIVERSAL

All classes in Perl implicitly inherit from a common base class—UNIVERSAL. The UNIVERSAL class provides three methods that can be used on all objects—isa(), can(), and VERSION().

The isa() method can be used to determine if an object belongs to a particular class or any child of that class. This is preferable to using ref() to check the class of an object since it works with inheritance. For example, the following code prints "Ok":

```
my $logger = BOA::Logger::Enhanced->new("logs/boa.log");
print "Ok" if $logger->isa('BOA::Logger');
```

but this similar code does not:

```
my $logger = BOA::Logger::Enhanced->new("logs/boa.log");
print "Ok" if ref($logger) eq 'BOA::Logger';
```

This is because ref() returns the name of the class that the object belongs to which is BOA::Logger::Enhanced. Even though BOA::Logger::Enhanced inherits from BOA::Logger, that won't make eq return true when comparing them as strings. The moral here is simple: Don't use ref() to check the class of objects, use isa() instead.

To check if an object supports a method call, use can(). You can use can() to provide support for older versions of modules while still taking advantage of the newer features. For example, imagine that at some point in the future BOA::Logger::Enhanced adds a method set_color() that sets the color for the next line in the log file. This code checks for the availability of the set_color() method and calls it if it is available:

```
if ($logger->can('set_color')) {
    $logger->set_color('blue');
}
$logger->write("This might be blue, or it might not!");
```

Another way to query the features provided by a module is to use the VERSION() method. With no arguments, this method looks at the $VERSION variable defined in the class package and returns its value. If you pass an argument to VERSION(), then the method will check if the class's $VERSION is greater than or equal to the argument and die() if it isn't. This form is used by use when use is passed a version number. For example, this statement calls BOA::Logger->VERSION(1.1) after BOA::Logger is compiled and exits with an error message if the call returns false:

```
use BOA::Logger 1.1;
```

To support this usage, BOA::Logger would need to be modified to initialize a $VERSION package variable:

```
package BOA::Logger;
$VERSION = 1.1;
```

Since these features are provided as method calls in a parent class, child classes can override them and provide their own implementations. This enables classes to lie to the rest of the world about their inheritance, capabilities, and even version. In Perl, things are not always as they appear.

Overloaded Modules

Object-oriented programming can be cumbersome. Everything is a method call, and sooner or later all your method calls start to look the same. Overloading your modules provides a way to simplify code that uses your module. It allows you to express code like the following:

```
$foo->add(10);
print "My favorite cafe is " . $cafe->name() . "\n";
```

in a more natural way:

```
$foo += 10;
print "My favorite cafe is $cafe\n";
```

Overloading enables your objects to work with Perl's existing math and string operators. When a Perl operator is used with an object of an overloaded class, a method is called. You specify which operators you are overloading and which methods to call using the overload pragma.[16]

```
package My::Adder;
use overload '+' => "add",
             '-' => \&subtract;
```

The overload pragma takes a list of key-value pairs as an argument. The keys are symbols representing the various operators available for overloading. The values specify the method to call when the operator is used; this can be expressed as a

---

16. A *pragma* is loosely defined as a module that functions as a compiler directive; it changes the way Perl compiles the code that follows. The pragmas that come with Perl all have lowercase names.

string or as a reference to a subroutine. The string form is preferred since it allows for a child class to override an overloaded method. Table 2-3 lists the overloadable operations.

Table 2-3. Overloadable Operations

Operation Type	Symbols
Conversion	`"" 0+ bool`
Arithmetic	`+ += - -= * *= / /= % %= ** **= ++ --`
String	`x x= . .=`
Numeric comparison	`< <= > >= == != <=>`
String comparison	`lt le gt ge eq ne cmp`
Bitwise	`<< >> <<= >>= & ^ | neg ~`
Logical	`!`
Transcendental	`atan2 cos sin exp abs log sqrt int`
Iteration	`<>`
Dereferencing	`${} @{} %{} &{} *{}`
Special	`nomethod fallback =`

This method will be called with three parameters—the object itself, the variable on the opposite side of the operator, and metadata about the operator call including the order of the arguments.

NOTE Overloading in Perl has little in common with overloading in other languages. For example, in C++ "overloading" refers to the ability to have two functions with the same name and different parameter types. Currently Perl does not have this ability, but rumor has it Perl 6 will change that.

Overloading Conversion

Overloading's most useful feature is not its ability to overload math operators. I'll be covering that in a moment, but unless you're inventing new mathematical types, it's not likely you'll be overloading addition in your modules. On the other hand, overloading conversion is quite common. An overloaded conversion operator is called when Perl wants to use your object in a particular context— string, numeric, or Boolean.

Overloading string conversion enables you to provide a method that Perl will call when it wants to turn your object into a string. Here are a few examples of places where a string conversion operator is used:

```perl
$string = "$object";
$string = "I feel like a " . $fly . " with its wings dipped in honey.";
print "Say hello to my little ", $friend, ".\n";
```

Without an overloaded string conversion operator, objects are converted to highly esoteric strings such as "IO::File=GLOB(0x8103ee4)"—just next door to useless. By providing a string conversion operator, a class can furnish a more useful string representation. This can enhance debugging and provide a simpler interface for some modules.

For example, one of my fellow BOA programmers is an exceptionally lazy individual. He's responsible for the networking code in BOA::Network. Each network connection is represented as an object in the BOA::Network class. Since he's such a lazy guy, he'd like to be able to use the BOA::Logger class with the absolute minimum work:

```perl
$logger->write(1, $connection);
```

His initial suggestion was that I modify write() to check for BOA::Network objects and pull out the relevant status information for logging. That would work, but sooner or later you'd have an if() for every module in BOA. Because BOA is a big ol' application, this wouldn't be a good idea. Instead, BOA::Network can overload string conversion:

```perl
package BOA::Network;
use overload '""' => "stringify";

sub stringify {
  my $self = shift;
  return ref($self) . " => read $self->{read_bytes} bytes, " .
        "wrote $self->{wrote_bytes} bytes at " .
        "$self->{kps} kps";
}
```

Now when BOA::Network calls

```
$logger->write(1, $connection);
```

the log file will contain a line like the following:

```
BOA::Network => read 1024 bytes, wrote 58 bytes at 10 kps
```

Nothing in BOA::Logger changes—the overloaded string conversion provides the method call to BOA::Network::stringify() automatically when BOA::Logger::write() prints its second argument.

Overloading *numification*, through the '0+' key, works similarly. Numification is the name for the process that coverts a variable to a number when the variable is used in a numeric context. This happens when an object is used with a math operator, as an array index or in a range operator (..). For example, the variable $number is *numified* in the second line in order to increment it:

```
$foo = "10"; # foo contains the string value "10"
$foo++;      # foo is numified and then incremented to contain 11
```

Overloading numification gives you control over how your variable is represented as a number.

Finally, a Boolean conversion method, using the bool overload key, is employed when the object is used in Boolean context. This happens inside an if() and with logical operations such as && and ||.

Unary Operators

A unary operator is one that applies to only one argument. It's very simple to provide an overloaded unary operator—there are no arguments to deal with and you only need to worry about implementing the required semantics. See Listing 2-1 for a module that overrides ++ and -- so that the object always contains an even number.

Listing 2-1. Overloading Unary Operations in the Even Class

```
package Even;
use overload
    '++' => "incr",
    '--' => "decr",
    '+0' => "numify",

sub new {
    my ($pkg, $num) = @_;
    croak("Even requires an even number to start with!") if $num % 2;
    return bless(\$num, $pkg);
}

sub incr {
    my $self = shift;
    $$self += 2;
    return $self;
}

sub decr {
    my $self = shift;
    $$self -= 2;
    return $self;
}

sub numify {
    my $self = shift;
    return $$self;
}

1;
```

This module also serves as a demonstration of an idea briefly discussed earlier: Objects need not be based on hashes but can be based on any reference. In this case objects in the Even class are implemented using a scalar as the underlying type. When new() creates a object, it simply blesses a reference to a scalar:

```
return bless(\$num, $pkg);
```

Then when object methods need access to the underlying scalar, they simply use a scalar dereference:

```
$$self -= 2;
```

Binary Operators

Most of the overloadable operators are binary operators. To implement a binary operator, you provide a method that takes three arguments. The first argument is always the overloaded object. The second is the other argument to the operator—it might be another object or a plain scalar. The third argument gives you information about the order of the arguments. When the third argument is true the arguments are in the same position as in the operation that generated the call; when it is false, the arguments are reversed.

Why do you need this third argument? Consider implementing subtraction. These lines will generate the same method call if $number is an object in a class that overloads subtraction with a method called subtract():

```perl
$result = $number - 7;    # actually $number->subtract(7, 0);
$result = 7 - $number;    # actually $number->subtract(7, 1);
```

By examining the third argument, the implementation for subtract can do the right thing:

```perl
sub subtract {
  my ($self, $other, $reversed) = @_;
  if ($reversed) {
    return $other - $$self;
  } else {
    return $$self - $other;
  }
}
```

Of course, this assumes that your module will obey the normal rules of arithmetic; it doesn't have to!

Your binary operators will need to be a little more complicated than the preceding simple example. Since the second argument to the operator could be a normal variable or another object, there needs to be logic to handle both cases. Also, a binary operator should function as a constructor so that the results of the operation are also members of the class. Here's an implementation of addition for the Even module that always produces even numbers, rounding up where necessary:

```perl
use overload '+' => "add";

sub add {
  my ($self, $other, $reversed) = @_;
  my $result;
```

```perl
    if (ref($other) and $other->isa('Even')) {
        # another Even object will always be even, so the addition
        # can always be done
        $result = $$self + $$other;
    } else {
        # make sure it's even
        $other += 1 if $other % 2;
        $result = $$self + $other;
    }

    # return a new object in the same class as $self
    return ref($self)->new($result);
}
```

This method will work with other objects that are either of the Even class or inherit from it. It also uses an inheritance-safe method for creating new objects by calling the new() method (implemented earlier in this section) on the result of calling ref() on the object. This means that the new() method will be called on whatever class $self belongs to, even if that's a child class of the class where add() is implemented.

Auto-Generation

As you can see from the preceding example, it takes a lot of work to write a safe overload method. Fortunately, it's usually not necessary to create methods for all the possible overloadable operations. This is because the overload module can *auto-generate* many overload methods from existing overloaded methods. Table 2-4 contains the rules for method auto-generation.

Table 2-4. Method Auto-Generation

Method(s)	Auto-Generation Description
Assignment forms of math operators	Can be auto-generated from the nonassignment forms (+= can be auto-generated from +, for example)
Conversion operators	Any conversion operator can be auto-generated from any other
++, --	Auto-generated from += and -=
abs()	Auto-generated from < and binary subtraction
Unary -	Auto-generated from subtraction
Negation	Auto-generated from Boolean conversion
Concatenation	Auto-generated from string conversion

Using method auto-generation generally requires that your module follow the normal rules of arithmetic. For example, if abs() is to be successfully generated by < and subtraction, your module will have to have fairly standard semantics.

You can provide your own auto-generation rules by overloading the special nomethod key. The method will receive four arguments—the normal three associated with binary operators (whether the called operator is binary or not), and a fourth argument containing the operator actually called.

Finally, you can turn off auto-generation altogether by setting the special overload key fallback to 0 (although nomethod will still be tried if it exists). Alternately you can set it to 1 to allow an unavailable overload method to be ignored— Perl will continue with whatever behavior it would have had if overloading had not been used at all. The default setting for fallback, undef, produces an error if an overloaded operation cannot be found.

Overloading "="—It's Not What You Think

Overloading = does not overload assignment. What overloading = does do is provide a copy constructor. For example, consider a class called Fraction that uses an array[17] of two elements to represent a fraction internally and provides all the normal overloaded math operators. Imagine it also provides an overloaded copy constructor with the copy() method. Here's an example showing how the copy constructor is used:

```
$x = Fraction->new(1, 2);  # create a new Fraction containing one half (1/2).

$y = $x;                    # assign the reference in $x to $y.  At this point
                            # both $x and $y reference the same object.

$x *= 4;                    # first implicitly calls the copy
                            # constructor: $x = $x->copy()
                            # then multiplies $x by 2 yielding 4/2

print "x = $x\n";           # prints x = 4/2
print "y = $y\n";           # prints y = 1/2
```

As you can see, the copy constructor is called implicitly before a mutating operator is used, *not* when the assignment operator is used. If Fraction did not provide an overloaded copy constructor, then this code would generate an error:

```
Operation '=': no method found, argument in overloaded package Fraction
```

---

17. It's important that this class be implemented using something other than a scalar because overload will actually auto-generate a copy constructor for scalars.

Implementing a copy constructor is usually a simple matter of pulling out the values needed for initialization and calling new() to create a new object. In this case the object stores the numerator and denominator in the first and second positions of the object array so the copy constructor is written as follows:

```
package Fraction;
use overload '=' => "copy";
sub copy {
  my $self = shift;
  return ref($self)->new($self->[0], $self->[1]);
}
```

The copy constructor is only activated for the mutating operators: ++, --, +=, and so on. If your object can have its value changed in other ways—through a method call or by a nonmutating operator, for example—then the user will need to call the copy constructor directly. In practice, this restriction makes the copy constructor suitable only for rather normal mathematical packages. If your module is playing outside the bounds of Perl's normal math, then it's probably not going to mesh well with an overloaded =.

Just to drive home the point that you're not overloading assignment, note that the copy constructor is never called if the object is the recipient of an assignment:

```
$object = 6;
```

After this assignment, $object contains the scalar "6" and is no longer a reference to an object, overloaded or not! If you really want to overload assignment, then what you need is a tied module. The next section will describe tied modules in all their glory.

Tied Modules

Tying enables a class to provide the implementation for a normal Perl variable. When a variable is tied to a class, all accesses to that variable are handled by methods in the class. This is similar to an overloaded class, but instead of returning a reference to a specially prepared object, tying enables a variable to be magically associated with a hidden object. This may sound complicated, but the implementation is quite simple—all the hard stuff is handled by Perl.

Tying Scalars

Sometimes a class is so simple that its entire interface can be represented by a tied scalar. For example, imagine that the BOA::Thermostat module implements an interface to a thermometer and a heater for the BOA spacecraft. If this class provided a tied scalar interface, then reads could correspond to checking the current temperature and writes could correspond to opening or closing the heating vents. Here's some example code that keeps compartment 10 of the spacecraft between 20 and 30 degrees:

```perl
use BOA::Thermostat;

# tie $thermo to temperator controls for compartment 10, the captain's quarters
tie $thermo, 'BOA::Thermostat', compartment => 10;

# enter infinite loop
while (1) {
   # check temperature
   if ($thermo <= 20) {      # too cool?
      $thermo = 1;           # open the vents
   } elsif ($thermo >= 30) { # too hot?
      $thermo = 0;           # close the vents
   }
   sleep(30);                # pause for 30 seconds
}
```

The code starts by using the BOA::Thermostat module. Next, a call to the `tie` function is made. This call tells Perl that the $thermo variable's implementation will be provided by the BOA::Thermostat class. Whenever the program accesses the $thermo variable, a method in the BOA::Thermostat class is called. The call also passes the compartment number to the BOA::Thermostat class using a named parameter style. The program then enters an infinite loop, checking the temperature and opening or closing the vents as appropriate.

This example highlights a key difference between tying and overloading—the ability to handle assignment. An overloaded class could not provide this interface because after the first assignment the $thermo variable would no longer contain a reference to an overloaded object. Tied variables provide *magic containers,* whereas overloaded objects provide *magic values* that can be assigned to variables. The difference is subtle but important to understand.

To implement a tied scalar class, you need to provide three methods—TIESCALAR(), FETCH(), and STORE(). The first, TIESCALAR(), is the constructor for the tied scalar class. It works just like the new() methods you've seen previously—it takes some parameters and returns a bless()'d reference. Here's a possible implementation for BOA::Thermostat::TIESCALAR():

```
package BOA::Thermostat;
sub TIESCALAR {
    my $pkg = shift;
    my $self = { @_ }; # retrieve named options into $self hash-ref

    # check for required 'compartment' option
    croak("Missing compartment number!") unless exists $self->{compartment};

    # the vent is initially closed
    $self->{vent_state} = 0;

    # bless $self and return
    return bless($self, $pkg);
}
```

This should look very familiar by now—it's just a simple variation on a normal constructor. The only difference is the name and the way it will be called—by tie() instead of directly. Notice that even though this code is emulating a scalar, there's no need to use a scalar underneath—the object itself is a hash in this example.

The remaining two methods are FETCH() and STORE(), which get called when the tied variable is read and written, respectively. Here's the FETCH() implementation for the BOA::Thermostat class:

```
# method called when scalar is read
sub FETCH {
    my $self = shift;
    return get_temp($self->{compartment});
}
```

FETCH() receives only the object as an argument and returns the results of calling the class method get_temp() with the compartment number as a parameter. This method will check the temperature in the given compartment and return it. I'll leave implementing this method as an exercise for budding rocket scientists in the audience.

The STORE() method is almost as simple:

```
# method called when scalar is written to
sub STORE {
   my ($self, $val) = @_;

   # return if the vent is already in the requested state
   return $val if $val == $self->{vent_state};

   # open or close vent
   if ($val) {
     open_vent($self->{compartment});
   } else {
     close_vent($self->{compartment});
   }

   # store and return current vent state
   return $self->{vent_state} = $val;
}
```

STORE() receives two arguments, the object and the new value. The code checks to see if it can return right away—if the vent is already in the requested position. It then calls the class methods close_vent() or open_vent() as necessary. Finally, it returns the set value. STORE() methods should return their new value so that chained assignment works as expected:

```
$foo = $thermo = 1;    # $foo == 1
```

It's possible to call object methods using a tied variable. There are two ways to get access to the underlying object. First, it's returned by tie(). Second, it can be retrieved from a tied variable using the tied() routine. For example, say you added a method to the BOA::Thermometer class called fan() to turn on and off a fan inside the vent. Client code could call this method as follows:

```
$thermo_obj = tie $thermo, 'BOA::Thermometer', compartment => 10;
$thermo_obj->fan(1);   # turn on the fan
```

This will also work:

```
tie $thermo, 'BOA::Thermometer', compartment => 10;
tied($thermo)->fan(1);   # turn on the fan
```

Using additional object methods, tied modules can provide enhanced functionality without giving up the simplicity of a tied variable interface.

Tying Hashes

By far the most commonly used tied interface is the tied hash. Hashes are so inherently flexible that they lend themselves well to representing an interface to a variety of data types. In fact, Perl's support for tied variables evolved from support for tying hashes to database files using dbmopen() into the general mechanism it is today.

One common use for tied hashes is to provide lazy computation and caching for some large dataset. For example, BOA::Network::DNS provides a tied hash interface for network name–to–IP mappings. Here's an example using the module:

```
use BOA::Network::DNS;

# tie hash to BOA::Network::DNS - provide nameserver as argument to constructor
tie %dns, 'BOA::Network::DNS', nameserver => '10.0.0.1';

# lookup IP address for www.perl.com
print "www.perl.com : ", $dns{'www.perl.com'} || "not found!", "\n";

# do a reverse lookup for the DNS server
print "The name for the DNS server is: ", $dns{'10.0.0.1'} || "not found!", "\n";
```

Obviously it would be impossible to prepopulate a hash with all the possible names and addresses on the Internet, but a tied hash allows you to pretend that you have. Also, as you'll see, the hash can very easily hold onto the results of past lookups to improve performance.

To implement a tied hash interface, you must provide eight methods— TIEHASH(), FETCH(), STORE(), DELETE(), EXISTS(), CLEAR(), FIRSTKEY(), and NEXTKEY(). Here's TIEHASH() the constructor:

```
package BOA::Network::DNS;
sub TIEHASH {
   my $pkg = shift;
   my $self = { @_ }; # retrieve named options into $self hash-ref

   # check for required 'nameserver' option
   croak("Missing nameserver address!") unless exists $self->{nameserver};

   # initialize cache to an empty hash
   $self->{cache} = {};

   # bless $self and return
   return bless($self, $pkg);
}
```

This should definitely look familiar by now—it's the same basic constructor pattern you've seen earlier in the chapter.

The rest of the methods are more interesting. FETCH() is similar to the methods in a tied scalar, but it receives an extra parameter—the key that's being requested. The implementation here is very simple:

```
# method called when an entry is read from the hash
sub FETCH {
   my ($self, $key) = @_;

   # check cache and return if found
   return $self->{cache}{$key} if exists $self->{cache}{$key};

   # make lookup using nameserver provided to TIEHASH
   my $result = _do_dns_lookup($self->{nameserver}, $key);

   # cache result and reverse mapping
   $self->{cache}{$key} = $result;
   $self->{cache}{$result} = $key;

   # return result
   return $result;
}
```

It's debatable whether BOA::Network::DNS should even provide a STORE() method—DNS entries are generally considered to be read-only! However, for the sake of completeness, let's provide one. STORE() takes two parameters, the key and the value to be set for that key:

```
# called when an entry is written to the hash
sub STORE {
   my ($self, $key, $value) = @_;

   # store the value in the cache, forward and reverse
   $self->{cache}{$key} = $value;
   $self->{cache}{$value} = $key;

   # return the value stored so that chained assignment works
   return $value;
}
```

Perl's hashes distinguish between an entry containing undef and an entry that doesn't exist at all. The defined() operator simply calls FETCH() on tied hashes, but exists() needs special support from the tied implementation in the form of EXISTS(). To complete the picture, DELETE() must be provided to remove a key from the hash, after which it is expected that EXISTS() will return false for that key. It is often difficult to decide what behavior to provide for these calls on a tied hash. In this case, you'd want to do the simple thing and just examine the underlying cache:

```perl
# method called when exists() is called on the hash
sub EXISTS {
    my ($self, $key) = @_;
    return exists $self->{cache}{$key};
}


# method called when delete() is called on the hash
sub DELETE {
    my ($self, $key) = @_;

    # delete both forward and reverse lookups if the key exists
    my $value;
    if (exists $self->{cache}{$key}) {
        $value = $self->{cache}{$key};
        delete $self->{cache}{$value};
        delete $self->{cache}{$key};
    }

    # return deleted value, just like the normal delete()
    return $value;
}
```

Perl provides a hook for a special case of delete() when the entire hash is being cleared. This is triggered by assigning an empty list to a hash:

```perl
%dns = ();
```

It's possible to implement this by looping over the keys and calling DELETE(), but there's usually a more efficient implementation. In this case you can just clear the cache:

```perl
sub CLEAR {
    my $self = shift;
    %{$self->{cache}} = ();
}
```

Finally, you must provide an iterator by implementing FIRSTKEY() and NEXTKEY().
The iterator functions are used when several Perl operators are called—keys(),
values(), and each(). The utility of allowing users to iterate over DNS lookups in
the cache is questionable, but here's a possible implementation:

```perl
sub FIRSTKEY {
  my $self = shift;

  # reset iterator for the cache
  scalar keys %{$self->{cache}};

  # return the first key from the cache
  return scalar each %{$self->{cache}};
}

sub NEXTKEY {
    my ($self, $lastkey) = @_;
    return scalar each %{$self->{cache}};
}
```

This implementation just proxies the call to each() on the underlying cache. As a
result, it doesn't use the second parameter to NEXTKEY()–the last key returned. This
can be useful if the underlying data store isn't a hash but rather something that
maintains an order.

Other Ties

In addition to scalars and hashes, you can also tie arrays and file handles. Once
you've grokked implementing tied scalars and hashes, it's just a matter of learning
the specific method names and interfaces. You can get this information from Perl's
documentation with the command perlpod perltie.

Tying and Overloading

You might imagine that you could combine tying and overloading to form the
ultimate magic Perl module. Unfortunately, due to a bug in the implementation of
overloading in the version of Perl I'm using (5.6.1) and older versions, this isn't
easily done. You can find the rather complicated details in the overload documentation, but suffice it to say that for the time being you should choose tying *or*
overloading, not both.

Read the Fine Manuals

Much of the information in this chapter is also available in the documentation that comes with Perl. As an added bonus, Perl's documentation will be kept up-to-date as Perl changes, so you might find information on features that don't even exist as I'm writing. Table 2-5 provides a list of documents in which you can expect to find more information about the areas I've covered.

Table 2-5. The Fine Manuals

Perldoc	Description
perlmod	Perl modules and packages
perlobj	Perl's object support explained
overload	Full documentation on overloading
perltie	Tying explained

Summary

This chapter has equipped you with the knowledge necessary to create modules in Perl. You've learned how to create both functional and object-oriented modules. Furthermore, you've been initiated into the magic art of tied and overloaded modules. In the next chapter, I'll show you how to take this technical knowledge and use it to create high-quality modules.

### CHAPTER 3

Module Design and Implementation

PROGRAMMING IS BOTH science and art. The last chapter equipped you with the science of modular programming in Perl—the syntax and behavior of modules. This chapter will present the other side—the art of designing and implementing modules.

Just by using modular programming you're ahead of the programming pack—the majority of working programmers spend their days desperately writing one-off scripts in a dialect of Perl akin to BASIC. That said, there are good modules and there are bad modules. This chapter will help you write modules that resemble the former more than the latter. I expect you to treat the advice given critically—the best design technique to use will depend on your aesthetics, and that's the last thing I want to dictate!

Ultimately, there's only one inviolate rule of software design: Do it. It's worth it. The satisfaction you gain from jumping into the fray with some impulse coding won't last when the first wave of bug reports and unexpected changes lands. I'll leave it to the management books to break out the charts and graphs; if you give it a try you'll soon convince yourself. Every moment of thought and planning you put into a project at the outset will be paid back in spades by the end. It's a rare task that's *really* so small that it's worth knocking off without consideration.

Check Your Slack

Before you start a new module, you should visit CPAN.[1] You may be able to avoid a lot of work (and thus gain a lot of slack) by reusing an existing module. If you need features that an existing module doesn't provide, consider extending the module. Object-oriented modules can usually be extended through inheritance. If you make changes to a CPAN module, consider contributing those changes back to the author.[2] Remember, one of the virtues of a Perl programmer is laziness; CPAN is the greatest enabler of programmer laziness since the terminal!

---

1. See Chapter 1 for copious instructions.
2. If you'll be distributing your module, then you may be required to release the source for any changes under the same license as the module. Be sure to read the license for the module *before* you start making modifications!

Size Matters

Many modules try to do too much. Instead of being useful tools, they're more like overflowing toolboxes. They're hard to learn, hard to implement, and painfully slow to load. Even if they provide undeniably useful services, their bulk limits their utility.

The best modules do one thing and do it well. As a result, they are easy to use and easy to implement. The trick is to break your problem down into pieces that are small enough to make good modules but no smaller. If you create too many small modules, you'll end up back in the spaghetti bowl where you started!

A good test for module complexity is to try to describe what the module does. If it takes more than a clause or two, then you've got something that's too complicated to be just one module. For example, "an interface to the Acme Products Database" would make a fine module. On the other hand, "an interface to the Acme Products Database that functions as its own Web server and accepts orders via CGI and e-mail" would not. Of course, it's possible to find a compact expression for an impossibly large module. For example, "a complete replacement for Linux" would not make a good Perl module! Although the description is simple, the scope of the module is vast.

The process of taking a system and breaking it down into component pieces is called *factoring*. It doesn't stop once you've decided to create a module. The next task is to break the functionality of your module down into subroutines (or methods in the case of an OO module) that will form the interface. At this point you might find that your module requires a large number of subroutines (or methods). This may be a sign that your module is trying to do too much.

Factoring may sound like a science, but in practice it is much closer to an art. It owes more to composition in the visual arts than it does to any particular engineering discipline. Over time you'll develop a taste in module size and shape that will guide you. Until then, keep it simple and don't be afraid to refactor when your modules grow!

Document First

The easiest way to make sure you've got a workable design is to start writing the documentation. If you can explain it in the docs, then there's a good chance you'll be able to code it. When you get stuck writing the documentation, there's a good chance you've discovered a flaw in your design. This is an excellent time to fix design flaws—there's no code to rewrite and very little effort wasted.

Plain Old Documentation

Perl provides a very simple code documentation system called **plain old docu-mentation**, or POD. POD allows you to place your documentation inline with your Perl code. POD can be translated into a number of formats—HTML, text, manual pages, PostScript, and more. The `perldoc` command that you've been using to read Perl documentation is a POD formatter that formats POD to be read on your screen.

The primary strength of POD is its ease of use. You only need to know a couple commands to get started. POD commands always begin with an equal sign (=) and must start at the beginning of a line. Here's a minimal example that documents the function `estimate()`:

```
=pod

($low, $high) = estimate($design_time, $loc)

This function computes an estimate for the amount of time required for
a project.  It takes two arguments - the amount of time spent on design in
hours and the expected number of lines of code.  The return value is a list
of two values, the lower and upper bounds on the time required in hours.

=cut
```

Everything between a `=pod` and a `=cut` is POD documentation. Perl knows to skip this stuff when it's compiling your module so you don't have to do any com-menting to have it ignored.

POD is a paragraph-oriented format. Paragraphs begin and end with blank lines. If the paragraph begins with white space, then it is considered a verbatim paragraph and no formatting is applied. This is useful for code examples where the spacing is important. The text in normal paragraphs will be automatically for-matted in a number of ways—the text will be wrapped and filled, plain quotes may be turned into smart quotes, and any embedded Perl identifiers will be made more visible. The actual details of the formatting are up to the individual formatter—what makes sense in HTML may not make sense in a man page.

Modules typically have at least five sections: NAME, SYNOPSIS, DESCRIPTION, AUTHOR, and SEE ALSO. The NAME section gives the module's name followed by a dash and a short description. The SYNOPSIS section shows some simple usages of the module. DESCRIPTION contains the bulk of the documentation, usually containing subsections for each function or method in the module. AUTHOR gives credit and contact information, and SEE ALSO contains references to external documents related to the module.

The best way to learn POD is by example—it's just too simple to be worth a lot of complicated explanation. Here's the start of some POD docs for BOA::Logger, the example module in the last chapter:

```
=pod

=head1 NAME

BOA::Logger - provides logging for the Big Ol' Application

=head1 SYNOPSIS

    my $logger = BOA::Logger->new("log_file");  # get new logger object
    $logger->level(10);                         # set log-level to 10
    $logger->write(1, "Hello log!");            # write a line at log-level 1

=head1 DESCRIPTION

BOA::Logger is an object-oriented class that provides access to a log file
with an associated log-level.  Users of the module create a new BOA::Logger
object with the new() method.  The level() method is used to set the log-level
and the write() method is used to write lines to the log file.

=head1 AUTHOR

Sam Tregar <sam@tregar.com>

=head1 SEE ALSO

L<BOA>

=cut
```

As you can see in this example, the =head1 command declares a top-level heading (=head2 is also available to create subheadings). Also notice the indenting for the code example in the SYNOPSIS section. This creates a verbatim paragraph—without the indenting the POD formatter would wreck the spacing and render the code unreadable. See Figure 3-1 for the output from running pod2html on the POD.

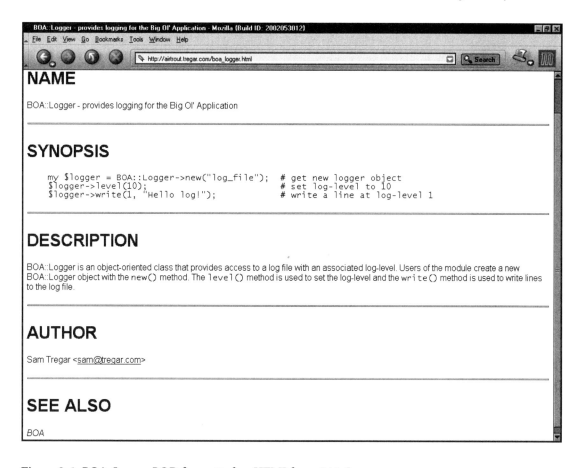

Figure 3-1. BOA::Logger POD formatted as HTML by `pod2html`

Inside normal paragraphs you can apply formatting to your text. POD formatting codes begin with a capital letter and the text to be formatted goes inside angle brackets. The formatting codes used purely for formatting are B<bold>, I<italic>, C<code-style>, and F<filename>. There are also codes for linking between documents (L<Pod::Parser> links to the Pod::Parser documentation), displaying special characters (for example, E<lt> for the less-than sign), and designating non-breaking space (S<text like this>).[3]

In general, it's best to avoid overusing the formatting codes. One of POD's best features is that it's generally readable even without a formatter; use too many of the code sequences, and that feature disappears.

---

3. There are some fairly complicated rules governing these nonformatting codes (linking in particular). When you're ready to start using them, you should read the perlpod documentation.

Indentation

You can indent a paragraph using the =over command and go back to the previous indentation using =back. The =over command takes a numeric argument that indicates how far to indent in characters, defaulting to 4. Here's a little indented paragraph:

```
=over
```

```
POD is so great that I need extra room to say it.
```

```
=back
```

Indenting is also used to layout lists. You start a list by indenting and then using the =item command for each list item. The argument to =item can be words, an asterisk to create a bulleted list, or numbers to create a numbered list. For example, here's a numbered list of some of my favorite things:

```
=head1 My Favorite Things
```

```
=over
```

```
=item 1
```

```
An ancient train stopped in a forest.
```

```
=item 2
```

```
Victor Hugo
```

```
=item 3
```

```
Watermelon Sugar
```

```
=back
```

Explicit Formatting

If you ever need to add some explicit formatting for a particular formatter, you can use =begin and =end. For example, to add an HTML table that will only show up when the POD is translated into HTML, do the following:

```
=begin html

<table>
    <tr><th>Name</th><th>Nickname</th></tr>
    <tr><td>Sam</td><td>Dave</td></tr>
</table>

=end html
```

You can add explicit formatting instructions for any POD formatter by using the appropriate format identifier. For example, to add special formatting for the pod2man formatter that translates POD into UNIX manual page format, you would use a =begin man command. These identifiers (html, man, and so on) are usually easy enough to guess, but you can also determine the identifier for a particular translator by reading its documentation.

That's all there is to it.[4] For the most part writing POD is no more difficult than writing comments—you rarely need to worry about formatting unless that sort of thing makes you happy. This is the key to its success; getting lazy programmers like us to write documentation is hard enough, so the format has to be as simple as possible.

Where to Start

Now that you have the tools for the job, you're ready to start designing your module. Start with a general description of what the module will do. Try to focus on *what* not *how* at this stage. Here's an example of a good description:

```
=head1 DESCRIPTION

This module will provide an interface to the BOA SETI satelite.  It
provides functions to send signals to distant star-systems as well as
functions to retrieve responses.
```

---

4. With some minor exceptions. See the perlpod documentation for the other 10 percent of POD that takes up 90 percent of the manual.

The reader is presented with a clear description of what the module is meant to do.

Here's an example of how *not* to describe the same module:

```
=head1 DESCRIPTION

This module will provide an interface to the BOA SETI satellite.  The
satellite communicates with the base station over a radio-IP link.  The
module uses a low-level UDP socket interface to communicate with the satellite
to maximize bandwidth utilization.  It also compresses larger packets with
Compress::Gzip for further saving.
```

This description also delivers useful information, but it leaves open the most important question—what does the module do? It can be tempting to jump directly into implementation details; after all, that's where the fun of programming is. However, even the most technically minded reader would be hard-pressed to figure out what BOA::SETI does from the preceding description.

Know Your Audience

Writing good documentation is a lot like any other kind of writing—to do a good job you need to think about your audience. Your primary audience at this stage is actually yourself. The best reason to start designing by writing documentation is to explain the module to yourself. You'll explore your design, find problems, and fill in the gaps long before the module is ever examined by anyone else. Later on when you return to the module, your documentation will help you remember how your module works.

Secondarily, think about the eventual users of the module, but be careful not to think only about the short term. In the near future the only user might be yourself or the guy in the next cubicle over who knows your brain like the back of his eyelids, but that won't last. Software frequently lives longer than you think it will. Your module should be designed to stand the test of time—make sure it has enough documentation to make its own introduction.

Make Your Case

Consider writing some documentation about why the module is being written. This may seem brutally obvious, but in many cases it's not. For example, if there is an existing CPAN module that provides similar functionality, you should explain why you're not using it. You might also use this as a chance to explain any design goals that might not be obvious from the module description. Such a section might look like this:

```
=head1 RATIONAL

The CPAN module Net::SETI seems on the surface to provide the same
functionality as BOA::SETI, but in actuality Net::SETI only works over a
TCP connection.  The BOA application requires greater performance than can
be achieved using TCP so the decision was made to implement our own module.
```

Writing down your rational for building the module forces you to critically examine your design choices before it's too late to reverse them. Also, your users will be less likely to reject your module if they understand why your wrote it in the first place. Any time you can spend convincing your fellow programmers to stop reinventing the wheel is time well spent!

Interface Design

Design a good interface, and everything else is negotiable. If your first pass at the implementation is flawed, no big deal; you improve it, and your users get a painless upgrade. Design a bad interface, and your module is doomed to use-lessness. It doesn't matter how fantastic your implementation is—no one can figure out how to use it and no one will.

This property of a module, that the internals may change without affecting users of the module, is known as *encapsulation*. Encapsulation is often associated with object-oriented programming, but any well-designed module can benefit from it. A module's interface is the barrier between users and the module's internals that allows for encapsulation.

Functions or Objects?

You might not have to think about this question—you might be an OO true believer. My introduction to the Church of Pure Objects came on my first day as a computer science student. The guy sitting next to me in CS201 greeted me with "Do you uphold the object model?" I thought for a moment and said "Ah, sometimes." His eyes narrowed. I was clearly the enemy.

Aside from fulfilling religious obligations, object-oriented modules do provide some benefits. If your module will need to maintain state between calls to the interface, then using objects might be a good idea. This was the case with the BOA::Logger example in the last chapter. Object-oriented modules are also easier to extend through the magic of inheritance, which sometimes allows OO modules to be reused in situations where a functional[5] module would be rewritten.

On the other hand, object-oriented code is usually more complicated than an equivalent functional implementation. Doing OO means dealing with references and occasionally thinking about difficult topics like garbage collection and inheritance. Sometimes a module is more naturally expressed as a set of functions that can be exported into the caller's namespace. One easy test for this is to ask yourself if more than one object will ever be created by this module in a typical usage. If the answer is no, then chances are you don't really need to go the OO route.

Regardless of which way you choose to go, you should read through both of following sections. The dividing line between a functional interface and an object-oriented one is exceptionally blurry in Perl. Topics in functional programming like parameter passing and subroutine naming have parallels in object-oriented programming. Conversely, object-oriented programming techniques like inheritance can be useful in functional programming. Ultimately Perl makes little distinction between functional and object-oriented modules; both are built on the same underlying technology—packages and subroutines.

Functional Interfaces

A functional interface is defined by the subroutines it provides and the ways in which users can access them. Designing a functional interface is similar to designing a small programming language. The subroutines you provide form a grammar that is used to write programs in your module's domain. If you design a powerful and flexible grammar, then your users will be able to write powerful and flexible programs.

Subroutine Naming

In general, subroutines should be named with an action verb and, optionally, a noun[6]—for example, `print_form()`, `connect()`, `find_cities()`, and `complain()`. This allows the arguments to be treated as subjects and direct objects of the activity

---

5. No need to send me angry e-mail—I know this isn't the best usage of "functional." I'm actually a big fan of LISP, so I know about the *real* functional programming. See Inline::Guile on CPAN for proof. Here I'm using the word as the opposite of object-oriented in terms of Perl module design.

6. For object-oriented methods, the noun is usually unnecessary—a well-named object does the trick. For example, `$logger->print_log()` has no advantages over `$logger->print()`.

expressed by the subroutine. For example, `connect($server_address)` is much easier to understand than `socket($server_address)`. Avoid ambiguous verbs like "process" and "handle."

An exception to the this rule are functions whose sole purpose is to return a particular value. In this case, dispensing with the superfluous "get" or "return" verbs is preferable. That is, `next_id()` is better than `get_next_id()`.

Try to use full words and avoid abbreviation. Some developers are under the impression that removing vowels from their subroutine (and module) names—for example `snd_cmd()` rather than `send_command()`–will enhance their usability. The time you spend typing the full name will be more than repaid by the time your users save remembering the name!

Capitalization is certainly a fruitful subject for flame wars, but there seems to be a rough consensus in the Perl community. Normal subroutines are all lowercase and multiple words are joined with underscores (for example, `encode_html()`). Constants and package variables are in all caps (such as `FORBIDDEN` and `$DEBUG`). Private subroutines are preceded by an underscore (such as `_parse()`). Consider carefully before violating these expectations.

Above all, be consistent. If you're determined to use innerCaps,[7] then at least do so consistently. It's far too easy to forget something like `printData_filter()` and instead type `print_data_filter()` or `printDataFilter()`.

Take advantage of conventions wherever you can—they reduce the time it takes a new user to learn to use your module. For example, if a subroutine prints to a file, consider using "print" or "write" in the name rather than inventing your own terms. You might also be able to follow the example of an existing module. If you're writing a CGI module that handles parameters, you might consider implementing a `param()` function that works like the CGI module's `param()`.

Subroutine Documentation

As you plan your interface, you should document each subroutine you plan to write. The documentation for a subroutine should specify possible arguments and return values. If the subroutine will make assumptions about its arguments, then these should be stated. Just like the module description, a subroutine description should focus on *what* and not *how*. Here's a good example of a well-documented subroutine:

---

7. aka StudlyCaps

```
=over

=item @msgs  = check_mail($imap_server, $username, $password)

=item @msgs  = check_mail($imap_server, $username, $password, $mailbox)

This routine checks for new mail on a IMAP server.  It takes three required
arguments - the server address (name or IP), the user name and the
password.  The fourth, optional, argument is the mailbox name,
which will default to "INBOX" if not set.  If an error is encountered -1 is
returned and an error message is printed to STDERR.  If successful, a list of
new message IDs is returned that can be used with retrieve_mail().  An empty
list indicates no new messages.

=back
```

Notice that an example is given for each possible call to the function—both with the optional $mailbox argument and without. This is a common convention that is worth following. Another possibility is to place the optional argument in square brackets (for example, [$mailbox]), but that risks confusion with a reference to an array containing the argument.

One common problem with subroutine documentation is ambiguous language. For example, "the subroutine *may* return undef on failure." The reader is left wondering what else it might do on failure. There are two crucial pieces of information that a user needs—how to check for an error and how to determine what the error was. Certainly there's more than one way to do it—just make sure you document which one you choose!

Parameter Passing

Simple subroutines are best served by simple interfaces. If you have only a couple parameters, then there's no good reason to do anything more complicated than take them directly from @_. However, when designing a subroutine that will take more parameters, you should consider using a named-parameter style. Here's a call to the check_mail() subroutine described earlier, redesigned to use a named-parameter style:

```
check_mail(imap_server => $imap_server,
           username     => $username,
           password     => $password);
```

Implementing a named-parameter subroutine is easy. Here's one way to do it:

```
sub check_mail {
    croak("Odd number of parameters to check_mail!") if @_ % 2;
    my %params = @_;
    # ... rest of sub uses %params to access parameters
}
```

The first line checks to make sure you have an even number of parameters. If you omit this test, then the next line will cause a confusing error if a user calls the routine with an odd number of parameters.

An alternate way to implement a named-parameter style subroutine is to require the calling code to pass a reference to a hash as a single parameter. If this were done with check_mail(), then the call would look like this:

```
check_mail({imap_sever => $imap_server,
            username    => $username,
            password    => $password});
```

As a result, the implementation of the subroutine changes a bit:

```
sub check_mail {
    croak("Bad call to check_mail - expected a single hash ref!")
      unless @_ == 1 and ref $_[0] eq "HASH";
    my $params = shift;
    # ... rest of sub uses %$params to access parameters
}
```

Which method you choose is largely a matter of taste.

One of the main benefits of using a named-parameter style, aside from the ease of use, is in extensibility. For example, let's imagine you need to add a couple new optional parameters to the previously documented check_mail()—$timeout and $retries. Since they're optional, they'll have some reasonable default if not specified. That makes a call using positional parameters look like the following:

```
check_mail($imap_server, $username, $password, $mailbox, $timeout, $retries);
```

The problem is that if you only want to specify one of the optional parameters, then you'll need to pad the preceding parameters with undefs. For example, to specify a number of retries but leave the other optional parameters alone, an ugly call is required:

```
check_mail($imap_server, $username, $password, undef, undef, $retries);
```

Add a few more optional parameters, and pretty soon the average call is using more undefs than values!

Contrast this to the call with named parameters:

```
check_mail(imap_sever => $imap_server,
           username   => $username,
           password   => $password,
           retries    => 3);
```

Named-parameter subroutines will automatically treat missing keys as undef so there's no need to put them in just for padding.

Return Values

If you need to return multiple values, return a list or a reference to an array. Avoid the tendency to slip into C mode and make your users pass in output parameters by reference. For example, the hobnob() subroutine sends a message to the BOA satellite and retrieves a response. It has two values to return—a status flag indicating success or failure and the received message. In C mode, it might look like the following:

```
sub hobnob {
    my ($message, $reply_ref) = @_;
    my $status = _send_message($message);
    $$reply_ref = _get_message();
    return $status;
}
```

It would be called like this:

```
$reply = "";
$status = hobnob("Hello out there!", \$reply);
```

The $reply variable is passed by reference and the retrieved message is filled in.

A simpler and more Perl-ish way to do the same thing is to simply return a list of two values:

```
sub hobnob {
    my ($message) = @_;
    my $status = _send_message($message);
    my $reply = _get_message();
    return ($status, $reply);
}
```

Now the subroutine can be called like this:

```
($status, $reply) = hobnob("Hello out there!");
```

This style makes it obvious that both $status and $reply are values returned by the subroutine.

Consider allowing your routines to behave differently in list and scalar context using the wantarray() built-in. It's much easier to use a subroutine that knows to return a count of its results in scalar context than to have to assign the results to an array and take its length. This also allows you to mimic the way many Perl built-ins use context to determine their behavior (such as localtime and split). Here's a subroutine that returns all the values currently in a message queue in list context and the number of messages in scalar context:

```
sub get_messages {
   if (wantarray) {
     return @MESSAGES;            # return all the messages in list context
   } else {
     return $MESSAGE_COUNT;       # return the message count in scalar context
   }
}
```

Using the Exporter

Many functional modules will use the Exporter to make their subroutines available in the user's package. This is very convenient, but doing it in the simplistic way presented in the last chapter has some drawbacks. To refresh your memory, the simplest way to use the Exporter is to export everything by default:

```
package BOA::Network;
require Exporter;
@ISA = qw(Exporter);
@EXPORT = qw(open_socket
             send_message
             receive_message
             close_socket
             start_server
             stop_server);
```

With this setup it's possible to selectively import just the symbols you need:

```
use BOA::Network qw(open_socket send_message close_socket);
```

But most users of the module will take the path of least resistance and import everything:

```
use BOA::Network;  # imports everything in @BOA::Network::EXPORT
```

The practice of exporting everything by default is known as *namespace pollution* and it has a justifiably bad name for a number of reasons. If a group of modules are all exporting symbols by default, there's a good chance some of the symbols will conflict. Even worse, upgrading a module that exports everything by default can suddenly cause client code to fail by exporting a new symbol that causes a conflict.

Exporting everything by default also makes deciphering code more difficult. For example, imagine you've been given the task of debugging this code:

```
use Some::Module;
use Some::Other::Module;
use Yet::Another::Module;
some_call('...');
```

If you're trying to figure out why some_call() is failing, you'll first have to search through each used module to determine where some_call() is being imported from. Contrast that to this case:

```
use Some::Module qw(some_call some_other_call);
use Some::Other::Module qw(foo bar);
use Yet::Another::Module qw(BIF BAZ);
some_call('...');
```

Now it's immediately obvious that some_call() is being imported from Some::Module.

Fortunately the Exporter comes equipped with an alternative to @EXPORT that can be used to enforce the preferred explicit importing. Just change @EXPORT to @EXPORT_OK and modules will have to declare their imports explicitly. For example, if BOA::Network is changed to use @EXPORT_OK as follows:

```
package BOA::Network;
require Exporter;
@ISA = qw(Exporter);
@EXPORT_OK = qw(open_socket
                send_message
                receive_message
                close_socket
                start_server
                stop_server);
```

then client code will have to list their imports explicitly. Using a module that exports with @EXPORT_OK won't trigger any unwanted namespace pollution.

The Exporter also supports a more advanced mechanism for managing your exported symbols: tags. By setting up export tags, you create shortcuts to importing a group of symbols. This is particularly helpful for large modules with many symbols to export. For example, here's a version of BOA::Network that sets up three tags— all, client, and server:

```perl
package BOA::Network;
require Exporter;
@ISA = qw(Exporter);
@EXPORT_OK = qw(open_socket
                send_message
                receive_message
                close_socket
                start_server
                stop_server);
%EXPORT_TAGS = (
                all    => [ @EXPORT_OK ],
                client => [ qw(open_socket
                               send_message
                               close_socket) ],
                server => [ qw(start_server
                               receive_message
                               stop_server) ],
               );
```

Now a user of the module can use a tag when they use BOA::Network and automatically pull in a set of symbols:

```perl
use BOA::Network qw(:client);
```

It's worth noting that using %EXPORT_TAGS has many of the same problems that using @EXPORT does. Debugging is just as difficult without an obvious source for each symbol, and an upgrade that adds a symbol to an existing tag can cause unexpected collisions. As a general rule, you should use @EXPORT_OK whenever you can and only resort to %EXPORT_TAGS for truly large modules.

Object-Oriented Interfaces

Object-oriented design is a large topic with many encyclopedic tomes dedicated to it. This section will give you an introduction to some of the more useful techniques that you can use to improve your OO module design.

Inheritance or Composition

Determining when and how to use inheritance is perhaps the hardest job in object-oriented interface design. Inheritance is a powerful tool—it can open up new avenues of extensibility for your users and allow you to reduce code size by exploiting polymorphism. On the other hand, inheritance can serve to greatly increase the complexity of otherwise simple designs.

The classic rule is deceptively simple—inheritance relationships should be used when classes exhibit an "is a" relationship. This is easy to demonstrate using real-world classes, Shape and Square being the usual examples. Since an object of the Square class "is a" Shape, inheritance is the right choice. Shape will naturally provide an area() method, and Square can inherit from Shape and provide an implementation of area() that uses Square's height and width attributes.

However, in the real world things tend to be a less clear-cut. Often there's no independent standard to judge whether an "is a" relationship applies. Does your brand new CGI::MailForm class enjoy an "is a" relationship with the CGI module? That's hard to know—it could or maybe it just "has a" CGI object. The latter possibility is known as *composition,* and the classic rule is that the classes in question should share a "has a" relationship.

The principal difference between inheritance and composition is the degree of coupling between the classes involved. Using inheritance, the objects *are* the same—they share the same underlying data structure. As a practical matter, this means that the child class needs to know intimate details about the implementation of the parent class: Does it use a hash underneath, what convention can be used to stake out a private namespace within the object, and so on. If the parent class changes its implementation, it could break child classes.

Composition, on the other hand, is a loose coupling. The two classes remain distinct, and their objects do not share the same underlying data structure. This loose coupling can also be exposed to the user by allowing the user to initialize the contained object directly. This is a powerful technique since it lets users access methods in the contained object without requiring an inheritance relationship. That said, composition usually requires more code to implement.

Classes using composition can approximate some of the advantages of inheritance by *proxying* calls to contained objects. This means that the class sets up a method that passes calls through to an equivalent method of a contained object.

In this example, the CGI::MailForm class proxies calls to the param() method in the contained CGI object:

```
package CGI::MailForm;
use CGI;

# basic constructor
sub new {
  my $pkg = shift;
  my $self = { query => CGI->new() };
  bless($self, $pkg);
}

# the proxying param method
sub param {
  my $self = shift;
  return $self->{query}->param(@_);
}


1;
```

Contrast this with an implementation using inheritance:

```
package CGI::MailForm;
use CGI;
@ISA = qw(CGI);
```

In both cases users of the module can use the param() method:

```
my $mailForm = CGI::MailForm->new();
$mailForm->param(foo => 'bar');
```

Composition also has the advantage of scaling better than inheritance. An object that contains five other objects of various types is no harder to write than one that contains one object. In contrast, doing five-way multiple inheritance is probably grounds for commission to a mental facility.

If you are going to use inheritance, keep it simple. Having worked on a Perl project with an inheritance hierarchy over six levels deep, I can safely state that here be dragons . Deep inheritance hierarchies make understanding the behavior of a particular class very difficult—either documentation is repeated at each level, or readers must perform a tedious search process up the inheritance tree to find the method they're looking for.

Even if you don't use inheritance in your module, you should be ready for it. You should design your module with the expectation that some users will use it as a parent class for their creations. At the very least, this means using the two-argument form of bless() and using isa() to check the type of objects rather than ref(). Better yet, document your private methods and object layout so that subclasses can avoid breaking the rules.

Designing a Method

Methods in Perl are subroutines, so all the advice about subroutine design and construction in the section on functional modules applies here. Of course, methods aren't *just* subroutines; depending on your outlook, they might be messages passed to the object, actions performed by the object, or actions performed on the object. Nailing your metaphors is the key to designing powerful methods. Be consistent and be explicit about your choices in your documentation.

Consider, as an example, an object-oriented implementation of the check_mail() function presented previously. To refresh your memory, this function is called as follows:

```
check_mail(imap_sever => $imap_server,
           username   => $username,
           password   => $password,
           retries    => 3);
```

One possible object-oriented approach to this functionality would encapsulate the parameters in attributes of a mail-checking object. For example:

```
my $checker = MailChecker->new();     # create a new MailChecker object
$checker->imap_server($imap_server); # set up attributes
$checker->username($username);
$checker->password($password);
$checker->retries(3);
$checker->check();                    # check mail
```

This design has a few problems. First, what happens if you call check() before calling imap_server()? Second, this system is considerably more verbose than the functional example. To solve these problems, the constructor should be written to take attributes as parameters:

```
my $checker = MailChecker->new(imap_sever => $imap_server,
                              username   => $username,
                              password   => $password);
$checker->check();
```

Now new() can be written to require the parameters that don't have sensible defaults. This demonstrates an important goal of OO design—your classes should make it impossible to put an object in an "illegal" state that can only cause problems later.

Method Documentation

Methods need much the same documentation as normal subroutines—return values, parameters, and error handling all need coverage. However, method documentation also needs to cover how the method affects the object it is called on. If a method has side effects on the object, then these need to be spelled out. For example, BOA::Network's send() method keeps statistics about how many bytes have been written and network speed. The documentation for this method would look like this:

```
=over 4

=item $success = $net->send($msg)

The send() method sends $msg along the network connection.  Returns true if
the send succeeded, false if the send failed.  Error details can be
retrieved using the error() method after a failure occurs.  This method
updates the read_bytes and kps attributes.

=back
```

If a method has no effect on the object, then this should be documented too. Methods that do not effect the state of the object are called *constant methods* in the OO texts. Perl doesn't have any syntax for enforcing constant methods, but documenting them can give your users valuable information.

Accessor-Mutators

Accessor-mutators are the bread and butter of object-oriented programming. The ability to examine and change the state of an object is the most basic service that a class can provide. In the last chapter I demonstrated how to provide accessor-mutators by writing a method for each attribute. When the method has no parameters, it returns the value of the attribute; with one parameter, it sets the value of the attribute.

It doesn't take long before writing accessor-mutator methods gets old. Every one is essentially the same. Fortunately, there are a number of better ways to choose from!

Auto-Rolling Your Own

The basic problem is simple—you have a number of subroutines to generate, and they all do the same thing on different data. Fortunately, Perl is a highly dynamic language, and it's easy to generate new subroutines at runtime. Here's an example that creates a simple accessor-mutator for a set of attributes stored in the package variable @ATTRIBUTES:

```
package BOA::Logger;

# initialize array of attribute names
@ATTRIBUTES = qw(filename level format);

# create a subroutine for each attribute
foreach my $attribute (@ATTRIBUTES) {
    *$attribute = sub {
        my $self = shift;
        $self->{$attribute} = shift if @_;
        return $self->{$attribute};
    }
}
```

This block of code works by assigning a closure to a symbol-table entry with the same name as the attribute. After this code runs, there will be three new methods available in the BOA::Logger package—filename(), level(), and format(). If you needed to add a new attribute to the package, it would be a simple matter of adding it to @ATTRIBUTES.

Another way to accomplish the same effect is to use AUTOLOAD(). When you call a method on an object that doesn't exist in the object's class or any parent classes, Perl looks to see if the class has a method in it called AUTOLOAD(). If not, Perl will traverse the inheritance hierarchy the same way it does when looking for normal methods. When Perl finds a suitable AUTOLOAD() method, the package global $AUTOLOAD is set to the full name of the method being called, and AUTOLOAD() is called.

Here's an example of creating accessor-mutators on demand using AUTOLOAD():

```perl
package BOA::Logger;
use Carp;

# initialize hash of attribute names
%ATTRIBUTES = map { $_ => 1 } qw(filename level format);

sub AUTOLOAD {
  return if $AUTOLOAD =~ /DESTROY$/;    # skip calls to DESTROY()
  my ($name) = $AUTOLOAD =~ /([^:]+)$/; # extract method name

  # check that this is a valid accessor call
  croak("Unknown method '$AUTOLOAD' called ") unless $ATTRIBUTES{$name};

  # create the accessor-mutator and install it as &$name
  *$name = sub {
    my $self = shift;
    $self->{$name} = shift if @_;
    return $self->{$name};
  };

  goto &$name;  # jump to the new method with the magic goto(&) call
}
```

This code is more complicated than just creating all the accessors upfront, but if you have many attributes that are rarely called, it might be more efficient. Notice that AUTOLOAD() will only be called on the first call to each accessor; after that the newly created subroutine is installed and will be called directly. You might be tempted to skip this step and simply do the access directly in the AUTOLOAD() method, but this will slow your module significantly since Perl will spend time checking for the missing method every time the accessor is called.

Either of the preceding options is a clean way of auto-generating methods.[8] However, they require you to do some unnecessary work, which no doubt offends your instincts as a Perl programmer. It's unnecessary because there are two excellent modules—Class::Struct and Class::MethodMaker—that use similar techniques but provide a much more convenient interface. As a bonus, they also handle writing those repetitive constructors too!

---

8. And efficient too—all the generated closures share the same compiled code.

Using Class::Struct

Class::Struct[9] exports a single subroutine, struct(), that allows you to build a class skeleton with a single subroutine call. You pass the struct() routine information about your attributes, and it generates and compiles the code for your new class, including a constructor called new() and an accessor-mutator for each attribute. For example, say you're building a class to manage the scientific probes aboard the BOA spacecraft. The BOA::Probe class has a number of attributes that describe an individual probe. Here's what the class file looks like using Class::Struct:

```
package BOA::Probe;
use Class::Struct;

# create accessors and constructor
struct(id       => '$',
       model    => '$',
       contents => '$',
       heading  => '$',
       status   => '$');
```

The struct() call takes a list of key-value pairs that describe the names of attributes and their types. The preceding class uses the "$" type, which indicates it is scalar. This provides the interface you're familiar with—the accessor-mutator created takes zero or one argument and gets or sets its value. After calling struct(), six new methods are created—one for each of the attributes and a new() method. This new() takes a list of key-value pairs to initialize the contents of the object. Here's an example of how to use the new class:

```
# create a new probe
my $probe = BOA::Probe->new(id => 10503, model => "BOA Mark 10");

# modify heading and status
$probe->heading([10, 20, 100, 50]);  # heading at (10,20,100) with at 50 kph
$probe->status("moving");
```

Class::Struct supports more than just scalar attributes. You can specify that an attribute will hold an array, a hash, or an object of a specific class. This may seem unnecessary—the scalar attributes can already hold a reference to any of these types—but declaring these type allows Class::Struct to generate more powerful

---

9. Written by Jim Miner, based on Class::Template by Dean Roehrich. The module is included with Perl.

accessors. For example, the preceding code uses the heading attribute to hold a reference to an array. Declaring it as an array creates a more powerful accessor:

```
package BOA::Probe;
use Class::Struct;

# create accessors and constructor
struct(id       => '$',
       model    => '$',
       contents => '$',
       heading  => '@',
       status   => '$');
```

Now the accessor can accept zero, one, or two parameters. With no parameters, it still returns a reference to the array. One parameter is treated as an index into the array, and the value is returned. With two parameters, the first is an index and the second is the value to be set. So, to reproduce the usage example shown previously, the code would now be as follows:

```
# heading at (10,20,100) at 50 kph
$probe->heading(0, 10);
$probe->heading(1, 20);
$probe->heading(2, 100);
$probe->heading(3, 50);
```

The result is that loading an array attribute with values becomes more verbose, but accessing a single index is simpler. For example, compare these two expressions to access the fourth element in the array—the speed of the probe:

```
${$probe->heading()}[3];  # access when heading is a scalar attribute
$probe->heading(3);       # access when heading is an array attribute
```

The difference is even more pronounced if you change heading to be a hash attribute with the keys "x", "y", "z", and "speed". Here's the call to struct:

```
struct(id       => '$',
       model    => '$',
       contents => '$',
       heading  => '%',
       status   => '$');
```

Now to set values in the hash, a two-argument form of the accessor is used:

```
# heading at (10,20,100) at 50 kph
$probe->heading(x     => 10);
$probe->heading(y     => 20);
$probe->heading(z     => 100);
$probe->heading(speed => 50);
```

There are some limitations to using Class::Struct. First, it can't be used to create child classes. Class::Struct goes to some truly amazing lengths to prevent this.[10] Second, if you need to do anything interesting when the constructor gets called, you'll need to write your own new().

Using Class::MethodMaker

When Class::Struct isn't enough, Class::MethodMaker[11] comes to the rescue. Class::MethodMaker supports all the same functionality as Class::Struct and a whole lot more. Class::MethodMaker can generate a wide variety of accessors that cover not only object methods, but also useful class methods. I'll cover the basic functionality, but you'll need to read the module documentation to discover the more esoteric bits. There's a *lot* in there!

Class::MethodMaker differs from Class::Struct in that you don't just tell it what kind of data you'll be storing in your attributes; you also get to pick what kind of accessor to provide. This also applies to the constructor, which Class::Struct doesn't even let you name! Here's an example of using Class::MethodMaker to generate some simple scalar accessor-mutators and a constructor called new():

```
package BOA::Probe;
use Class::MethodMaker
    new     => 'new',
    get_set => [ qw(id model contents heading status) ];
```

Class::MethodMaker works by taking arguments to the use statement in key-value pairs. The key is a method in the Class::MethodMaker module, and the value is either a single string or a reference to an array of strings. These strings are the names of the methods to be created. After the preceding call, the eleven methods are created—two for each of the five attributes given for the get_set key and new().

The two methods created for each get_set attribute are a normal accessor-mutator for the attribute and a method to clear the attribute called clear_id(),

---

10. Class::Struct ties your @ISA to a private class that croaks on STORE()! How rude.

11. Available on CPAN. Class::MethodMaker was written by Peter Seibel and is being refurbished and maintained by Martyn J. Pierce.

clear_model(), and so on. This extra method is unnecessary, since you can always call $obj->id(undef) to clear the value of an attribute. Fortunately, Class::MethodMaker is highly configurable. Here's a few variations on the default get_set:

```
package BOA::Probe;
use Class::MethodMaker
    new     => 'new',
    get_set => 'id',                    # creates id() and clear_id()
    get_set => [ -noclear => 'model' ], # creates just model() ala Class::Struct
    get_set => [ -java =>[("Contents",  # creates getContents() and setContents()
                          "Heading")]   # creates getHeading() and setHeading()
            ];
```

You can also design your own get_set method templates, but I won't go into the syntax here. Suffice it to say that if you have an accessor-mutator scheme in mind, Class::MethodMaker can save you the trouble of coding it.

Similar flexibility is available for the generated constructor. When using Class::Struct, doing anything at all during object creation requires you to replace the generated new() method. Class::MethodMaker has a more elegant solution:

```
package BOA::Probe;
use Class::MethodMaker
    new_with_init => 'new',
    get_set       => [ qw(id model contents heading status) ];

# called from the generated new()
sub init {
    my $self = shift;
    croak("Required id parameter missing!") unless @_;
    $self->id(shift);
    return $self;
}
```

Using new_with_init creates a constructor that calls init() in your module. You receive as arguments the arguments passed to new(). One thing you might want to do with init() is take a list of key-value pairs and assign their values to the named attributes. With Class::MethodMaker you can actually auto-generate a constructor that does this too:

```
package BOA::Probe;
use Class::MethodMaker
    new_hash_init => 'new',
    get_set       => [ qw(id model contents heading status) ];
```

Or if you need a call to your own init() *and* want to accept an initializer hash, you could implement the following:

```
package BOA::Probe;
use Class::MethodMaker
    new_with_init => 'new',
    new_hash_init => 'hash_init',
    get_set        => [ qw(id model contents heading status) ];

# called from the generated new()
sub init {
  my $self = shift;
  $self->hash_init(@_);
  # do other initialization stuff...
}
```

The method generated by new_hash_init is specially designed to be called as both a class method and an object method. Isn't that cool?

Class::MethodMaker sports some truly comprehensive support for list and hash attributes, generating common class methods as well as many useful variations on the normal accessor-mutators. To top it all off, Class::MethodMaker can itself be extended using inheritance. For this and more, see the Class::MethodMaker documentation.

Visual Modeling

Complex object-oriented systems are often easier to design visually than textually. The Unified Modeling Language (UML)[12] specifies a popular notation for doing visual design of object-oriented systems. There are numerous tools available to aid in the task from simple drawing applications to complex software design tools that generate code (although they rarely support Perl).

However, in my experience, these tools are usually unnecessary. Visual modeling done on a whiteboard or on paper is just as valuable as that done on a computer. Seeing your design laid out visually can help clarify your thinking and reveal dangerous complexity problems that aren't apparent from your documentation. The key to using visual modeling successfully is to keep it simple; don't get caught up in trying to represent the entirety of a working system in a diagram.

Figure 3-2 shows a simple UML class diagram of a few of the BOA classes I've used as examples earlier. The diagram shows three classes—BOA::Logger, BOA::Logger::Enhanced, and BOA::Network. The items in the top half of the class

---

12. See http://www.uml.org for details.

boxes are the attributes of the class. Under that are the methods, with the class methods underlined. The diagram uses the open arrow to show inheritance between BOA::Logger::Enhanced and BOA::Logger. The dashed arrow from BOA::Network to BOA::Logger::Enhanced says that BOA::Network uses BOA::Logger::Enhanced.

Figure 3-2. UML class diagram example

If this small introduction piques your interest, I suggest you invest in a good book on the UML[13] and give it a try on your next project.

---

13. There are many to choose from, but I've found *The Unified Modeling Language User Guide* by Booch, Rumbaugh, and Jacobson (Addison-Wesley) to be readable and engaging.

Summary

Software design is a slippery subject—doing it well relies as much on aesthetic sense as it does on technical ability. Hopefully this chapter has given you some new ideas and techniques that you can use to design and build high-quality Perl modules. The next chapter will take you into the heart of the topic—creating a module distribution for CPAN.

### CHAPTER 4

CPAN Module Distributions

A CPAN MODULE IS released into an unpredictable environment. Nothing is certain—operating system, version of Perl, and the availability of other modules will vary from user to user. To combat this variability, CPAN modules come packaged in *module distributions*. A module distribution includes all the files necessary to build, test, and install your module.

The portability of module distributions is at the core of what makes CPAN so extraordinarily successful. Many languages have repositories containing freely available code modules. But only Perl's has the capability to automatically install these modules on every supported platform with no appreciable work required on the user's part. This chapter will show you how your modules can be packaged to take full advantage of this remarkable capability.

Chapter 1 included examples of installing modules from module distributions; in this chapter, I'll briefly expand on how CPAN module installation works. Then I'll explain how to build them. Along the way, I'll also describe refinements in constructing the module itself for maximum portability.

Module Installation

Modules are installed from module distributions using a few simple steps. The CPAN module automates these steps, but let's look at how they work manually. I'll be demonstrating this process on a UNIX system (Redhat Linux to be precise), but with the proper tools listed in Chapter 1 installed, the examples should work on Windows too.

First, you download and uncompress the module. For example, I use lwp-download[1] to download the Memoize[2] module from CPAN:

```
$ lwp-download http://www.cpan.org/authors/id/M/MJ/MJD/Memoize-1.00.tar.gz
Saving to 'Memoize-1.00.tar.gz'...
46.2 KB received in 1 seconds (46.2 KB/sec)
```

---

1. lwp-download is installed with the LWP module by Gisle Aas.
2. Written by Mark-Jason Dominus

Then you decompress the module distribution. For example, I decompress Memoize with Gnu `tar`:

```
$ tar zxf Memoize-1.00.tar.gz
```

Then I enter the directory created:

```
$ cd Memoize-1.00
```

To build the `Makefile`, I run the Perl script `Makefile.PL`. This script examines my system and builds a `Makefile` appropriate for my system:

```
$ perl Makefile.PL
Checking if your kit is complete...
Looks good
Writing Makefile for Memoize
```

Using the `Makefile` just created, I build the module. The `make` command follows the instructions in the `Makefile`. It copies the Perl modules into a staging area called `blib` that's used to assemble the module before installation. It also builds manual pages from POD source.

```
$ make
cp Memoize.pm blib/lib/Memoize.pm
cp Memoize/ExpireTest.pm blib/lib/Memoize/ExpireTest.pm
cp Memoize/Saves.pm blib/lib/Memoize/Saves.pm
cp Memoize/Expire.pm blib/lib/Memoize/Expire.pm
cp Memoize/AnyDBM_File.pm blib/lib/Memoize/AnyDBM_File.pm
cp Memoize/Storable.pm blib/lib/Memoize/Storable.pm
cp Memoize/SDBM_File.pm blib/lib/Memoize/SDBM_File.pm
cp Memoize/ExpireFile.pm blib/lib/Memoize/ExpireFile.pm
cp Memoize/NDBM_File.pm blib/lib/Memoize/NDBM_File.pm
Manifying blib/man3/Memoize.3
Manifying blib/man3/Memoize::ExpireTest.3
Manifying blib/man3/Memoize::Saves.3
Manifying blib/man3/Memoize::Expire.3
Manifying blib/man3/Memoize::AnyDBM_File.3
Manifying blib/man3/Memoize::Storable.3
Manifying blib/man3/Memoize::ExpireFile.3
Manifying blib/man3/Memoize::SDBM_File.3
Manifying blib/man3/Memoize::NDBM_File.3
```

Next, I test the module with `make test`:

```
$ make test
PERL_DL_NONLAZY=1 /usr/local/bin/perl -Iblib/arch -Iblib/lib            \
-I/usr/local/lib/perl5/5.6.1/i686-linux -I/usr/local/lib/perl5/5.6.1 -e        \
'use Test::Harness qw(&runtests $verbose); $verbose=0; runtests @ARGV;' t/*.t
t/array_confusion...ok
t/array............ok
t/correctness.......ok
t/errors...........ok
t/expfile..........ok
t/expire...........ok
t/expmod_n.........ok
t/expmod_t.........ok
t/flush............ok
t/normalize........ok
t/prototype........ok
t/speed............ok
t/tiefeatures.......ok
t/tie_gdbm.........ok
t/tie_ndbm.........skipped test on this platform
t/tie_sdbm.........ok
t/tie_storable......ok
t/tie..............ok
t/unmemoize........ok
All tests successful, 1 test skipped.
Files=19, Tests=175, 43 wallclock secs (14.74 cusr +  0.17 csys = 14.91 CPU)
```

Finally, I install the module and documentation using `make install` as root.
This takes the contents of `blib` created previously and moves them into the appropriate places in my system:

```
$ su root
Password:
# make install
Installing /usr/local/lib/perl5/site_perl/5.6.1/Memoize.pm
Installing /usr/local/lib/perl5/site_perl/5.6.1/Memoize/ExpireTest.pm
Installing /usr/local/lib/perl5/site_perl/5.6.1/Memoize/Saves.pm
Installing /usr/local/lib/perl5/site_perl/5.6.1/Memoize/Expire.pm
Installing /usr/local/lib/perl5/site_perl/5.6.1/Memoize/AnyDBM_File.pm
Installing /usr/local/lib/perl5/site_perl/5.6.1/Memoize/Storable.pm
Installing /usr/local/lib/perl5/site_perl/5.6.1/Memoize/SDBM_File.pm
Installing /usr/local/lib/perl5/site_perl/5.6.1/Memoize/ExpireFile.pm
Installing /usr/local/lib/perl5/site_perl/5.6.1/Memoize/NDBM_File.pm
```

```
Installing /usr/local/man/man3/Memoize.3
Installing /usr/local/man/man3/Memoize::ExpireTest.3
Installing /usr/local/man/man3/Memoize::Saves.3
Installing /usr/local/man/man3/Memoize::Expire.3
Installing /usr/local/man/man3/Memoize::AnyDBM_File.3
Installing /usr/local/man/man3/Memoize::Storable.3
Installing /usr/local/man/man3/Memoize::ExpireFile.3
Installing /usr/local/man/man3/Memoize::SDBM_File.3
Installing /usr/local/man/man3/Memoize::NDBM_File.3
Writing /usr/local/lib/perl5/site_perl/5.6.1/i686-linux/auto/Memoize/.packlist
Appending installation info to
/usr/local/lib/perl5/5.6.1/i686-linux/perllocal.pod
```

The amazing thing about this procedure is that it works for nearly every module on CPAN on nearly every operating system supported by Perl. Virtually every module on CPAN supports the exact same installation procedure. This chapter will explain in detail how each of these steps works and show you how to build a distribution that your users will be able to install as easily as Memoize.

Always Begin with h2xs

The Perl documentation on building a module distribution[3] contains the excellent advice, "Start with h2xs." The documentation for ExtUtils::MakeMaker,[4] the module responsible for making Makefile.PL work, elaborates:

> Always begin with h2xs.
>
> Always begin with h2xs!
>
> ALWAYS BEGIN WITH H2XS!

This is good advice because using h2xs can save you a lot trouble, and I'll show you how to follow it. Perl comes with a program called h2xs[5] that can be used to generate the skeleton[6] of a module distribution. Its rather obscure name comes from the fact that it was originally designed as a tool to generate XS[7] modules from C header files.

---

3. perlnewmod, written by Simon Cozens

4. Written by Andy Dougherty, Andreas Köenig, Tim Bunce, Charles Bailey, and Ilya Zakharevich. It is included with Perl.

5. Written by Larry Wall and others. I'm using version 1.21.

6. No black magic required—this just means that h2xs creates a set of mostly empty files for you to flesh out to complete your module distribution.

7. XS is the name for Perl's C language extension system. See Chapter 9 for details.

As an example, I'll create a module distribution for a fictitious module called Data::Counter. To use h2xs to generate the module skeleton for Data::Counter, I use the following command:

```
h2xs -XA -n Data::Counter
```

This command creates the directory structure shown in Figure 4-1 and Table 4-1 beneath the directory where the command was run. The –X option tells h2xs not to generate any XS files and the –A option causes h2xs to omit Autoloader support. The –n option tells h2xs the name of the module to be created. h2xs uses the module name to create a directory to hold the generated files.

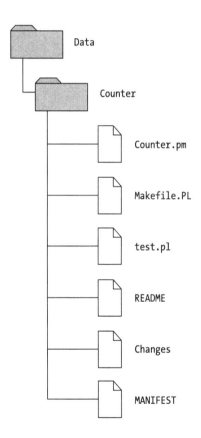

Figure 4-1. Directory structure created by h2xs -XA -n Data::Counter

Table 4-1. Files Generated by h2xs

File	Description
Counter.pm	The module file itself, containing Perl code and POD documentation
Makefile.PL	A script that uses ExtUtils::MakeMaker to generate a Makefile
test.pl	A test script run when a user enters "make test" or installs your module with the CPAN module
README	A quick description of your module and how to install it
Changes	A change-log where you can describe differences between versions of your module
MANIFEST	A list of all the files in your distribution

Counter.pm—The Module File

The module file generated by h2xs (see Listing 4-1) is a generic template into which I'll place the code and documentation for Data::Counter. However, before I blow away what's there, let's look at the generated template; it uses some features that might be new to you.

Listing 4-1. Counter.pm *File Generated by* h2xs

```
package Data::Counter;

use 5.006;
use strict;
use warnings;

require Exporter;

our @ISA = qw(Exporter);

# Items to export into callers namespace by default. Note: do not export
# names by default without a very good reason. Use EXPORT_OK instead.
# Do not simply export all your public functions/methods/constants.

# This allows declaration       use Data::Counter ':all';
# If you do not need this, moving things directly into @EXPORT or @EXPORT_OK
# will save memory.
our %EXPORT_TAGS = ( 'all' => [ qw(
```

```perl
) ] );

our @EXPORT_OK = ( @{ $EXPORT_TAGS{'all'} } );

our @EXPORT = qw(

);
our $VERSION = '0.01';


# Preloaded methods go here.

1;
__END__
# Below is stub documentation for your module. You better edit it!

=head1 NAME

Data::Counter - Perl extension for blah blah blah

=head1 SYNOPSIS

  use Data::Counter;
  blah blah blah

=head1 DESCRIPTION

Stub documentation for Data::Counter, created by h2xs. It looks like the
author of the extension was negligent enough to leave the stub
unedited.

Blah blah blah.

=head2 EXPORT

None by default.

=head1 AUTHOR

A. U. Thor, E<lt>a.u.thor@a.galaxy.far.far.awayE<gt>

=head1 SEE ALSO

L<perl>.

=cut
```

First, h2xs encourages you to be explicit about the version of Perl required by your code:

```
use 5.006;
```

If this module were used in a version of Perl older than 5.6.0,[8] an error message would be generated stating that a newer version of Perl is required. Actually, as you'll see later, it's better to put this check in Makefile.PL, but the intent is the same.

Next h2xs includes the following use lines:

```
use strict;
use warnings;
```

So far, I've avoided the strict and warnings pragmas in order to keep the examples simple, but the buck stops here. All CPAN modules should include use strict and use warnings, and Data::Counter won't be an exception! By using these two pragmas, your module will be free from the most common problems occurring in Perl programs. For more information on these most useful of pragmas, see the documentation for strict and warnings as well as the coverage in most good introductory Perl books.

The next section of code deals with using the Exporter correctly. It not only sets up @ISA but also includes helpful commentary about how to use the various package variables employed by Exporter—@EXPORT, @EXPORT_OK, and %EXPORT. This might seem like overkill, but there was once a time when Exporter abuse was rampant throughout CPAN. If you don't need to export any symbols, then you can delete the entire section, until the $VERSION line.

The next line sets up $VERSION:

```
our $VERSION = '0.01';
```

This variable is needed by all CPAN modules. Without it, the CPAN module won't know which version of your module to install, and make dist (discussed later) won't be able to create a distribution archive. By convention most CPAN modules start their lives at version 0.01, but you are free to use any number you like.

---

8. So why doesn't it say "use 5.6.0"? Support for X.Y.Z format numbers, called *v-strings*, is itself a feature of modern versions of Perl. Since the purpose of this line is to produce a sensible error message in old versions of Perl, it can't use a v-string to express the version number.

CAUTION   You might be tempted to start with a version like 0.1 instead of 0.01, but that can cause problems later when you want to release a version after 0.9 but aren't ready for the psychological impact of releasing 1.0.

After the $VERSION assignment, h2xs includes the cryptic comment "preloaded methods go here." You can read that as "your module code goes here." The term "preloaded" is a reference to h2xs's support for the AutoLoader module, which makes a distinction between "preloaded" and "autoloaded" subroutines and methods

Finally, h2xs includes some example POD documentation after the requisite final true statement. The example POD contains the sections that most CPAN modules will need—NAME, SYNOPSIS, DESCRIPTION, EXPORT, AUTHOR, and SEE ALSO. Of course, unless your module is very simple, you'll need to add sections that describe the available subroutines and methods. Also, unless your module uses the Exporter, it's safe to remove EXPORT.

An edited version of Counter.pm containing the code and documentation for the module is shown in Listing 4-2.

Listing 4-2. Modified Counter.pm *for Data::Counter*

```
package Data::Counter;

use 5.006;  # this will be checked in Makefile.PL too
use strict;
use warnings;


# make count() available for optional exporting
require Exporter;
our @ISA = qw(Exporter);
our @EXPORT_OK = ( 'count' );

our $VERSION = '0.01';

# return a count of arguments
sub count {
  return scalar @_;
}

1;
__END__

=head1 NAME
```

```
Data::Counter - Perl extension to count data items.

=head1 SYNOPSIS

  use Data::Counter qw(count);
  print count("one", "two", "three");  # prints 3

=head1 DESCRIPTION

This module provides a single function, count(), that counts its arguments.

=over 4

=item $num = count($item1, $item2, ...)

This subroutine returns the number of items passed as arguments.

=head2 EXPORT

The 'count' routine is available for optional export.

=head1 AUTHOR

Sam Tregar <sam@tregar.com>

=head1 SEE ALSO

L<perl>.


=cut
```

Makefile.PL—The Makefile Generator

The core of a CPAN distribution is the Makefile.PL script. Running Makefile.PL generates a Makefile that drives the rest of the build, test, and installation procedure. You might wonder why a module couldn't just include a Makefile outright—the reason is portability. Most operating systems have some kind of make utility, but the format and syntax of their Makefiles differ significantly. Also, the Makefile needs to know how Perl was configured in order to do its job. Hence, the solution is to have a Perl script that generates a Makefile appropriate for the system where the module is being installed.

What's a Makefile?

If you don't come from a UNIX programming background, you might not be familiar with Makefiles. A Makefile is a script processed by a program called make.[9] When make is run, it automatically looks for a file called Makefile in the current directory. make uses the information stored in the Makefile to perform the steps necessary to build and install programs from source files. To accomplish this task, a Makefile specifies a set of *rules* and *dependencies*.

A Makefile rule is a particular step in the build process—examples of rules you've seen so far include "test" and "install". When you run the command make test, you're instructing make to run the "test" rule in the Makefile. Makefiles also support the notion of a default rule that is run when no rule is explicitly specified, usually called "all".

Aside from rules that specify activities such as make test and make install, Makefiles also have rules for creating files. One example of this type of rule is the one used to turn a module's POD documentation into a UNIX manual page through the pod2man program.

Makefiles combine rules by laying out rule dependencies. For example, the "all" rule depends on the rule to build manual pages from POD documentation, among others. Dependencies work in two ways. First, they specify a series of steps describing how to complete a requested rule. Second, they allow make to intelligently skip rules when it can tell that the target is up-to-date. For example, make can tell that it doesn't need to rerun pod2man unless the module file containing the POD has been changed since the last time pod2man was run.

For more information about how Makefiles work on your system, see the documentation for your make command.

The Makefile.PL that h2xs generates (see Listing 4-3) for Data::Counter is a simple Perl script. The script uses a single module—ExtUtils::MakeMaker.[10] The subroutine WriteMakefile() is exported from ExtUtils::MakeMaker by default.

---

9. Or, on Microsoft Windows systems, possibly dmake or nmake. See the "Installing CPAN Modules" section in Chapter 1 for details.

10. Written by Andy Dougherty, Andreas Köenig, Tim Bunce, Charles Bailey and Ilya Zakharevich. It is included with Perl.

Listing 4-3. `Makefile.PL` *Generated by* `h2xs`

```
use ExtUtils::MakeMaker;
# See lib/ExtUtils/MakeMaker.pm for details of how to influence
# the contents of the Makefile that is written.
WriteMakefile(
    'NAME'              => 'Data::Counter',
    'VERSION_FROM'      => 'Counter.pm', # finds $VERSION
    'PREREQ_PM'         => {}, # e.g., Module::Name => 1.1
    ($] >= 5.005 ?      ## Add these new keywords supported since 5.005
      (ABSTRACT_FROM    => 'Counter.pm', # retrieve abstract from modul
       AUTHOR           => 'A. U. Thor <a.u.thor@a.galaxy.far.far.away>') : ()),
);
```

WriteMakefile() employs the named-parameter style discussed in Chapter 3 using the parameters NAME, VERSION_FROM, PREREQ_PM, ABSTRACT_FROM, and AUTHOR. The first parameter, NAME, is the name of your module. The second parameter here is VERSION_FROM, which tells ExtUtils::MakeMaker where to look for the $VERSION setting. This is necessary because a module distribution may have more than one module. I will discuss multimodule distributions in depth later in the chapter.

The next parameter, PREREQ_PM, is initially empty, but is important enough that h2xs includes it as a reminder. PREREQ_PM specifies your module's dependencies. By including information on which other modules your module uses, you allow the CPAN module to do its job much better. For example, if Data::Counter uses CGI::Application, I would change the PREREQ_PM line to read as follows:

```
'PREREQ_PM' => { 'CGI::Application' => 0 },
```

The keys of the PREREQ_PM hash are module names, and the values are version numbers. By specifying a version number of zero, I'm telling ExtUtils::MakeMaker that I need some version of CGI::Application installed, but I don't care which one. To specify that I need *at least* version 1.3 installed, I would use this setting:

```
'PREREQ_PM' => { 'CGI::Application' => 1.3 },
```

Now when a user tries to install Data::Counter using the CPAN module, CGI::Application will be automatically installed. Using PREREQ_PM prevents users from discovering a dependency when they try to use the module by advising them when the module is installed. This ensures that the system is not cluttered with half-working code.

CAUTION   It is important to include *all* modules that your module uses in PREREQ_PM, even ones that come with Perl. Unfortunately, many packagers of Perl choose to not include some or all of the optional modules usually included with Perl. Thus, even if a module is installed by default on your system, some of your users may need to install the module from CPAN.

NOTE   There is no way to specify that your module needs an exact version of another module and won't work with a later, higher-numbered version. To do this you'll need to add code to your Makefile.PL to explicitly check for the version you need.

The next section is somewhat curious:

```
($] >= 5.005 ?     ## Add these new keywords supported since 5.005
  (ABSTRACT_FROM   => 'Counter.pm', # retrieve abstract from module
   AUTHOR          => 'A. U. Thor <a.u.thor@a.galaxy.far.far.away>') : ()),
```

It checks to see if the Perl version is 5.005 or greater and then defines some parameters if it is. This seems to be at odds with the module file that h2xs generates. Although Makefile.PL goes out of its way to support older versions of Perl, the generated module file will only work with rather new versions! In fact, it would be better if the required Perl version were checked in Makefile.PL rather than in the module file itself. That way version incompatibility is discovered as early as possible, saving users from downloading prerequisite modules for a module that they won't be able to use. For example, to include a version check for Perl 5.6.0, I add this line at the top of Data::Counter's Makefile.PL:

```
use 5.006;
```

This is needed since Data::Counter uses the new our keyword, which isn't available before version 5.6.0.

The parameters that are set inside the check for 5.005 are ABSTRACT_FROM and AUTHOR. ExtUtils::MakeMaker uses ABSTRACT_FROM to search for a one-line description of your module. It does so by looking for a line that starts with your module name and a dash. Everything after the dash is the module's abstract.[11] For example, here's the section from Data::Counter's module file where the abstract would be extracted:

```
Data::Counter - Perl extension to count data items.
```

Finally, the AUTHOR parameter gives the name and e-mail address for the author of the module.

The Makefile.PL for Data::Counter is in Listing 4-4. This is a simple Makefile.PL; for more information about Makefile.PL techniques, see the "Exploring the Distribution" section later in this chapter.

Listing 4-4. Modified Makefile.PL *for Data::Counter*

```
use ExtUtils::MakeMaker;

use 5.006;  # this module requires Perl 5.6.0
WriteMakefile(
    NAME               => "Data::Counter",
    VERSION_FROM       => "Counter.pm",
    ABSTRACT_FROM      => "Counter.pm",
    AUTHOR             => 'Sam Tregar <sam@tregar.com>'
);
```

test.pl—The Test Script

h2xs generates a simple test script that you can use to build *regression tests* for your module. A regression test is a test that proves a described feature performs the way it is supposed to work. By developing regression tests for your module, you'll be sure that your module works the way your documentation says it does. Also, when you fix a bug, you can add a regression test to prove that it's fixed—after which you can be sure that the bug will never be reintroduced into your module. Similarly, when you add a new feature, you can add a new test so that you can be sure the feature works as advertised.

The generated test script (see Listing 4-5) is a normal Perl script that uses a module called Test.[12] The Test module exports a subroutine called plan(), which must be called before any tests. In this case, plan() is called inside a BEGIN block with a single named parameter, tests, giving the number of tests to be run. When you add a test to the script, you'll need to update this number.

---

11. For the regex literate: /^$package\s-\s(.*)/
12. Written by Joshua Nathaniel Pritikin

Listing 4-5. `test.pl` *Generated by* h2xs

```
# Before 'make install' is performed this script should be runnable with
# 'make test'. After 'make install' it should work as 'perl test.pl'

#########################

# change 'tests => 1' to 'tests => last_test_to_print';

use Test;
BEGIN { plan tests => 1 };
use Data::Counter;
ok(1); # If we made it this far, we're ok.

#########################

# Insert your test code below, the Test module is use()ed here so read
# its man page ( perldoc Test ) for help writing this test script.
```

The default test script includes one test—it attempts to load Data::Counter and automatically succeeds if that didn't cause the script to die. Another use of the ok() function is to test that a returned value is what it should be. For example, Data::Counter has a test for the count() subroutine that checks whether count() returns 3 when it is called with three arguments:

```
ok(count("one", "two", "three") == 3);
```

After adding this test case, a make test run looks like the following:

```
$ make test
PERL_DL_NONLAZY=1 /usr/local/bin/perl -Iblib/arch -Iblib/lib \
-I/usr/local/lib/perl5/5.6.1/i686-linux -I/usr/local/lib/perl5/5.6.1 test.pl
1..2
ok 1
ok 2
```

If count() were broken, the output would look like this:

```
1..2
ok 1
not ok 2
# Failed test 2 in test.pl at line 18
```

The last line tells you which test failed and where to look in `test.pl` for the failing test.

The complete test script for Data::Counter is included in Listing 4-6.

Listing 4-6. Modified `test.pl` *for Data::Counter*

```
use Test;
BEGIN { plan tests => 2 };
use Data::Counter qw(count);
ok(1); # If we made it this far, we're ok.

# make sure count works
ok(count("one", "two", "three") == 3);
```

README

The `README` file is often a potential user's first contact with a module. When you upload a module to CPAN, the `README` file is extracted and placed alongside the module. Its job is to introduce the module and give information about installation. The generated `README` (see Listing 4-7) is self-explanatory. Some of the information is redundant—the header contains the version number that you'll also specify in your module file, and the list of dependencies should be the same as the information in your `Makefile.PL PREREQ_PM` setting. This means that you'll have to be careful to keep the information in the `README` up-to-date as your module changes. Don't worry about the `COPYRIGHT AND LICENSE` section for now—I'll be covering this in detail later in this chapter.

Listing 4-7. `README` *Generated by* h2xs

```
Data/Counter version 0.01
=========================

The README is used to introduce the module and provide instructions on
how to install the module, any machine dependencies it may have (for
example C compilers and installed libraries) and any other information
that should be provided before the module is installed.

A README file is required for CPAN modules since CPAN extracts the
README file from a module distribution so that people browsing the
archive can use it get an idea of the modules uses. It is usually a
good idea to provide version information here so that people can
decide whether fixes for the module are worth downloading.
```

```
INSTALLATION
```

```
To install this module type the following:
```

```
    perl Makefile.PL
    make
    make test
    make install
```

```
DEPENDENCIES
```

```
This module requires these other modules and libraries:
```

```
  blah blah blah
```

```
COPYRIGHT AND LICENCE
```

```
Put the correct copyright and licence information here.
```

```
Copyright (C) 2001 A. U. Thor blah blah blah
```

Changes

The Changes file (see Listing 4-8) provides a place for you to record changes to your module as you release new versions. Using this file to record bug fixes and new features will help your users stay up-to-date on the module's development.

Listing 4-8. Changes *File Generated by* h2xs

```
Revision history for Perl extension Data::Counter.
```

```
0.01  Sat Dec  1 17:10:07 2001
            - original version; created by h2xs 1.21 with options
        -XA -n Data::Counter
```

MANIFEST

The MANIFEST file (see Listing 4-9) contains a list of all the files in your module distribution. ExtUtils::MakeMaker uses this list to build the distribution file itself (described later in this chapter) and to check to make sure that the module distribution is complete on the user's system before installation. You'll need to keep this file up-to-date as you add files to your distribution.

Listing 4-9. MANIFEST *Generated by* h2xs.

```
Changes
Makefile.PL
MANIFEST
Counter.pm
README
test.pl
```

Exploring the Distribution

Like most things Perl, there's more than one way to build a module distribution. The module skeleton generated by h2xs is designed to be simple and generic enough to be useful for all sorts of modules. It's a great place to start, but there are some modifications that will be helpful for you to know. I'll also explore some of the useful things that the build system can do for you without any modifications at all.

Testing

The test script generated by h2xs is simply a Perl script that uses the Test module to run tests. Adding a new test is very simple—just add a few lines to the script that call ok() and update the plan number accordingly. This works well for simple modules, but a complicated module that uses this system will end up with a very large test script. Also, some modules contain features that are difficult to test in a single script.

Fortunately, ExtUtils::MakeMaker allows you to have as many separate test scripts as you need. To use this functionality, create a directory in your module distribution called t. Then create your test files, ending with the extension .t, inside this directory. For example, a typical t directory might contain the files 01load.t, 02basic.t, and 03errors.t. The resulting directory structure is shown in Figure 4-2. Using this layout, make test looks a little different.

```
$ make test
PERL_DL_NONLAZY=1 /usr/local/bin/perl -Iblib/arch -Iblib/lib \
-I/usr/local/lib/perl5/5.6.1/i686-linux -I/usr/local/lib/perl5/5.6.1 \
-e 'use Test::Harness qw(&runtests $verbose); $verbose=0; runtests @ARGV;' t/*.t
t/01load......ok
t/02basic.....ok
t/03errors....ok
All tests successful.
Files=3, Tests=6,  0 wallclock secs ( 0.20 cusr +  0.04 csys =  0.24 CPU)
```

This output is a summary of the output for each of the test scripts. Also included is some timing information that can be useful in performance optimization.[13]

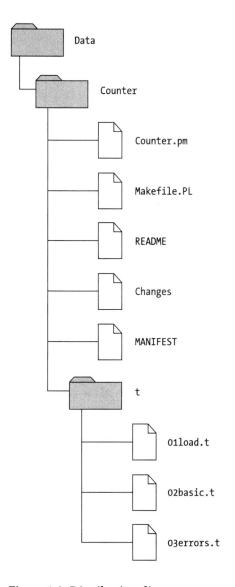

Figure 4-2. Distribution directory structure using a test directory

13. See `Devel::DProf` for a better way.

If one of the tests has failures, then the output will look like the following:

```
$ make test
PERL_DL_NONLAZY=1 /usr/local/bin/perl -Iblib/arch -Iblib/lib \
-I/usr/local/lib/perl5/5.6.1/i686-linux -I/usr/local/lib/perl5/5.6.1 \
-e 'use Test::Harness qw(&runtests $verbose); $verbose=0; runtests @ARGV;' t/*.t
t/01load......ok
t/02basic.....FAILED test 2
        Failed 1/2 tests, 50.00% okay
t/03errors....ok
Failed Test Stat Wstat Total Fail  Failed  List of Failed
-------------------------------------------------------------------------------
t/02basic.t                   2    1  50.00% 2
Failed 1/3 test scripts, 66.67% okay. 1/6 subtests failed, 83.33% okay.
```

Here test number 2 in t/02basic.t has failed. The test output is clear enough, but it doesn't include any line numbers. To get the actual output from each of the test scripts, you can add the TEST_VERBOSE=1 option to the make test run:

```
$ make test TEST_VERBOSE=1
PERL_DL_NONLAZY=1 /usr/local/bin/perl -Iblib/arch -Iblib/lib \
-I/usr/local/lib/perl5/5.6.1/i686-linux -I/usr/local/lib/perl5/5.6.1 \
-e 'use Test::Harness qw(&runtests $verbose); $verbose=1; runtests @ARGV;' t/*.t
t/01load......1..1
ok 1
ok
t/02basic.....1..2
ok 1
not ok 2
# Failed test 2 in t/02basic.t at line 5
FAILED test 2
        Failed 1/2 tests, 50.00% okay
t/03errors....1..3
ok 1
ok 2
ok 3
ok
Failed Test Stat Wstat Total Fail  Failed  List of Failed
-------------------------------------------------------------------------------
t/02basic.t                   2    1  50.00% 2
Failed 1/3 test scripts, 66.67% okay. 1/6 subtests failed, 83.33% okay.
```

Now the filename and line number where the test failed is visible—t/02basic.t, line 5.

NOTE Numbers are added to the front of the t/*.t test script names because make test runs the test files in sorted order. By ordering your test scripts, you can test basic functionality at the start of the test run and reduce the time it takes to detect simple errors.

Another way to improve your testing is to use the Test::More module instead of Test. Test::More[14] lets you write your tests in such a way that failing tests provide much more information. For example, consider a test case that verifies that the count() function returns a count of its arguments:

```
ok(Data::Counter::count('foo', 'bar') == 2);
```

If this test fails, then all you're told is that the test failed.

If instead you used Test::More's is() function, then you'll get a much more useful error:

```
is(Data::Counter::count('foo', 'bar'), 2);
```

The is() function takes two arguments—the operation to be tested and the expected value. If count() returns 3 instead of 2, then the test will fail with the following message:

```
#     Failed test (t/testname.t at line 3)
#          got: '3'
#     expected: '2'
```

Armed with the expected results and the actual return value, you may not even need to look at the test script to start debugging. Test::More includes testing functions for applying regular expressions (like()), comparing complex data structures (eq_array(), eq_hash(), eq_set(), and is_deeply()), and examining objects (can_ok() and isa_ok()). Test::More also contains support for skipping tests when they are known to fail under certain environments and marking tests as *todo* items that are not expected to pass. See the Test::More documentation for details on all this and . . . well, *more*!

---

14. Written by Michael Schwern and available on CPAN

Debugging

Perl comes with a command-line debugger similar to the popular gdb C debugger. If you've never used the Perl debugger before, you should look at the perldebug documentation to get started. To run the Perl debugger on a single test.pl test script, use the command make testdb:

```
$ make testdb
PERL_DL_NONLAZY=1 /usr/local/bin/perl -d -Iblib/arch -Iblib/lib \
-I/usr/local/lib/perl5/5.6.1/i686-linux -I/usr/local/lib/perl5/5.6.1 test.pl
Default die handler restored.

Loading DB routines from perl5db.pl version 1.07
Editor support available.

Enter h or 'h h' for help, or 'man perldebug' for more help.

1..1
main::(test.pl:4):      ok(1); # If we made it this far, we're ok.
  DB<1>
```

However, if you're using a t directory of test scripts, then a simple make testdb won't work. This is because the debugger will only work on a single script. To use the debugger on a single .t file, include the option TEST_FILE. For example, to run t/02basic.t under the debugger, you would use the following command:

```
make testdb TEST_FILE=t/02basic.t
```

Multimodule Distributions

A module distribution can contain more than one module file. A common use for packaging multiple files in a distribution is to install a family of modules in a common namespace. For example, the HTML::Template::JIT[15] module distribution contains the three modules HTML::Template::JIT, HTML::Template::JIT::Compiler, and HTML::Template::JIT::Base. The main module file, JIT.pm, is placed where you would expect it—in the module distribution directory. The other two, Compiler.pm and Base.pm, are placed in a directory called JIT. Makefile.PL automatically finds the two submodules and installs them along with JIT.pm.

---

15. HTML::Template::JIT provides a just-in-time compiler for HTML::Template. The module was written by myself, Sam Tregar, and is available on CPAN.

An alternate method of packaging multiple modules within a distribution is to create a `lib` directory inside your distribution. Inside `lib` you then create the full module path for each included module. If this were done with HTML::Template::JIT, then the path to `JIT.pm` inside the module distribution would be `lib/HTML/Template/JIT.pm`. Note that you would have to modify `Makefile.PL`'s `VERSION_FROM` and `ABSTRACT_FROM` to point to the new location of `JIT.pm`. Using `lib` provides a more flexible system since it allows a distribution to contain modules with different root names collected under a common tree.

Executable Scripts

Module distributions can contain more than just modules, they can also contain executable scripts. For example, the LWP[16] module distribution contains a script called `lwp-download` that uses the LWP modules to download files from the Web. When you install the LWP distributions on your system, this script and others are installed alongside Perl's executable scripts, usually somewhere in your `PATH`.

Including scripts with your modules can serve two useful purposes. First, they allow nonprogrammers to access the functionality of your module. Second, they can provide examples for programmers of how to use your module to accomplish a simple task.

By default ExtUtils::MakeMaker installs any file ending in `.pl` other than `test.pl` in the top-level module directory as an executable script. See the ExtUtils::MakeMaker documentation for details and a description of the `PM` option to `WriteMakeFile()` that can be used to search for `.pl` files (and `.pm` files) in other locations.

Self-Modifying Code

If you look at the LWP distribution, you'll see that the scripts aren't distributed as `.pl` but as `.PL` files. The reason for this is that they need to be processed before they can be installed on the user's machine. To see why this is necessary, consider the script file in Listing 4-10, `count_args.pl`, that counts its arguments. If this file were distributed as-is with Data::Counter, it wouldn't work on many users' systems. This is because the first line contains the path to the `perl` executable. Since this path varies from system to system, `count_args.pl` would only work on other systems where `perl` is installed in `/usr/bin`.

---

16. LWP provides client and server modules for all manner of network communication. LWP was written by Martijn Koster and Gisle Aas and is available on CPAN.

Listing 4-10. Nonportable count_args.pl

```perl
#!/usr/bin/perl -w
use Data::Counter qw(count);
print count(@ARGV), "\n";
```

The solution to this problem is shown in Listing 4-11. ExtUtils::MakeMaker will execute any script ending in .PL at build time and use the output as the source for the script to install. The name of the file to be generated must be the name of the script preceding the .PL. This follows the pattern set by Makefile.PL generating Makefile. In the example shown, to generate count_args.pl, I created a file named count_args.pl.PL. This script uses the Config module to generate the correct perl execution line for the start of the script file.

Listing 4-11. Portable count_args.pl.PL

```perl
use Config; # used to get at startperl
# open output script and make it executable
open OUT,">count_args.pl" or die "Can't create count_args.pl: $!";
chmod(0755, "count_args.pl");

# output perl startup line
print OUT $Config{startperl}, " -w \n";

# output the rest of the script
print OUT q{
  use Data::Counter;
  print Data::Counter::count(@ARGV), "\n";
};
```

This mechanism can be used to do more than just extract platform information from the Config module. Some overly clever module authors use .PL scripts in zany code-generation schemes to gain flexibility and performance. I'll admit to being guilty of this charge, but I hesitate to suggest the practice to the sane!

Building the Distribution Archive

Building the distribution archive with ExtUtils::MakeMaker is as simple as running make dist (after running perl Makefile.PL, of course). This is the command that generates all those nice .tar.gz files available on CPAN. The make dist command is the payoff for all the hard work that goes into using h2xs and Makefile.PL.

Here's what the make dist output looks like on my Linux system:

```
$ make dist
rm -rf Data-Counter-0.01
/usr/local/bin/perl -I/usr/local/lib/perl5/5.6.1/i686-linux \
-I/usr/local/lib/perl5/5.6.1 -MExtUtils::Manifest=manicopy,maniread \
-e "manicopy(maniread(),'Data-Counter-0.01', 'best');"
mkdir Data-Counter-0.01
mkdir Data-Counter-0.01/t
tar cvf Data-Counter-0.01.tar Data-Counter-0.01
Data-Counter-0.01/
Data-Counter-0.01/t/
Data-Counter-0.01/t/03errors.t
Data-Counter-0.01/t/01load.t
Data-Counter-0.01/t/02basic.t
Data-Counter-0.01/README
Data-Counter-0.01/MANIFEST
Data-Counter-0.01/count_args.pl.PL
Data-Counter-0.01/Changes
Data-Counter-0.01/Makefile.PL
Data-Counter-0.01/Counter.pm
rm -rf Data-Counter-0.01
gzip --best Data-Counter-0.01.tar
```

A .tar.gz distribution file is created called Data-Counter-0.01.tar.gz. The contents of the file are taken from your MANIFEST file. (Here's where all your hard work keeping it up-to-date finally pays off!) Conveniently, the format for the distribution filename is exactly what CPAN expects.

ExtUtils::MakeMaker also provides a convenient way to make sure your new distribution will pass a make test after being unpacked in an empty directory— make disttest. Running make disttest will catch missing files in your distribution, although be aware that it won't catch a missing test file from your test directory since make test doesn't know what it's missing. To explicitly check your MANIFEST file, use the command make distcheck. The output will list files in your distribution that aren't in your MANIFEST file.

Do It Yourself

Sometimes the way ExtUtils::MakeMaker does things isn't the way you want to do them. One common example is that your module can *optionally* use some other modules (as opposed to prerequisite modules that are *required* for your module to work) to provide advanced functionality. It wouldn't be appropriate to place such modules in PREREQ_PM since that will cause them to be installed by people who don't intend to use the advanced features. However, you might not want to be totally silent about the choice either.

An example of this situation can be found in the Net::FTPServer[17] module. If the user installs the Archive::Zip[18] module, then Net::FTPServer will enable FTP clients to request zipped versions of files. To alert users during installation to this option, Net::FTPServer includes code inside Makefile.PL that checks for Archive::Zip and prints a message if it's not found:

```
Checking for optional module Archive::Zip >= 0.11 ... not found.

*** Archive::Zip is missing. This module is required if you want to
enable archive mode, which allows users to create ZIP files on
the fly from directories on the server.
```

The code in Net::FTPServer's Makefile.PL then calls sleep(1) to give the user the chance to read this message before the usual flurry of make output continues. Some modules handle this situation by prompting the user, asking whether to continue without the optional module or abort the installation process. This ensures that users will read the message, but at the cost of breaking unattended installation. If you've ever had the experience of firing up a lengthy CPAN.pm installation, getting a cup of coffee, and coming back to find that the first module stopped the installation to ask a question, then you'll probably avoid this path!

Adding custom code in Makefile.PL works fine for checking module dependencies, but if you need to modify the generated Makefile, then you'll need to extend ExtUtils::MakeMaker itself. ExtUtils::MakeMaker provides a simple way to do this: Just define subroutines in the MY package, and they'll be called automatically instead of the normal ExtUtils::MakeMaker methods.[19]

I ran into a situation like this while developing the Guile[20] module. As you may have noticed earlier, the default make test implementation sets the PERL_DL_NONLAZY environment variable when it runs the test scripts. For reasons best left unexplored, this setting makes testing the Guile module impossible; the underlying

---

17. Available on CPAN, this module implements an FTP server (almost) entirely in Perl. It was written by Richard Jones, Rob Brown, Keith Turner, Azazel, and many others.

18. Written by Ned Konz and available on CPAN

19. This works because the MY package inherits from the MM package that ExtUtils::MakeMaker uses to abstract platform dependencies. See the ExtUtils::MakeMaker documentation for the details.

20. This module provides a Perl binding to the GNU Guile Scheme interpreter. It is available on CPAN.

libguile libraries I was using don't pass the PERL_DL_NONLAZY tests. What I needed to do was to filter out the PERL_DL_NONLAZY setting but otherwise leave the make test code in the Makefile as-is. To accomplish this, I added a subroutine called MY::test to the end of my Makefile.PL:

```
package MY;
sub test {
  my $pkg = shift;
  my $test = $pkg->SUPER::test(@_);   # call the real test() from MY parent
  $test =~ s/PERL_DL_NONLAZY=1//g;     # filter out PERL_DL_NONLAZY setting
  return $test;                        # return the modified test block
}
```

This subroutine filters the output of the real test() subroutine and removes the troublesome PERL_DL_NONLAZY setting. To get a list of subroutines that you can extend in MY, see the documentation for the ExtUtils::MM_Unix module.

Alternatives to h2xs

In Perl, there is nearly always more than one way to do any given task, and building a module distribution is no exception. It's a good bet that most of the module distributions on CPAN were built with h2xs, but that hasn't stopped people from trying to build better tools.

ExtUtils::ModuleMaker is intended to bring generating module templates "into the 21st century," according to its author, R. Geoffrey Avery. The module offers the ability to operate from the command line similarly to h2xs or to be called from a script file to access more advanced functionality. One unique feature of ExtUtils::ModuleMaker is its ability to generate license text and a full LICENSE file based on a selection of open-source licenses. For more details, see the module documentation, available on CPAN.

Sean M. Burke's makepmdist script offers an entirely different take on building a module distribution from h2xs and ExtUtils::ModuleMaker. Instead of generating templates for you to edit and maintain, it offers a fast path to building a module distribution from a single module file. You simply give it your module file as an argument, and out pops a .tar.gz file ready to upload to CPAN. The module file must be the only module in the distribution, and in order to specify prerequisites and tests it must adhere to a POD convention specified by makepmdist. However, for very simple modules it offers a time-to-upload that just can't be beat! You can find the script in Sean's author directory on CPAN—authors/id/S/SB/SBURKE/.

However, even with these working alternatives some modules require the services of h2xs. For example, XS modules (introduced in Chapter 9) are only supported by h2xs. I suggest you learn to use h2xs and then explore these alternatives once you're familiar enough to draw your own conclusions.

Portability

Perl is perhaps the most portable programming language ever created. Perl modules can be written to work on virtually every modern computer system.[21] Similarly, Perl modules can also be written to work with a range of versions of Perl. In general, this is accomplished by limiting your use of certain Perl features—be they features that work differently on different operating systems or features that are broken or nonexistent in older versions of Perl. This section will give you information on the most commonly seen portability problems in CPAN modules; for an exhaustive list, take a look at the perlport document that comes with Perl.

Operating System Independence

Writing operating system–independent code requires you to know which features might behave differently when used on different operating systems. This topic alone would be enough to fill a book at least as large as this one, but next you'll find information on the most commonly encountered portability problems.

Line Endings

Historically operating systems have had different ideas about what to put at the end of a line in a text file. UNIX systems use a single byte—\012 or LF. MacOS also uses a single byte—\015 or CR. Microsoft's operating systems (DOS and Windows) use 2 bytes—\015\012 or CRLF. However, in Microsoft's stdio[22] implementation, CRLF is translated into LF on input and back into CRLF on output, but only when reading or writing text files. As a result, in memory the lines have UNIX line endings but on disk they have the distinctive 2-byte format.

Perl provides the \n escape code for strings and regular expressions that matches what the platform thinks of as a line-ending—be it CR or LF—so you usually don't need to think about it when reading and writing text files. However, the issue has implications for the handling of binary data. Consider the following CGI code that reads in a binary image file from disk, smoothes it, and prints it to STDOUT:

```
open(IMAGE, "image.jpg") or die $!; # open the image file
my $image = join('',<IMAGE>);       # read the image data into $image
smooth($image);                     # smooth the image
print STDOUT $image;                # print out the image to the client
```

---

21. With the notable exception of small-scale embedded systems too small for Perl 5. Perl 6 aims to address this deficiency. See the perlport documentation for a full list of currently supported systems.

22. The system library used by Perl to do file I/O

This code will work fine under UNIX and MacOS, but may result in a corrupted image under Windows. The reason is that by default Windows handles files in text mode. That means translating all CRLFs into CRs on input and the reverse on output. The problem is that since image.jpg is a binary file, it might well have CRLF sequences that aren't meant to be line endings. To safely handle binary data, you need to use the binmode() function:

```
open(IMAGE, "image.jpg") or die $!; # open the image file
binmode(IMAGE);                      # the image file is binary data
my $image = join('',<IMAGE>);        # read the image data into $image
smooth($image);                      # smooth the image
binmode(STDOUT);                     # about to print binary data on STDOUT
print STDOUT $image;                 # print out the image to the client
```

Notice that in this case binmode() is necessary on both IMAGE and STDOUT to avoid corrupting text-mode translations.

Another place where line endings rear their ugly heads is in network programming. Many network protocols state that lines must end in CRLF. The *only* way to be sure that you're ending your lines properly is to explicitly add the line-ending bytes:

```
print SOCK "GET / HTTP/1.1\015\012";
```

In particular, using \r\n will *not* work since the setting for \n varies from system to system.

File Systems

Nothing varies as much between operating systems as file system usage. Everything is up for grabs—the path separator, maximum size of filenames, characters allowed in filenames, the number of "root" directories or "volumes," the way network resources are named in the file system, and so on. Listing out all the variations would only serve to convince you that producing portable code that accesses the file system is impossible. Instead I'll just cut to the good news—it is possible and it's not very hard at all.

Perl comes with a module called File::Spec[23] that provides functions for manipulating filenames and paths. To get a list of available methods, read the documentation for the File::Spec::Unix module—all the available subclasses support the same methods.

---

23. This module comes with Perl and was written by Kenneth Albanowski, Andy Dougherty, Andreas Köenig, Tim Bunce, Charles Bailey, Ilya Zakharevich, Paul Schinder, Shigio Yamaguchi, and Barrie Slaymaker.

The only aspect of file naming that File::Spec doesn't treat is the constraints on the actual names themselves. The rule here is keep them short and simple. To be maximally portable, your filenames shouldn't be longer than 11 characters and should contain only one dot (.). Also, you can't count on a case-sensitive file system, so having both test.pl and TEST.pl in the same directory is out. Spaces in filenames are generally verboten, as are punctuation characters aside from under-scores and hyphens.

Portable modules should never contain hard-coded paths. If you need to refer to an external file, you should provide a way for users of the module to specify it. Of course, when they do, they'll be using the filenaming conventions of their platforms, so use of File::Spec is necessary.

On Self-Reliance

Think of a user's system as a strange and alien land—you don't know where any-thing is, you don't know who to ask for help, and you don't speak the language well enough to understand the user's reply if you did. In Perl terms, don't expect to be able to call external programs. Even if you could reliably locate the program you want, there's probably a version out there that produces output you aren't expecting. A classic example is the ps utility found on many UNIX systems. Every ps accom-plishes the same basic task: displaying information about running processes. Unfortunately, every flavor of ps is different—each takes different options and produces different output formats.

If you need a particular service in a portable module, you have two options—code it yourself in pure Perl, or find a module that has it. The latter solution is def-initely preferable—portability problems are common ground shared by the entire CPAN community. The chances are quite good that the service you need is already available on CPAN.

Coding Around the Problem

One way to address portability is to build it into your module's design. A good example of this is in the way the File::Spec module works. File::Spec provides a standard API across all platforms using an object-oriented inheritance strategy. File::Spec is con-ceptually a virtual base class from which the concrete File::Spec subclasses inherit.[24] When you perform a use File::Spec, code inside File::Spec determines which

---

24. Notice that I said "conceptually." The implementation is actually the reverse—File::Spec dynamically chooses one of the "subclasses" as its parent class. Perl OO is fantastic!

OS you're running under[25] and loads the appropriate File::Spec subclass, be it File::Spec::Unix or File::Spec::OS2. This pattern, breaking out OS-specific implementations of a standard API, is an excellent one for portable code. One major advantage is that it allows the code to start small—supporting only a few systems—and grow in portability as additional subclasses are added.

Be Explicit

It's good to be portable; but if you can't, then you should be explicit about it. One way to do this is to put code in your Makefile.PL that explicitly checks the OS at installation. For example, if you know that your module can't possibly work under Microsoft Windows, you could use code like this:

```
if ($^O eq 'MSWin32') {
    die "Sorry, the Data::Counter module doesn't support Windows yet!\n";
}
```

This is much nicer than allowing a user to install your module and realize that it doesn't work later. That said, this technique is hard to get right since you have to either know all the $^O strings where your module will work or all the $^O strings where it won't work. Neither piece of knowledge is easy to come by considering the large number of possibilities.

Perl Version Independence

Another type of portability is compatibility with older versions of Perl. There are many reasons why people don't upgrade their Perl, some good and some bad. Ignore older versions of Perl at your own peril—you never know when you'll end up in a job where the hoary old sys admin insists that Perl 5.004 is as good today as the day it was born!

Supporting older versions of Perl means avoiding new Perl features like the plague. In particular, you'll need to watch out for using the newer syntactic features of modern Perl—our, use warnings, v-strings (numbers of the form 1.2.3), unquoted hash strings, unquoted strings on the left-hand side of a =>, new-fangled regex extensions, and much more. Some of these will merely cause warnings under old versions of Perl, but many will break the module unequivocally.

---

25. Using the $^O variable, which carries a short identifier specifying the OS. See the perlport documentation for a complete list.

Sometimes it's possible to take advantage of newer features while maintaining backwards compatibility. For example, if your module is intended to work with 5.003, then you'll need to avoid using File::Spec[26] since it wasn't included with Perl until 5.004_05. On the other hand, it's hard to support MacOS and VMS without using File::Spec. To solve this problem, you might conditionally include File::Spec if the version of Perl you're using is high enough. For example:

```
if ($] > 5.00405) {
    require File::Spec;
    $path = File::Spec->catfile($foo, $bar, $baz);
} else {
    $path = join('/', $foo, $bar, $baz);
}
```

The key to maintaining compatibility with older versions of Perl is testing. Perl has changed greatly over the years, and it's not easy to keep up with all those changes. If you're serious about supporting older versions of Perl, then you'll need to keep versions around to test your module against. It's either that or release it, and sit back and wait for the bug reports!

Choosing a License

In the first part of the chapter, you saw that the README file generated by h2xs contains a section to indicate the copyright and license information for your module. You should include license information with your module so that people know what they're allowed to do with your module. It's a good idea to include your copyright and license information in your module's POD documentation as well as in your README.

The success of the entire open-source and free-software movements, in which CPAN exists, is founded on licenses. Free-software and open-source licenses grant the user the right to view, modify, and redistribute the code for a given piece of software. Contrast this to the licenses that come with proprietary products where you are neither allowed to see the source code nor redistribute it if you did. Clearly, CPAN can only function within the context of open-source and free software.

---

26. Okay, you could put it in your PREREQ_PM setting in Makefile.PL, but let's imagine you don't want to do that because you're a kind and giving person who believes in playing along with an author's examples.

Perl's License

Most CPAN modules are licensed under the same license as Perl. In their documentation they contain something like the following:

```
Copyright (c) YEAR, NAME.  All rights reserved.  This module is free software;
you can redistribute it and/or modify it under the same terms as Perl itself.
```

Perl's license is a bit unusual—it is a *hybrid license*. A hybrid license is one that allows users to choose between more than one license. In this case, the user is offered the choice between the *GPL* and the *Artistic License*. The GPL is the *GNU General Public License* created by the Free Software Foundation.

Perl's license is included in the Perl distribution in a file called README. You can view a copy of the GPL on the Web at http://www.gnu.org/copyleft/gpl.html. The Artistic License was created for Perl and can be found on the Web at http://www.perl.com/language/misc/Artistic.html.

Using Other Licenses

Using Perl's license for your module is generally a good idea. Since your users are already using Perl, you know that the license will be acceptable to them. When most modules use the same license, it makes life easier for users since they don't have to worry about whether using a module will put them in danger of legal troubles. In addition, module authors benefit since they can share code without needing to worry about incompatible[27] licenses. However, CPAN doesn't place any restrictions on the license you apply to your module. The only practical requirement is that the module must be freely distributable; otherwise CPAN itself would be violating your license by distributing your module among the CPAN mirrors!

If you choose to use a license other than Perl's, you should make sure that users will know about it. Consider putting a large warning at the top of your module documentation and README to get their attention. Better yet, consider just using Perl's license. It's the best thing for the Perl community.[28]

---

27. Licenses are *incompatible* when the terms of one license specify restrictions that are not allowed by the other.

28. Even the Free Software Foundation, usually a proponent of pure GPL usage, agrees: "We recommend you use [the Perl] license for any Perl 4 or Perl 5 package you write, to promote coherence and uniformity in Perl programming." See http://www.gnu.org/philosophy/license-list.html for this quote and more.

I Am Not a Lawyer

Licenses are legal documents, and you should consult a lawyer if you need help deciding which one to use.

Summary

This chapter has shown you how to package a module inside a module distribution. The next chapter will show you how to submit your module to CPAN for inclusion in the archive.

### CHAPTER 5

Submitting Your Module to CPAN

AMONG THE MANY GIFTS Larry Wall gave the Perl community is an aversion to rules and regulations. This is reflected in the Perl language as well as by the Perl community—there's always more than one way to do it, and freedom of choice reigns. However, CPAN requires a different approach. As a shared resource, it would quickly dissolve into anarchy without a few rules to govern submissions.

A modicum of order is maintained on CPAN by a group of Perl elders who share a single mailing address—modules@perl.org. The group that runs modules@perl.org is responsible for two important tasks—registering new CPAN authors and accepting new CPAN modules for inclusion in the Module List. This address isn't a mailing list (you can't subscribe to it), but it does have a Web interface where you can read messages sent there: http://www.xray.mpe.mpg.de/mailing-lists/modules.

This chapter will show you the best way to make requests to modules@perl.org and what to expect in response. I'll also cover the automated services offered by the Perl Author Upload SErver (PAUSE). Once you're registered as a CPAN author you'll use PAUSE to upload your modules.

Requesting Comments

The first step in submitting a new CPAN module is to introduce your idea to the Perl community. A common way to do this is to post a Request For Comments (RFC). An RFC is a message that describes your module and publicly solicits responses. It's common to post RFCs for new modules to the comp.lang.perl.modules Usenet[1] newsgroup as well as any e-mail mailing lists that are relevant to your module. A typical RFC message looks something like:

---

1. Usenet is a distributed messaging system that's been around almost as long as the Internet itself. You might have access to Usenet through your Internet service provider; if not, there are several Web sites that provide gateways to Usenet. One good one is http://groups.google.com.

```
From: sam@tregar.com
Subject: [RFC] Data::Counter

Hello all - I've written a new module called Data::Counter that I'm planning to
put on CPAN.  Take a look at the documentation and tell me what you think.

NAME
    Data::Counter - a module that counts your data

DESCRIPTION
    ...
```

An easy way to produce the content for the message is to use the pod2text script that comes with Perl to create a plaintext copy of your module's POD documentation.

 CAUTION   The perl5-porters mailing list is *not* a good place to send your RFC. The perl5-porters are responsible for developing Perl itself and are not very patient with people who mistake their mailing list for a general Perl discussion area.

If your RFC receives any replies, then it's likely that some of them will be negative.[2] You should treat criticism seriously, but don't let it prevent you from releasing your module—there are plenty of successful CPAN modules that began their lives with controversy! On the other hand, if you receive no replies, you should take that as a sign that you haven't found your user community yet. Keep looking—your module will only be a success if people use it, and they'll need to hear about it first!

One of the most sensitive issues for a new CPAN module is the module's name. Since all CPAN modules share a global namespace, everyone has a stake in making sure modules are named appropriately. If you're not certain that you have the right name for your module, then you should include a section in your RFC discussing possible alternatives. Avoid the most common mistakes in module naming— creating new top-level namespaces needlessly (such as Profile::DBI instead of DBIx::Profile), cute or funny names (for example, D'oh), or ego-based names (for example, Sam::Template).

---

2.   Particularly true on Usenet!

Your goal in naming your module is to provide potential users with a clear picture of what your module does even before they look at your documentation. This is often a difficult task, but it is so critical to your module's success that you should spend the time to do it right.

Be aware that some module namespaces are administrated by a particular person or group (Tk::, Apache::, and DBI::, among others). This information is usually contained in the documentation for the "root" module—for example, the DBI module contains contact information regarding the DBI:: and DBIx:: namespaces. Even when the author of a module hasn't explicitly laid claim to the module namespace, you should contact him or her before uploading. For example, it would be polite to contact that author of CGI::Application before releasing CGI::Application::BBS.

Requesting a CPAN Author ID

After shopping around your RFC, the next step is to request a CPAN Author ID. To do this, send an e-mail to `modules@perl.org` containing the following information:

- Your name

- Your e-mail address

- Your home page (optional)

- Your preferred Author ID (4 to 9 characters, uppercase letters only, one dash allowed)

- A short description of what you plan to contribute to CPAN

The description of your contribution doesn't need to be more than a single sentence per module. Later, when you submit a namespace registration request, you'll have a chance to fully describe your work.

When one of the `modules@perl.org` maintainers registers you, you'll receive an e-mail explaining how to activate your PAUSE account. Usually registration happens in under a week; if you're waiting longer than that, it's occasionally necessary to send a reminder e-mail. However, remember that CPAN is run by volunteers—keep it friendly!

Registering Your Namespace

Once you have an Author ID, you can log in to the PAUSE system at
http://pause.cpan.org. There you'll find a link to the namespace registration form
under the User Menu (see Figure 5-1). In the form, you'll fill out the information
necessary to register your module in the Module List (described in Chapter 1). The
result of filling out this form is a message sent to modules@perl.org.

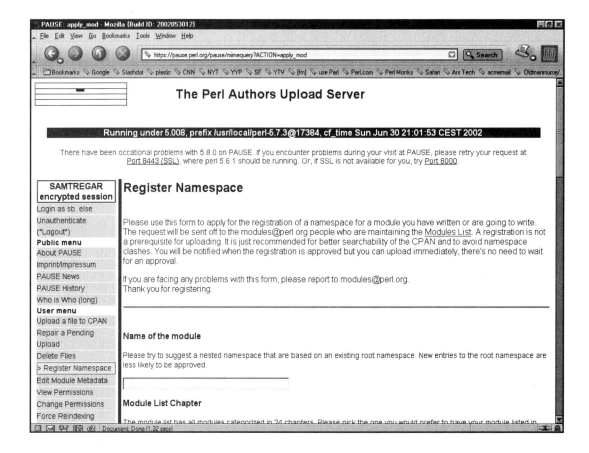

Figure 5-1. The PAUSE namespace registration form

The namespace registration form requires the following information:

- The module name

- The module list chapter

- The DSLIP code information:

  - D: The development stage (i—idea, c—pre-alpha, a—alpha, b—beta, R—released, M—mature, S—standard, or ?—unknown)

  - **S:** The support-level (n—none, d—developer, m—mailing list, u—comp.lang.perl.*, or ?—unknown)

  - **L:** The language used (p—Perl, c—C, +—C++, o—other, h—hybrid, or ?—unknown)

  - **I:** The interface style (f—functions, r—references and ties, O—object-oriented, p—pragma, h—hybrid, n—none, or ?—unknown)

  - **P:** The public license (p—standard Perl, g—GPL, l—LGPL, b—BSD, a—Artistic, o—open source, d—distribution allowed, r—restricted distribution, n—no license, or ?—unknown)

- A short description of the module (up to 44 characters)

- A list of places where the module has been or will be discussed publicly

- A list of modules with similar functionality

- Rational

Although highly recommended, filling out this form isn't strictly necessary. Once you have a CPAN Author ID, you're able to upload any module you like so long as you're not uploading a module containing a package name that's already been registered to another author. However, by not registering your module name, you run the risk that someday the folks on modules@perl.org will decide to let another author register the namespace out from under you.[3]

You should expect to receive a reply to your namespace registration request within three weeks. Or you might never receive a reply at all, which means acceptance of your registration request. Yes, really.[4] As a result, it's common for experienced authors to register and upload in one fell swoop.

---

3. This has never happened, to my knowledge, but if it scares just one author into registering his or her namespace, then it was worth mentioning.

4. A search of the modules@perl.org archive will reveal that I had to learn this one the hard way. Learn from my mistake!

Pre-Upload Checklist

Uploading a new module is an exciting experience. It's the culmination of a great deal of planning and development. Unfortunately, that excitement can make for some fantastic blunders. Here's a checklist to help you avoid some of the more common errors.

- Check your MANIFEST. Make sure your MANIFEST file contains all the files in your distribution directory. One way to do this is to run a make disttest, but this will only work if your module's tests are complete enough to notice a missing file. It won't catch a missing README, for example, so it's best to check by hand.

- Make sure your module distribution filename contains a version number. This is a no-brainer if you're using make dist to generate your distribution (and why wouldn't you?). It's worth adding here because PAUSE won't let you upload the same file more than once. If you upload, for example, My-Module.tar.gz, then you'll have a hard time uploading a new version when you fix your first set of bugs.

- Make sure you've updated the version number everywhere. A common error is leaving old version numbers in README or Changes files. This can be confusing for your users.

- Remember to update the Changes file. Savvy (and/or lazy) users will use this file to decide whether or not to upgrade right away. If you fix a problem that might cause the premature heat death of the universe, then you want to make sure your users know to upgrade immediately.

- Test the distribution on at least one other machine. This step can be time consuming, but it definitely pays off. In choosing a test machine, try to find a machine as different from your own as possible. If you're developing on Linux, try installing your module under Windows and vice versa.

Uploading Your Module Distribution

When you have a new version of your module to release, you'll use the PAUSE upload file form (see Figure 5-2), found in the User Menu sidebar at http://pause.cpan.org. There are three ways to upload your module distribution to CPAN: using HTTP upload, providing a URL, and via FTP.

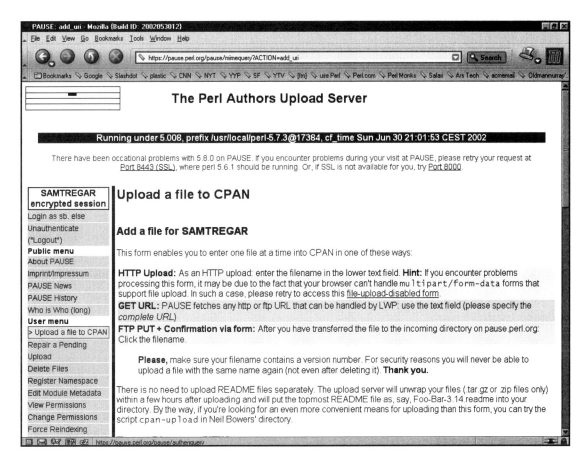

Figure 5-2. The PAUSE file upload form

HTTP Upload

Using HTTP upload is the easiest method in most situations. You'll need a modern[5] Web browser since many older browsers don't implement file upload correctly. To use this method, simply click the Browse button next to the file upload box and find the module distribution file you wish to upload. Then click the Upload this file from my disk button.

---

5.   Netscape Navigator 4.0+ or Microsoft Internet Explorer 4.0+, but other browsers will certainly work.

GET URL

The GET URL option allows you to tell PAUSE where to find your module on the Web. PAUSE will then go and retrieve this file for you. This option might be useful for projects that distribute modules on CPAN but also maintain a Web site that contains their module distributions. To use this method, enter the URL in the box and click the Upload this URL button.

FTP PUT

The FTP PUT method allows you to use FTP to upload a file to PAUSE. This is useful when you're doing development on a machine that can't run a modern Web browser. To use this method, first connect to the FTP server at `pause.cpan.org` via an FTP client. Log in as anonymous and use your e-mail address as your password. Change into the `incoming` directory and upload your file.

Next, use a Web browser to visit the upload form on the PAUSE Web interface. At the bottom of the form, you'll see a list of module distributions—these are all the distributions waiting in the `incoming` directory. Select yours and click the Upload the checked file button.

 CAUTION Make sure you transfer your file in binary mode. Transferring a distribution in ASCII mode will result in a broken distribution. In command-line FTP clients, the `binary` command is used to switch to binary mode.

Dealing with a Broken Upload

One way or another you'll eventually upload a broken file to CPAN. Either you'll transfer the file in ASCII mode FTP, or you'll forget to update some key piece of your distribution. There's only one way to deal with this situation—release a new version. This is because PAUSE will never allow you to upload a file with the same filename twice. Once you've uploaded `MyModule-0.02.tar.gz`, release 0.02 is set in stone. To fix a problem, you'll need to increment the version number and release `MyModule-0.03.tar.gz`.

Post-Upload Processing

After you upload a file to PAUSE, you'll be presented with links that you can use to monitor the progress of your module (see Figure 5-3). An FTP link provides access to the temporary directory where CPAN moves your module while processing. A link is also provided to the final destination for your module—from here it will be mirrored by the root CPAN server and from there out to the network of CPAN servers. Finally, links are provided to a program that tails the logs generated by the PAUSE scripts in action. Using these links, you can watch PAUSE do its work.

NOTE   Different CPAN mirrors update their contents at different intervals. Some mirrors may get a copy of your new module within a few hours of your upload, whereas others might take several days.

When PAUSE processes your upload, it performs several checks. First, the module distribution is checked for module files containing package declarations. The first time a particular package name is uploaded, it is assigned to the author who uploaded it. If a package declaration is found matching an already uploaded package, then the upload will be rejected. Next, if your module contains a README file, it is extracted and renamed by appending .readme to your distribution filename minus the .tar.gz or .zip extension. For example, the README for HTML::Template version 2.4 is available as HTML-Template-2.4.readme. Finally, the module distribution is moved to a directory where the CPAN mirroring scripts will find it. When this process is complete, you'll receive an e-mail from PAUSE.

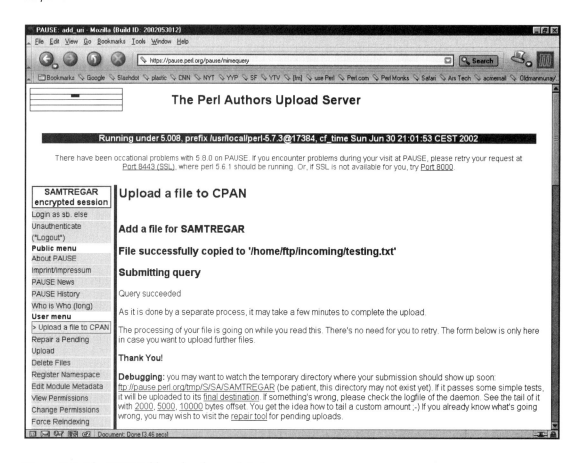

Figure 5-3. The PAUSE file upload completed screen

Summary

This chapter explained the process of uploading a new module to CPAN. Using this information you can now join the CPAN community and contribute your modules to the archive. The next chapter takes you into the life cycle of maintaining a CPAN module.

CHAPTER 6

Module Maintenance

As SOON AS YOU RELEASE your first module, you become the *maintainer* of your creation. A maintainer is the person in charge of the continued development of an open-source project. As maintainer you'll receive bug reports, requests for new features, and contributions from other developers. It's your job to make decisions about the direction of the project and release new versions. This chapter will introduce some useful tools and strategies that can make your job as maintainer easier.

Growing a User Community

Every successful CPAN module is fed by an active user community. A developer working alone on a project with no other users has a shelf life of approximately three releases before moving on to more entertaining work. This can be artificially extended with various enticements—revolutionary zeal, a weekly paycheck, caffeine, and so on—but ultimately an active community is an absolute requirement for the continued life of a module.

An active user community confers a number of benefits. Users will employ your module in ways you won't have anticipated. This can be both entertaining and inspirational; as you and your users see new uses for your module, you'll naturally come up with new features to make those uses more convenient. More fundamentally, users of your module will provide crucial testing for your module, identifying bugs that you would never have run into on your own.

Although having users is essential, it's not uncommon for a successful CPAN module to have a single author throughout its life. CPAN modules are by nature on the small side of open-source endeavors and are usually within the capabilities of a single developer. However, a module whose only developer is also its only user will not evolve beyond its original conception; it may be a technical marvel, but without a user community it's doomed to a short and uneventful life.

Since user communities are so valuable, it's worthwhile to spend some time thinking about what can be done to create one and get the most out of it. More than half of the effort of building a user community is marketing. The effort starts with picking a good name for your module, and continues in how you promote your module, how you involve users, and how you make subsequent releases. Your users are your customers, and as we all know, customer service is job one.

Manning the Help Desk

As the maintainer, you are the default destination for any questions or complaints concerning your module. Even if you didn't include your e-mail address in your module documentation (you hermit!), CPAN has it on record. Suffice it to say that if your module is used, you will receive e-mail about it.

The e-mail you'll receive falls roughly into two categories—useful and bewildering. The useful e-mail will contain feature requests, bug reports, and questions. In the second category, you'll find e-mail that sounds like a bug report but doesn't contain nearly enough information for you to be sure—usually something along the lines of "it doesn't work!!!" In this case you need to do a little coaching; explain what information you need in a bug report and how such users should go about getting it. You may have to repeat your advice several times, but hang in there. Sometimes there's a real bug to be found, and the sooner you find it the better. Also, it's sometimes necessary to point out that you're providing this service for free; people with limited experience in the open-source community will occasionally slip into "irate-customer mode". The sooner you correct that behavior, the better, for you and for them!

Running a Mailing List

Running a help desk is a useful service, but it doesn't tend to foster much of a community. The interaction is entirely one-to-one with you and each user carrying on private conversations. This is time-consuming and often thankless work. In order to get the most out of your user community, you need a more inclusive system. Running a mailing list can help turn individual users into a user community.

On a mailing list, users can interact with one another rather than solely with you. When you answer a question on the mailing list, your answer will be read by all the list members. This can help reduce the number of questions you receive. Over time members of the mailing list will be able to help you answer questions from new users.

Experienced users on your mailing list can help you answer questions about your module's development. When you have an idea for a new feature, you can post it to the mailing list and get reactions from your users. Your mailing list is also a good place for you and your users to float RFCs for related modules (see Chapter 5 for an explanation of RFCs) and make announcements of general interest.

A mailing list also attracts a class of users who wouldn't use a help desk—*lurkers*. A lurker is a user who doesn't say much—that user will subscribe to a mailing list for a project just to listen and learn. However, that doesn't mean lurkers are totally useless; they will still occasionally submit bug reports and every once in a while shed their cloaks of silence and join the discussion. When this happens, you'll certainly be surprised at the depth of knowledge their surveillance has produced!

When you run a mailing list, you become the *moderator*. A moderator is responsible for maintaining a certain level of civility as well as keeping the discussion reasonably on topic. Being a good moderator takes practice, but you can learn a lot by joining other mailing lists and observing how the moderators deal with problems.

Establishing a New Mailing List

There are many free resources available for creating a new mailing list. Those listed in the following text are popular with CPAN module authors at present, but you should be aware that their services might have changed by the time you read this.

Once you've set up a mailing list, you can put the subscription information into your module documentation, since your users will hopefully look there when they have questions. CPAN also maintains a list of Perl-related mailing lists. You can view the collection and register your new list at `http://lists.cpan.org`.

SourceForge

SourceForge is a site that provides a number of services, including free mailing lists, to open-source developers using their homegrown, open-source SourceForge software. To register a new SourceForge project, you must submit a description of your project. The process is similar to registering a namespace with CPAN, although SourceForge tends to act on registration requests more quickly and probably won't care if you've chosen a bad module name. You can find instructions by going to the SourceForge site at `http://sourceforge.net`.

Once you've registered a SourceForge project, you'll have access to a number of free services—mailing lists, Web-based discussion areas, CVS, Web site space, a public FTP site, bug tracking, task lists, news, and more! I'll be discussing some of these later, but it's definitely worth checking out to see what they've added since this book was published.[1]

The SourceForge mailing lists are of the GNU Mailman[2] variety and come with a Web archive set up automatically. Administration is performed through a Web interface where you can manage user subscription and mailing-list policy.

---

1. SourceForge also markets a proprietary, commercial version of its site software for sale to large organizations. Depending on your politics, this might seem like an interesting possibility or a damning impurity. If you like the software but curse the wayward business model, the Free Software Foundation runs an entirely free version of the SourceForge software at `http://savannah.gnu.org`.

2. See `http://www.list.org` for details.

Yahoo Groups

Yahoo offers free mailing lists as part of their Yahoo Groups service. The mailing list is run using proprietary software created by Yahoo and supports access through both e-mail and a Web interface. Note that only Yahoo members can join the list, and the Web interface is obscured by numerous advertising screens. For more information see `http://groups.yahoo.com`.

Rolling Your Own

It's not hard to set up your own mailing list if you have a UNIX machine handy that can send and receive e-mail. If you run qmail[3] as your mail handler, then Ezmlm[4] may be your answer. It allows users with normal e-mail accounts to set up their own mailing lists. Alternately, if you run Sendmail (available at `http://www.sendmail.org`) then you might find the venerable Majordomo (see `http://www.greatcircle.com/majordomo/`) meets your needs. Another popular package is GNU Mailman (see `http://www.list.org`), which works with both Sendmail and qmail. Of course, these are just a few of the more popular alternatives—there are far too many mailing-list packages to list here!

Managing the Source

As maintainer, you are solely responsible for the code in your module. A maintainer has to act as both an editor and a librarian. This section will describe solutions, both technological and social, to some of the most common problems you'll face managing the source code of your module.

Feeping Creaturism

All software, open source and closed, is vulnerable to a disease known as *feeping creaturism*. Once referred to by the less frightening *creeping featurism,* a new name was devised to more effectively render its hideous properties. A project suffering from feeping creaturism will exhibit symptoms of wild growth—new features sprouting from old at a wild rate. Typically the project will grow less stable with each passing release as new features create new bugs. A simple module thus afflicted becomes complex and finally moribund with features.

---

3. Written by Dan J. Bernstein and available at `http://qmail.org`. You can learn more about qmail by reading the excellent book *The qmail Handbook* by Dave Sill (Apress).

4. Also written by Dan J. Bernstein and available at `http://ezmlm.org`.

You can fight this disfiguring disease by keeping careful control of the growth of your modules. This is considerably harder than it sounds—every module must grow, and every feature request meets *someone's* need. Your only defense is to adhere to a strict definition of your module's place in world. When a request for a new feature arrives, you must evaluate it against this definition. Ask the questions, "Is it a natural extension that merely allows the module to function better in its problem space? Or is it a move into another problem space entirely, a symptom of the disease?"

Saying no isn't easy. Particularly when a developer has gone to the trouble of coding a patch, it can be very hard to turn him or her away. Your best defense is to be clear about what you see as the mission of the module and why you think his or her proposed addition is outside those bounds. Another useful strategy is to try to determine the motivation behind the change—there may be another module that user could use in conjunction to yours that would yield the desired behavior. This is in no way a failure on the part of your module—no module can be all things to all people.

Often a request that must be denied can point the way towards adding extensibility. Adding extensibility means giving the person requesting a new feature a means to achieve their goals, *even though you aren't going to implement it for the person making the request*. Of course, if each time you add extensibility you only deal with one feature request, then you haven't gained much. Instead your goal should be to deal with a whole *class* of requests.

As an example of adding extensibility, a key turning point in HTML::Template's development came with the addition of the `filter` option, which allows users to extend the supported template syntax. All throughout HTML::Template's life users had been asking for this or that special tag, each for its own special purpose. In the early days, I had no recourse but to respond that their special tag wasn't going to be part of HTML::Template and try to let them down as lightly as possible. But once the `filter` option was implemented, I could show them how to add support for the tag themselves. Not only has this improved HTML::Template's utility for its users, but it has also allowed a small number of extension modules to be developed that use the `filter` option to implement new functionality. All that, and the fundamental simplicity of the module itself was not harmed at all! By adding extensibility to address a class of problems, I was able to divert requests that could easily have resulted in feeping creaturism.

Another useful technique is to appeal to the silent majority of conservative users who populate most module mailing lists. Often a new feature will attract a number of radical proponents who will flood the mailing list with supportive arguments. If you allow your judgment to be swayed by the appearance of unanimity, you'll be doing the larger user community a disservice. Instead, appeal to them directly. Say publicly, "Do you guys agree with these nuts, or what?" I've found that when faced with the possibility that some craziness is about to be accepted, the wise hermits in the audience will come out of their shells.

Although uncommon, you should also be on the lookout for the opposite of feeping creaturism—stagnation. Every module must change with time to remain vital. Don't let a fear of wild growth prevent perfectly reasonable additions. After all, seeing your module grow in ways you never anticipated is part of the fun of open-source development!

Working with Patches

Accepting code contributions from other developers means working with *patches*. A patch is a text file that encodes the differences between two versions of the same file. Patch files are meant to be used with the patch program, written by Larry Wall (yes, that Larry Wall). Patch files are generated by the diff program.[5] diff looks at two versions of a file and outputs the differences. For this reason, patches are often called diffs, causing much confusion for the uninitiated.

A typical use of diff and patch is as a way to transmit a change to the source from a developer to a maintainer. The developer uses diff to produce a patch file that describes the changes made to the files. The patch file is then submitted to the maintainer of the project, often by e-mailing it to a mailing list or directly to the maintainer. If the maintainer accepts the change, then he or she uses the patch program to apply the changes described in the patch file. The end result is that the change made by a developer is transmitted to the project maintainer without requiring the entire set of changed files to be exchanged.

 TIP The patch program is able to skip any leading junk in a file containing a valid patch. This means that developers can append patches to e-mails, and you can send the entire e-mail to patch without needing to manually extract the patch file! This is also why maintainers often prefer patches to be appended to e-mail rather than attached.

Creating a Single-File Patch

The simplest type of patch describes changes to a single file. As an example, I'll make a small change to the Data::Counter module introduced in previous

---

5. Most Unix systems come with diff and patch installed. If your system is missing these utilities, you can find the GNU versions at http://www.gnu.org. Windows users can get diff and patch by installing the CygWin toolkit available at http://cygwin.com. Note that patch is an optional package, and you'll have to select it manually from setup.exe

chapters. I'll change the count() routine in Counter.pm to work as a class method rather than as a simple function. First, I copy Counter.pm to Counter.pm.orig:

```
$ cp Counter.pm Counter.pm.orig
```

Next I edit Counter.pm, changing the definition of count() from

```
sub count { return scalar @_ }
```

to this:

```
sub count {
  my $pkg = shift;
  return scalar @_;
}
```

Now I can produce a patch file by running the diff command on the files and redirecting the output to a file called newcount.patch. The order of the arguments is important—always put the old file first and then the new file:

```
diff Counter.pm.orig Counter.pm > newcount.patch
```

The diff program describes the differences in terms of what parts of the file would have to change to get from one version to a different version. Since you want to be able to see how to get from the original version to the new version, the original version goes first. Reversing the filenames would tell you exactly how to get from the new version back to the old version.

After this command, newcount.patch contains the following:

```
32c32,35
< sub count { return scalar @_ }
---
> sub count {
>   my $pkg = shift;
>   return scalar @_;
> }
```

Lines that begin with < are the lines that have been removed from the old file, and the lines beginning with > are the lines that have been added in the new file.

The diff program can represent differences between files in a number of different formats. The patch program can be used with the diff format shown previously, but it's not the preferred format. To produce a better patch, use the -u option:

```
diff -u Counter.pm.orig Counter.pm > newcount.patch
```

Now `newcount.patch` contains the following:

```
--- Counter.pm.orig  Sat Jan 26 17:37:29 2002
+++ Counter.pm       Sat Jan 26 17:44:10 2002
@@ -29,7 +29,10 @@

 # Preloaded methods go here.

-sub count { return scalar @_ }
+sub count {
+  my $pkg = shift;
+  return scalar @_;
+}

 1;
  __END__
```

This format is known as a *unified diff*. In a unified diff, lines that begin with a +
(plus sign) are the lines that have been added, and lines beginning with a – (minus
sign) are the lines that have been removed. Lines without a leading character are
context—lines that are unchanged between old and new that surround the changes.[6]
Including context enables `patch` to work even if the original files have changed
since the patch was created. The additional context lines also help human readers
understand the patch; with a little practice, you'll be able to read and understand
patches as easily as reading the original source.

Unified diffs also contain a header listing the old and new filenames and their
modification dates. As I'll demonstrate later, this allows changes to multiple files
to be included in one patch.

Applying a Single-File Patch

Applying patches is usually an easy process. The `patch` program accepts the patch
file on standard input (known in Perl as `STDIN`). By default, it finds target files automatically by examining the patch header and modifies them in place.

---

6. You can also get context in the normal diff format using the –c option, but unified patches are
   usually easier to read.

TIP Include the --backup option to patch when you're first using patch to avoid losing data. This creates a backup file before patch changes the file.

To apply the patch created previously to the original version of Counter.pm, I can use this command:

```
$ patch < newcount.patch
patching file 'Counter.pm'
```

The second line is output from patch—the name of the file to patch was correctly deduced from the patch file header.

There are many reasons that patches can fail to apply cleanly, from file corruption to changes made in the target file that conflict with the patch. When patch can't apply a patch file, it will issue an error message and create a reject file containing the pieces of the patch, known as *hunks,* that could not be applied. For more information about how patch deals with failure, see the patch manual page.

Creating Multifile Patches

It's common to need to change more than one file to bring about a single change. For example, you might need to add a new test to a module's test script to accompany a change in the module code. Although it is possible to use the technique introduced earlier and simply include multiple diff files, this will quickly become unmanageable both for the sender and the receiver. Instead, you'll probably want to use diff's support for creating diffs between two directories, as I'll demonstrate here.

For example, since I changed the way Data::Counter's count() routine is called, I need to change the test suite accordingly. Simply, I must modify the t/02basic.t file to call count() as a class method rather than a simple function. Since this will now be a multifile patch, I prepare by copying the entire Counter directory to Counter.orig (in contrast to simply copying the Counter.pm file to Counter.pm.orig as shown earlier):

```
cp -rp Counter/ Counter.orig/
```

Now I'll make the change to the two files and generate the diff with this command:

```
diff -ur Counter.orig Counter > newcount.patch
```

The additional –r option tells `diff` to operate recursively. The contents of `newcount.patch` after this command are as follows:

```
diff -ur Counter.orig/Counter.pm Counter/Counter.pm
--- Counter.orig/Counter.pm  Sun Jan 27 14:59:49 2002
+++ Counter/Counter.pm       Sun Jan 27 15:00:00 2002
@@ -29,7 +29,10 @@

 # Preloaded methods go here.

-sub count { return scalar @_ }
+sub count {
+  my $pkg = shift;
+  return scalar @_;
+}

 1;
 __END__
diff -ur Counter.orig/t/02basic.t Counter/t/02basic.t
--- Counter.orig/t/02basic.t  Sun Dec  9 21:29:35 2001
+++ Counter/t/02basic.t       Sun Jan 27 15:00:51 2002
@@ -1,3 +1,3 @@
 use Test::More tests => 1;
 use Data::Counter;
-is(Data::Counter::count('foo', 'bar'), 2);
+is(Data::Counter->count('foo', 'bar'), 2);
```

As you can see, this patch contains differences to both `Counter.pm` and `02basic.t`.

Applying Multifile Patches

To apply the multifile patch created using the technique shown in the preceding section, you need to use the –p1 option. This option tells `patch` to strip a single leading directory from the filenames specified in the diff headers. For example, the header for the changes to `02basic.t` reads as follows:

```
--- Counter.orig/t/02basic.t  Sun Dec  9 21:29:35 2001
+++ Counter/t/02basic.t       Sun Jan 27 15:00:51 2002
```

When `patch` reads this, it will look for `Counter/t/02basic.t`, but since you'll be applying the patch from inside your source directory, this file won't exist. By using the –p1 option you tell `patch` to look for `t/02basic.t` instead:

```
patch -p1 < newcount.patch
```

NOTE   When you send a patch that will require a –p1 option to be applied, you should specify that in your message. In general, it's a good idea to include application instructions when you submit a patch.

Read the Fine Manuals

For more information on `diff` and `patch`, see the manual pages on your system. Both programs support far more options than can be adequately described here.

Using CVS

Using the Concurrent Versions System (CVS) can make your life as a module maintainer significantly easier while also enhancing community interaction. In particular, CVS can make it easier for other developers to contribute to your module and for you to manage their contributions. As a bonus, CVS also functions as a powerful backup system for your code—no more self-flagellation after a careless deletion!

CVS is a revision control system, which means that it stores every version of your project source code and enables retrieval and comparison of arbitrary versions. You can think of it as a file server that doesn't overwrite a file when it is changed; instead, it saves the new revision alongside the old. Then when you want to know what changed between version X and version Y of the source, you can ask CVS for a diff that indicates these changes between the two versions.

Obtaining CVS

Many UNIX systems come with CVS. If you need to install CVS, you can download the software at `http://www.cvshome.org`.

Windows users can install the CygWin[7] toolkit, which supports CVS (it's an optional package, so be sure to choose it during installation). Additionally, a

---

7.   Available at `http://cygwin.com`

number of GUI clients for Windows are available, the best of which is definitely WinCVS. You can find WinCVS here: http://wincvs.org.

I'll be showing you how to use CVS through the command-line client, but it should be easy to adapt this knowledge to WinCVS.

The CVS Program

All CVS commands are run using a single program called cvs. The program always requires a command name specifying the action to perform. It can take options before the command and options after the command. Here's a few examples of CVS commands to give you an idea of what I'm talking about:

```
$ cvs -q update -d
$ cvs diff -u
$ cvs log Template.pm
```

Anything after the command that isn't an option is usually treated as a filename argument—for example, in the last command Template.pm is a filename argument. Without a filename argument, most CVS commands operate recursively on all files and directories below the current directory.

Repositories

CVS refers to the place where it stores your project's files as the *repository*, or sometimes the CVS *root*. A repository is simply a directory containing CVS files. You can use a repository on your local machine, or you can connect to one on a different machine. CVS supports two ways of connecting to remote CVS servers—using CVS's native pserver protocol or through an rsh-compatible service, such as ssh.[8] I'll cover two possibilities: setting up a local repository on your machine and connecting to a CVS repository using ssh. These are by far the most common uses of CVS.

Using a Local Repository

All you need to set up your own local repository is a directory for CVS to store its files. Once you've picked a directory for your repository, you must prepare it for CVS using the cvs init command. For example, to create a new repository in my

---

8.   rsh stands for remote shell, a common utility for running commands on remote hosts available in most UNIXes. ssh stands for secure shell, an rsh-compatible utility that also encrypts all communication between client and server.

home directory, /home/sam, called /home/sam/cvsroot, I would issue the following command:

```
$ cvs -d /home/sam/cvsroot init
```

Once you've initialized the repository, you need to tell CVS about it. You could specify a –d option to all your commands as I did with cvs init earlier, but that would get very tiresome. Instead, set the CVSROOT environment variable in your shell to the name of the repository directory. For example, I use the bash shell and I have a line in my .bash_profile file like this:

```
export CVSROOT=/home/sam/cvsroot
```

After this step, all your cvs commands will use /home/sam/cvsroot as the repository.

Using a Remote CVS Repository with SSH

The most common usage of CVS via the Internet is through ssh. This is the way the free CVS server on SourceForge works, and I'll use it as an example. Since the folks at SourceForge have already initialized your CVS repository, you don't need to do a cvs init operation. All you need to do is set up two environment variables—CVSROOT and CVS_RSH. For example, to access a repository stored on the machine cvs.foo.sourceforge.net in the path /cvsroot/foo using ssh with the username "sam", I would make these settings:

```
$ export CVSROOT=:ext:sam@cvs.foo.sourceforge.net:/cvsroot/foo
$ export CVS_RSH=ssh
```

The first line tells CVS where to look for the repository, and the second tells CVS to use ssh instead of rsh to connect to the server. If you're using SourceForge, you can find the values for both these variables on your project's CVS page.

The SourceForge servers also provide access using CVS's pserver protocol for *anonymous* access. Anonymous CVS access is a read-only service—it allows external developers to access the CVS tree and produce patches from it without being able to alter its state. See the SourceForge project's CVS page for details on connecting as an anonymous user.

Importing Your Module

To start using CVS with your module, you'll need to *import* your source into CVS. When you import your module into CVS, space is created in the CVSROOT for your project. To get started, make sure you have just the files you want to store in CVS in your module distribution directory. You shouldn't include derivative files such as Makefile or the contents of blib in CVS, so make sure you run a make clean first to remove them.

Next, you'll need to choose a CVS module name and import your source. CVS module names are unique identifiers that you'll use to access you files in CVS. By including module names, a single CVS repository can house any number of independent source trees. An easy way to create a name that CVS will accept is to use your module's distribution filename minus the version information. For example, to import the source for Data::Counter into CVS, I would use this command in the Data::Counter distribution directory:

```
$ cvs import -m "Import of Data::Counter" Data-Counter vendor start
```

The –m option specifies a log message for the import—if you leave it out, then CVS will open an editor for you to enter a log message. Most CVS commands accept a log message that can later be viewed with the cvs log command. After that comes the module name—Data-Counter. The last two arguments are the "vendor" tag and the "start" tag. Unless you're a total CVS nerd, you'll never use either of these, so you can set them to whatever you want. They're theoretically useful in tracking third-party sources through CVS. Or something like that.

Getting a Working Copy

To use CVS to manage the files you just imported, you need to check out a working copy of your source. To do so, use the cvs checkout command:

```
$ cvs checkout Data-Counter
U Data-Counter/Changes
U Data-Counter/Counter.pm
U Data-Counter/MANIFEST
U Data-Counter/Makefile
...
```

The output from the checkout command will show you the files and directories being created from the CVS repository; the leading U stands for updated. Your working copy contains all the same stuff that your module distribution does except that each directory also has a CVS directory that contains special CVS files. I won't go into the contents of these files, but you should be careful not to delete them or you'll have to check out a new working copy.

A CVS checkout does not lock the files being checked out, as is the case in some version control systems. CVS allows many developers to work on the same files simultaneously and will automatically merge changes. If changes cannot be merged, then a conflict results. See the CVS documentation for information on merging and conflict resolution.

Making Changes

Now that I have Data::Counter in CVS, let's take it out for a spin. To demonstrate making changes, I'll add a new subroutine to Data::Counter—count_char(), which counts the occurrences of character in a string:

```
sub count_char {
  my ($pkg, $char, $string) = @_;
  return $string =~ tr/$char/$char/;
}
```

I'll also add a new test to t/02basic.t:

```
is(Data::Counter->count_char('a', 'abababa'), 4);
```

After making the changes, I can get a list of changed files using the cvs update command:

```
$ cvs -q update
M Counter.pm
M t/02basic.t
```

The –q option stands for "quiet," and in this case suppresses the printing of unchanged files. The M in front of Counter.pm and t/02basic.t means "modified." This tells you that the files have been modified since the last time they were committed to the repository. Another useful CVS feature is the ability to request a diff against the version in the repository with cvs diff:

```
$ cvs diff -u
cvs diff: Diffing .
Index: Counter.pm
===================================================================
RCS file: /home/sam/cvs/Data-Counter/Counter.pm,v
retrieving revision 1.1.1.1
diff -u -r1.1.1.1 Counter.pm
--- Counter.pm        2002/02/04 01:31:54        1.1.1.1
+++ Counter.pm        2002/02/04 06:24:41
@@ -34,6 +34,11 @@
   return scalar @_;
 }
```

```
+sub count_char {
+  my ($pkg, $char, $string) = @_;
+  return $string =~ tr/$char/$char/;
+}
+
 1;
 __END__
 # Below is stub documentation for your module. You better edit it!
cvs diff: Diffing t
Index: t/02basic.t
===================================================================
RCS file: /home/sam/cvs/Data-Counter/t/02basic.t,v
retrieving revision 1.1.1.1
diff -u -r1.1.1.1 02basic.t
--- t/02basic.t      2002/02/04 01:31:54          1.1.1.1
+++ t/02basic.t      2002/02/04 06:24:55
@@ -1,3 +1,4 @@
-use Test::More tests => 1;
+use Test::More tests => 2;
 use Data::Counter;
 is(Data::Counter->count('foo', 'bar'), 2);
+is(Data::Counter->count_char('a', 'abababa'), 4);
```

By specifying the –u option to cvs diff, you can produce the same unified diff format as the diff -u you met earlier.

Once you're happy with your changes, you can save them to the repository with the cvs commit command, which takes a log message using the –m option just like cvs import did:

```
$ cvs commit -m "Added the count_char() method"
cvs commit: Examining .
cvs commit: Examining t
Checking in Counter.pm;
/home/sam/cvsroot/Data-Counter/Counter.pm,v  <--  Counter.pm
new revision: 1.2; previous revision: 1.1
done
Checking in t/02basic.t;
/home/sam/cvsroot/Data-Counter/t/02basic.t,v  <--  02basic.t
new revision: 1.2; previous revision: 1.1
done
```

Now the current version in the CVS repository matches the contents of the working copy. In CVS terms the changes have been committed to the repository.

This creates a new *revision* in the repository—in this case 1.2 for both files. Each file carries its own revision number, which is incremented each time it is updated. You can examine the history of a file in CVS using the `cvs log` command. For example, here's the `cvs log` output for `Counter.pm` after the commit operation:

```
$ cvs log Counter.pm

RCS file: /home/sam/cvsroot/Data-Counter/Counter.pm,v
Working file: Counter.pm
head: 1.2
branch:
locks: strict
access list:
symbolic names:
        start: 1.1.1.1
        vendor: 1.1.1
keyword substitution: kv
total revisions: 3;     selected revisions: 3
description:
----------------------------
revision 1.2
date: 2002/02/04 06:31:48;  author: sam;  state: Exp;  lines: +5 -0
Added the count_char() method
----------------------------
revision 1.1
date: 2002/02/04 01:31:54;  author: sam;  state: Exp;
branches:  1.1.1;
Initial revision
----------------------------
revision 1.1.1.1
date: 2002/02/04 01:31:54;  author: sam;  state: Exp;  lines: +0 -0
Import of Data::Counter
=============================================================================
```

At the bottom, listed in reverse chronological order, are the revisions that exist in the CVS repository—1.2, 1.1, and 1.1.1.1 in this case—along with log messages.

Adding and Removing Files and Directories

CVS needs to be told about new files and directories. This is done with the `cvs add` command. For example, if I created an INSTALL file in the Data::Counter project, I would run the `cvs add` command:

```
$ cvs add INSTALL
cvs add: scheduling file 'INSTALL' for addition
cvs add: use 'cvs commit' to add this file permanently
```

As the output indicates, a cvs commit is needed to add the new file to the repository:

```
$ cvs commit -m "Added new INSTALL file." INSTALL
RCS file: /home/sam/cvsroot/book/INSTALL,v
done
Checking in INSTALL;
/home/sam/cvsroot/Data-Counter/INSTALL,v  <--  INSTALL
initial revision: 1.1
done
```

Similarly, cvs remove removes files from the repository. Simply deleting a file from a working copy is not enough to remove a file from CVS—the next time you update, it will come back again! For example, to remove the newly create INSTALL file, three commands are required, rm, cvs remove, and finally cvs commit, to make the change in the repository:

```
$ rm INSTALL
$ cvs remove INSTALL
cvs remove: scheduling 'INSTALL' for removal
cvs remove: use 'cvs commit' to remove this file permanently
$ cvs commit -m "Removed INSTALL" INSTALL
Removing INSTALL;
/home/sam/cvsroot/book/FOO,v  <--  FOO
new revision: delete; previous revision: 1.1
done
```

However, INSTALL is not gone from the repository. You can still examine its history, request diffs, and even call it back into existence by checking out an old version and adding it to the project.

 NOTE Directories cannot be removed using normal CVS commands. The best you can do is make a directory empty and then check out a working copy with –P, which omits empty directories. To make matters worse, running cvs add on directories takes effect immediately—no cvs commit command is required. Thus you should very carefully consider your directory structure before running cvs add on a directory.

Staying Up-to-Date

A single project in CVS can support any number of working copies, which allows multiple developers to work on a project simultaneously. When you make changes in one working copy and commit them, your fellow developers will need to perform a cvs update to synchronize their working copies with the repository. For example, if I performed the cvs add INSTALL operation previously in one working copy, then my coworker Jesse would need to run cvs update in his working copy to get the new file as follows:

```
$ cvs -q update -d
U INSTALL
```

The –q ("quiet") option suppresses printing all the files and directories in the project. The –d option isn't strictly necessary in this case, but it's a good option to use when updating a project directory—it allows CVS to create new directories that have been added to the project since the last update.

Time Travel

Most often you'll be working on the most recent version of your module, and CVS makes that very convenient. Other times you'll need to travel back in time, and that's when CVS becomes nearly indispensable. For example, imagine that Bob Dobbs sends me a patch to Data::Counter that adds a new feature. I apply the patch and commit the change:

```
$ cvs commit -m "New feature from Bob Dobbs" Counter.pm
Checking in Counter.pm;
/home/sam/cvsroot/Data-Counter/Counter.pm,v  <--  Counter.pm
new revision: 1.3; previous revision: 1.2
done
```

Time passes, and a few weeks later I start having trouble with the function that Bob patched. In order to determine if Bob's patch is to blame, I need to roll back to the version before the patch and try my test case. Now, one option would be to dig out Bob's patch and reverse it using patch -R, but CVS offers an easier solution. Using cvs update with the –r argument, you can update a file to an arbitrary revision. For example, this command brings Counter.pm back to the state it was in before Bob's patch:

```
$ cvs update -r 1.2 Counter.pm
U Counter.pm
```

The 1.2 is the revision number for the version I want to update to, which can be determined by looking at the output of `cvs log`.

Another way to use `cvs update` to travel into the past is to include the –D option to specify a date to travel back to. For example, to update the entire tree to the state it was in on Monday, May 28th, you'd do something like this:

```
$ cvs update -D "5/28/2002"

cvs update: Updating .
U Changes
U Counter.pm
U INSTALL
...
```

As you can see, this has the advantage of working across the entire project. Since revision numbers (used with the –r option) are specific to a single file, they can't be used with multiple files.

To get back to the most recent version, you need to use the –A option to `cvs update`:

```
$ cvs update -A
cvs update: Updating .
U Counter.pm
cvs update: Updating t
```

This allows you to begin making changes to your files and committing them. In CVS you can examine the past but you can't change it.[9] Until you update with –A, CVS will prevent you from committing changes to files from the past.

Getting the Most out of CVS

You can get a lot out of CVS with only a little knowledge, which is fortunate since that's all I have space to impart. However, CVS supports many more useful features than I've had space to cover—tags, branches, conflict resolution, and much more. This section has introduced you to CVS and demonstrated a few common tasks. Hopefully you now see what a useful tool CVS can be in your development. It can allow you to work with patches and changes much more intelligently, as well as opening the door to multideveloper projects.

---

9. Thus CVS has solved the age-old science-fiction paradox: You can neither kill Hitler nor prevent your own conception with CVS, for better or worse.

To complete your CVS education, you should read the online documentation available at http://cvshome.org.

Or, if you'd prefer the details in book form, *Open Source Development with CVS* by Fogel and Bar (Coriolis) is an excellent read. As a bonus, it also includes another take on many of the topics presented in this chapter. See their site for more details: http://cvsbook.red-bean.com/.

Bug Tracking

Every piece of software has bugs, and your modules will be no exception. The usual way of dealing with bugs is via e-mail. A user spots a bug and writes to you or to the project mailing list with a description. After some discussion, you verify the bug and fix it, or if you're really lucky someone else does and sends you a patch. The problem with this approach is that it's all too easy for a bug to slip through the cracks. E-mail also lacks visibility—it's hard for your users to get an accurate picture of the status of a bug.

Bug-tracking software provides a better solution. Users typically fill out a Web-based bug submission form describing the bug. The bug enters the bug-tracking system as a new bug. At some later point you (or another developer with the appropriate permissions) verify the bug and move it to an accepted state. If any discussion is necessary to verify the bug, then it can be carried out through the bug tracker, which automatically e-mails the participants. Finally, when the bug is fixed, it is marked closed. This makes it exceedingly hard to lose track of a bug, and some systems will even remind you of neglected bugs periodically. It also allows users to keep track of bugs they care about.

The same software that you use to track bugs can also be used to track other types of development—feature development and ideas, for example. This can increase the visibility of the project and help organize development among developers.

Of course, there are far more bug-tracking packages available than I have space to list (or even time to learn about!). The following are some of the most popular in the open-source community and should be on your list when you're ready to start tracking your bugs.

CPAN's Request Tracker

CPAN offers a free bug-tracking service for all registered CPAN authors. You can log in to the system at http://rt.cpan.org.

When you log in you'll see a list of your CPAN modules along with status information on open bugs (see Figure 6-1). From here you can get to detail pages for each bug as well as pages to enter new bug reports.

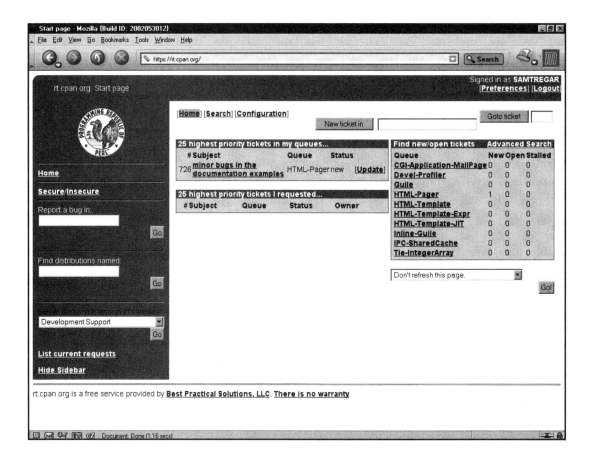

Figure 6-1. rt.cpan.org author home page

At the moment rt.cpan.org is very new and still under development. It definitely has some kinks left to work out. I recommend you check it out and see how things are shaping up; if all goes as planned, it will be the standard place for reporting bugs in CPAN modules by the time this book is printed.

SourceForge

SourceForge provides free bug-tracking for registered projects through a generalized "Tracker" system. In addition to bugs, the Tracker handles support requests, patches, and feature requests. SourceForge also provides a separate task-list application that functions as a lightweight progress tracker for use by developers.

The SourceForge bug-tracking facility is well integrated into the larger SourceForge system. When a SourceForge user creates a bug report, status information on the bug is available on that user's home page as long as the bug is live. If you're already using SourceForge for CVS and mailing lists, then this may be the ideal solution for you.

Bugzilla

Bugzilla is a popular, open-source bug-tracking system created to support the Mozilla[10] project. It's written entirely in Perl and uses MySQL[11] to hold its data. If you're considering setting up your own bug tracker, then you should definitely take a look at Bugzilla. You can find more information about this bug-tracking system at `http://www.mozilla.org/projects/bugzilla/`.

Making Releases

As Eric Raymond famously advised, "release early, release often."[12] There are a number of good reasons to follow his advice. Releases keep your user community engaged—users have a new release to download, test out, and critique. Frequent releases also mean that bugs have a shorter lifespan. If you hold onto bug fixes for long periods, you increase the chances that more people will run into the bug that's already fixed in your development tree.

Releasing real, working software is the most effective way to battle FUD[13] and head off competitors who might be close to a release themselves. Even in open source software, being the first to market has its benefits!

Finally, by releasing your module, you make it clear that your module is still being supported. It's unfortunate, but when people see that a module hasn't been updated in a few months they don't think "stable," they think "abandoned!"[14]

---

10. A Web-browsing, mail-and-news-reading, IRC-chatting, calendar-having mega-application. See `http://www.mozilla.org` for details.

11. An open-source relational database system. See `http://www.mysql.com` for details.

12. The Cathedral and The Bazaar, `http://tuxedo.org/~esr/writings/cathedral-bazaar`.

13. FUD stands for Fear, Uncertainty, and Doubt. It is the result of announcing a new feature, but not releasing the code. Commercial software companies (most famously Microsoft) use this technique to prevent their customers and potential customers from jumping ship to a competing product.

14. Mark-Jason Dominus, from an interview by the author via e-mail in the spring of 2002

Stable and Development Releases

Despite all that good advice I just laid out, some of you aren't going to feel comfortable releasing a new version of your module with every new bug fix and feature. The reason usually is that you feel that your software should live up to a certain level of stability that requires long periods of testing to establish. This is laudable goal, and it doesn't have to be in conflict with the "release early, release often" credo.

In order to satisfy your need for stability while still reaping the benefits of frequent releases, you can divide your releases into frequent development releases and infrequent stable releases. CPAN even has support for this built in. If your version number ends with an underscore followed by numbers, CPAN won't index it for automatic download by the CPAN module. For example, say I make a stable release of Data::Counter version "1.2" and then I want to release a development version—if I give it the version number "1.2_01", CPAN won't index it for download. Then when users run the following command:

```
$ perl -MCPAN -e 'install "Data::Counter"'
```

they'll get the stable version. To get the development version, they'll have to download it directly from CPAN—the CPAN shell cannot be used to download development versions of modules.

 CAUTION The *only* way to create a development version that CPAN will recognize as such is to append an underscore and a number to the version. It won't work to add words to the end; for example, "1.01_alpha" will get indexed as a normal release.

Be careful not to use making development releases as an excuse to put off stable releases indefinitely. This may sound obvious, but many open-source projects have been caught by this trap—even Perl itself, by some accounts. All your users deserve the fun of a new release, not just the thrill seekers!

Making Announcements

When you do issue a new release, you should make sure people hear about it. Write to mailing lists where potential users hang out. (As long as such partially off-topic posts are allowed—perl5-porters is a good example of a mailing list where you *should not* send your announcements.)

Many CPAN authors are in the bad habit of simply forwarding the acknowledgement e-mail from PAUSE to various mailing lists. This isn't much of an enticement to download unless you already happen to be a user of the module. I recommend you post a stripped-down version of your README along with download instructions and the most recent snippet of your change log. If you've included patches from other developers, be sure to list them in the announcement—crediting your contributors will help encourage them to keep contributing and might even inspire others to join their lauded company.

freshmeat

freshmeat is a Web site dedicated to collecting release announcements of open-source projects. Thousands of potential users read through the announcement list every day looking for new and interesting projects. Registering your modules at freshmeat is easy; just visit the site, which is at `http://freshmeat.net`, and read the instructions there.

Usenet

The `comp.lang.perl.announce` mailing list was set up specifically as a place to post announcements of Perl-related projects. Your CPAN modules, no matter how bizarre, certainly qualify.

Summary

Maintaining a module on CPAN is a challenging but rewarding occupation. I've given you the tools to maintain your modules and cultivate your user communities to the limit of your modules' potential. Now it's your job to go out and create the next CPAN hit. But what makes a module into a huge success? I'll address that question in the next chapter, where I'll examine the most successful CPAN modules.

CHAPTER 7

Great CPAN Modules

CPAN HOUSES A WIDE VARIETY of modules, from 10-line modules created by a single author to massive 10,000-line multifile modules created by teams of programmers. In fact, size and complexity are just one measure of variety in CPAN modules. Along every conceivable axis—design, documentation, implementation, testing, packaging—there exists great variety. CPAN is a virtual jungle teeming with biodiversity.

And, like a real jungle, CPAN hosts a struggle for survival. Modules on CPAN don't compete for food and shelter, but they do compete for equally scarce resources: users and developers. Open-source projects depend on users to grow and evolve. Without a group of users and at least one dedicated developer, even the best module on CPAN will soon find itself growing obsolete.

Of course, failure in this struggle isn't quite as perilous as it is in the real world; modules that fail to find a user community are never killed.[1] Also, it must be stressed that although modules are pitted in competition, their *authors* are not. Nearly every CPAN author has a couple duds in their module directories, but that doesn't detract from the success of their better works.

This chapter will examine the properties of a "great" CPAN module by examining particularly successful modules. These modules have attracted large numbers of users and are often supported by a number of programmers. Since CPAN doesn't collect statistics on module usage,[2] I've chosen modules to look at based on my own experience as a CPAN user. There are, of course, many excellent modules that I didn't have the time to include.

One of the best ways to learn how to create great CPAN modules is to read other great modules. Consider this chapter an annotated reading list and you'll be well on your way.

What Makes a Great CPAN Module?

The essential question of this chapter seems simple. So simple, in fact, that there's a single answer poised on the tip of every CPAN author's tongue: Great modules come from addressing a common problem in a reliable and efficient way.

---

1. Although some people think they should be! As Lincoln Stein, author of the CGI and GD modules, put it when asked what changes he would like to see in CPAN, "Purge the cruft!"

2. See the CPAN FAQ for an answer to the question, "Why not?"

How do I know what's on the tip of every CPAN author's tongue? I don't really, but I do know about a representative sample. I sent a set of questions to 30 of CPAN's most prolific authors. Their answers, for which I am very grateful, guided me in my quest for CPAN greatness. See the Acknowledgments at the front of the book for a full list.

But back to their single overwhelmingly shared sentiment—that great CPAN modules come from high-quality solutions to common problems. This has the ring of truth to it; after all, if success is partially measured by the size of the user community, then solving a problem that many users have is certainly a good start. And the quality of the module itself is also an obvious factor. If a module isn't reliable or doesn't perform well, then other developers will be tempted to create alternative implementations that will compete for user attention.

That said, it is my premise that there additional factors at work. I think the best CPAN modules certainly solve common problems and provide reliable, efficient solutions. However, they also encourage extension, allowing users to develop add-on modules in response to their particular needs. Furthermore, great modules are invariably supported by clear documentation with plenty of examples. Finally, great modules must possess the ability to grow over time to meet the changing needs of their users.

Some of the purported attributes of a great module are not necessarily accurate. For example, some commonly heard advice is to never create a new module that does the same job as an existing module. However, as I'll show in the upcoming sections, many of CPAN's most successful modules began their lives as better implementations of already solved problems. That said, if you're going where others have gone before, it makes sense to ensure that your solution really will be a better one. The only way to do that is to take a close look at the competition—give them a try and read their code before you set yourself the task of replacing them.

CGI.pm

The CGI module, often written "CGI.pm" to distinguish it from the standard it supports, is the granddaddy of successful CPAN modules.[3] Perl is the most popular environment for CGI programming,[4] and CGI.pm is the most popular way to go about it. CGI.pm was created by Lincoln Stein[5] as a Perl5 implementation of the facilities provided by the venerable Perl4 library `cgi-lib.pl`. It leveraged the new

---

3. So successful, in fact, that it's now included with Perl! But it was once a CPAN module, so I feel justified including it here.

4. Otherwise known as *Web programming*. CGI, or Common Gateway Interface, is used by programmers to create interactive applications for the Web.

5. See Lincoln Stein's site at `http://stein.cshl.org/`.

OO support in Perl 5 to provide a simpler way to write CGI scripts. CGI.pm also included many new features, particularly extensive support for HTML generation.

The most obvious reason CGI.pm is so popular is that it represents a complete solution to a difficult problem. Nearly every capability you could want in a CGI environment is present, from parameter parsing to file uploads to cookie handling to HTML form generation. All of these capabilities are documented clearly with full examples of nearly every possible usage.

Another highlight is the interface design. Lincoln Stein has embraced TMTOWTDI[6] to a degree that few have managed. For example, a critical task in CGI is parameter parsing and processing. CGI.pm provides *five* different ways to access the CGI parameters. Many of these are supplied to allow for backwards compatibility with older libraries and older versions of CGI.pm. Stein has always focused on keeping older scripts working even as he enhances CGI.pm with new features.

Furthermore, CGI.pm provides its functionality through *both* object-oriented and functional interfaces. This is accomplished by starting each and every subroutine in CGI.pm as follows:

```
sub method_foo {
   my($self,@p) = self_or_default(@_);
```

The self_or_default() routine extracts $self from @_, or if $self is not found uses a globally defined CGI object instead. This means that users can pick either an object-oriented style:

```
use CGI;
my $cgi = CGI->new;
print join "\n", $cgi->param();
```

or functional calling style:

```
use CGI qw(param);
print join "\n", param();
```

People writing quick scripts can benefit from the brevity of the functional interface, whereas those developing more intensive CGI code can benefit from the extensibility of the OO interface.

---

6. Short for "There's more than one way to do it."

For all that is great about the CGI module, it has its detractors. The usual complaints fall along the lines of memory consumption, performance and sheer code size. For these reasons there are many competitors to CGI.pm on CPAN—CGI::Lite,[7] CGI::Minimal,[8] and CGI::Thin,[9] to name a few. These modules tend to start by implementing just the core CGI functionality and grow slowly from there as the author realizes that this or that CGI.pm function is really quite useful after all. Ultimately they may perform better and use less memory, but CGI.pm remains more popular for a good reason—it does everything a CGI programmer needs and it does it well.

DBI

The DBI module, by Tim Bunce, provides Perl with an object-oriented interface to virtually every relational database system under the sun (MySQL, PostgreSQL, Oracle, Sybase, and many more). DBI accomplishes this Olympian feat by relying on database driver (DBD) modules to interface with individual databases. For example, when you use DBI to talk to a PostgreSQL database, DBI loads the DBD::Pg[10] module. If you want to connect to MySQL, the DBD::mysql[11] module is loaded. Even CSV[12] files can be accessed through the DBD::CSV[13] module. There are DBD modules available for all of the commonly used databases, and many of the less common ones too.

Before DBI, uneven database connection libraries were the norm—each database had its own modules and they all worked (or didn't work) differently. Perl was struggling to be useful for serious database software development. DBI provided a great platform for database interface libraries, and turned Perl into a serious database application programming environment.

DBI defines two interfaces—a front-end interface for users and a back-end interface for DBD module programmers. Regardless of the underlying DBD module being used, the DBI front-end interface remains the same. The benefit of this system is that users can learn to use the DBI module and employ those skills to access any database with a DBD driver. Also, code written to the DBI interface can be easily ported between databases.[14]

---

7. Written by Benjamin Low

8. Written by Benjamin Franz

9. Written by R. Geoffrey Avery

10. Written by Jeffrey Baker

11. Written by Jochen Wiedmann

12. Stands for Comma Separated Values, a text format commonly used to store tabular data

13. Written by Jeff Zucker

14. This would be much easier if databases all spoke the same dialect of SQL, but unfortunately that is not the case.

The DBI back-end interface for DBD creation is a rather complicated mix of composition and inheritance. Learning to create a DBD module is an arduous task, but that hasn't stopped the brigade of DBD developers from supporting nearly every database available today! This is an interesting point—front-end interfaces must be kept simple, but a back-end extension interface can be challenging and yet it will still be used if the module is successful enough. All DBD authors have to go through the difficult task of mastering the back-end interface, but once they do, their work immediately benefits from the elegance of the front-end interface. And their users are none the wiser.

If DBD modules can be viewed as back-end extensions, DBI also supports front-end extensions through the DBIx namespace. DBIx modules often work through composition. They proxy normal DBI methods to an internally held object and add new methods to perform common tasks. Other DBIx modules provide entirely new interfaces to DBI through tying.

DBI contains excellent documentation. The SYNOPSIS section shows an example of every available method call, all using a common convention in variable naming. This naming convention has become pervasive in DBI programming— virtually all database handles are called `$dbh`, statement handles `$sth`, and so on. This makes learning DBI and reading other programmers' DBI code easier.

The DBI user and developer community is perhaps one of the most active in all of Perldom. They maintain the `dbi-users@perl.org` mailing list where users and developers discuss problems and future development. See `http://dbi.perl.org` for more information.

The DBI and DBD modules have been responsible for turning Perl into the best platform for rapid database application development in existence today. They demonstrate the best results (if not the cleanest implementation) that modular and object-oriented programming has to offer. DBI was designed with reusability and extensibility as top priorities, and the results speak for themselves.

Storable

The Storable module provides *serialization* and *deserialization* of arbitrary Perl data structures. Serialization is the process of transforming a data structure into a string, and deserialization is the reverse—transforming a string back into a data structure. Serialization is a precursor to many other interesting programming projects—mobile agents, object persistence, persistent caching, and more.

When Raphael Manfredi created Storable, there were existing solutions to data serialization on CPAN already. Chief among them was the excellent Data::Dumper by Gurusamy Sarathy, which is still used frequently today. The problem with Data::Dumper, and other serialization systems, as Raphael saw it, was that they were too slow. Storable solved this problem by digging deep into the guts of Perl with C code (which you'll learn about in the next few chapters). As a result, Storable was able to offer serialization at a greatly reduced runtime cost.

Storable is a great example of doing one thing and doing it well. As such, Storable has become the basis for many other modules that add services on top of basic serialization.

Another key to Storable's success is the simplicity of its interface. All you need to get full use out of the module are two functions—`store()` and `retrieve()`—both of which are exported by default. More complicated usages are supported by a handful of extra functions that can be imported by request. Contrast this with Data::Dumper, which offers a slightly greater range of functionality, but at the price of a confusing functional and OO interface that uses an odd convention for subroutine naming (`Dumper()` and `Data::Dumper->Dump()`, for example).

A testament to Storable's success is that when Raphael recently announced his retirement from the Perl community, the perl5-porters[15] took over maintenance of Storable. Storable is now included as a core Perl module.

Net::FTP

The Net::FTP module by Graham Barr is just one of a collection of modules offered in the libnet package. Net::FTP offers an object-oriented interface to the client side[16] of the FTP[17] protocol. With Net::FTP, users can write scripts that upload and download files from FTP servers with extreme ease.

Net::FTP is successful first and foremost because it answers a very common need. However, the module also benefits from an exceptionally clear interface. Learning the module is easy, and, better yet, the payoff is bigger than just learning to FTP files with Perl. This is because Net::FTP is implemented as a child class of both Net::Cmd and IO::Socket::INET (both also by Graham Barr). Once a user has learned Net::FTP, the other modules in the libnet distribution—Net::SMTP, Net::POP3 and Net::NNTP to name a few—will be easy for that user to pick up.

Net::FTP demonstrates the power of a careful use of inheritance to create a group of modules that share common base functionality. Overall Graham's modules are models of code clarity and object-oriented design. Anyone interested in implementing network protocols in Perl would benefit from a close examination of Net::FTP and the other modules in libnet.

---

15. The perl5-porters are responsible for the maintenance and development of Perl 5.

16. For the server side, see the excellent Net::FTPServer module by Richard Jones, Rob Brown, Keith Turner and Azazel.

17. File Transfer Protocol, an internet protocol for transferring files. See RFC 959, available at `http://rfc-editor.org`.

LWP

The LWP module collection, written by Martijn Koster and Gisle Aas,[18] provides an interface to the network protocol of the World Wide Web—HTTP.[19] The project was originally based on Roy Fielding's[20] libwww-perl library for Perl 4. After the release of Perl 5, both Martijn and Gisle built their own Perl 5 version of libwww-perl. They decided to combine forces, and the result is the LWP module of today.

LWP modules have done for HTTP what Net::FTP did for FTP. It provides a simple and extensible implementation for writing HTTP clients. Given the explosive growth of the internet, LWP has come to hold a central place in the toolbox of many Perl hackers. If the data you want is on the Web, then you can use LWP to access it.

Another reason that LWP has been successful is that it goes to extreme lengths to make easy things easy while still making hard things possible. The LWP::Simple module that comes with LWP embodies this philosophy. For example, to fetch a copy of the `cpan.org` home page, this is all the code that's needed:

```
use LWP::Simple qw(get);
$contents = get('http://cpan.org');
```

It just doesn't get much simpler than that! But LWP doesn't end with LWP::Simple; for more complicated uses, it implements a fully object-oriented interface with classes for every component of the request and response (LWP::UserAgent, HTTP::Request, HTTP::Response, and so on). By providing two interfaces, one simple enough to learn in a day and the other powerful enough to address nearly any need, LWP can be used by both novices and experts.

LWP's object-oriented interface has provided a fruitful ground for extension modules. One popular example is LWP::Parallel by Marc Langheinrich, which extends LWP to allow users to make multiple requests simultaneously. Existing code that uses LWP can be modified to use LWP::Parallel very easily as most of the interfaces remain the same.

The LWP project has a homepage at `http://www.linpro.no/lwp/`. There you'll find links to the SourceForge-hosted CVS repository and bug tracker, development mailing list, and a list of applications built with LWP. You'll also find links to the LWPng project, which Gisle Aas started to revise the implementation of LWP to better support HTTP/1.1.

---

18. With lots of help—see the Acknowledgments section of the LWP documentation for a virtual who's who of Perl development.

19. LWP also supports HTTPS, FTP (using Net::FTP), Gopher, and NNTP, but HTTP is by far the most commonly used.

20. See Roy Fielding's site at `http://www.ics.uci.edu/~fielding/`.

XML::SAX

The Perl XML[21] community has come a long way in recent years. In the beginning there was XML::Parser, created by Larry Wall and maintained by Clark Cooper. XML::Parser provides a thin wrapper around the Expat XML parsing library written in C.[22] At the same time, the Perl XML mailing list, perl-xml@listserv.ActiveState.com, got started to provide a place to discuss using XML with Perl.

XML::Parser did (and still does) an excellent job of parsing XML. But it suffers from a quirky interface that is difficult to learn to use effectively. As a result, many wrapper modules grew up around XML::Parser—XML::Twig, XML::Simple, and XML::TokeParser, to name a few. These modules have helped the situation a great deal and are basically the "state of the art" in Perl XML usage.

XML::SAX[23] may not be the most popular module at present, but it represents an evolutionary step forward in the development of Perl's capabilities. It provides an interface for XML parser usage in the same way that DBI provides an interface for SQL database usage. Individual XML parsers can be plugged into the back-end API provided by XML::SAX. Much like using MySQL through DBI means loading the DBD::MySQL module, using Expat through XML::SAX loads XML::SAX::Expat. On the front-end modules can make use a of consistent and standardized[24] interface to whichever parser is in use.

XML::SAX is an object-oriented module, and it provides much of its functionality through inheritance. To start building a SAX parser or filter, the user creates a module that inherits from XML::SAX::Base and overrides methods as required to implement the desired functionality. It is interesting to note that although XML::SAX is tackling a similar problem to DBI, the choice of object-oriented methods differs— DBI chooses a complex mix of composition and inheritance, whereas XML::SAX chooses a pure inheritance model.

One of the most interesting front-end modules to make use of XML::SAX thus far is XML::SAX::Machines by Barrie Slaymaker. XML::SAX::Machines provides a layer over XML::SAX-based parsers and filters that allows the end user to easily construct XML processing pipelines. Using XML::SAX::Machines, XML::SAX components can be assembled into systems of almost limitless capability. Typically, input XML enters one end of the pipeline through a SAX parser, is transformed and processed by the configured SAX filters, and is output by a SAX writer at the end.

---

21. XML stands for the eXtensible Markup Language. See http://www.w3c.org/XML for details.

22. Written by James Clark. See http://expat.sourceforge.net for details.

23. Written by Matt Sergeant. See http://sergeant.org.

24. XML::SAX implements the SAX standard, versions 1 and 2. See http://www.saxproject.org for details.

Given the proliferation of SAX filters, I expect this to become a popular system for XML processing in Perl.

The Perl XML community is interesting aside from any particular module. Using the Perl XML mailing list as a hub, the community is unusual for its cohesion. Module ideas are vigorously discussed and the community even shares a Source-Forge project and Web space. It may be that this cohesion has come as a response to the largely uphill battle facing the Perl XML developers. As Matt Sergeant put it, "Right now our biggest battle seems to be for acceptance within the Perl community as a whole. People completely accept things like the DBI, Tk/Gtk, and LWP as a vital part of Perl, but are quick to dismiss XML as something they just don't need and really don't like. We're kind of the bastard child of the Perl community. But we're winning small battles quite often now."

Parse::RecDescent

No discussion of great CPAN modules would be complete without at least one module by the "Mad Scientist of Perl," Dr. Damian Conway.[25] His Parse::RecDescent module generates recursive descent parsers from a vaguely yacc-like grammar. If you've never used yacc, the concept is simple: you write a description of the grammar you want to parse and the parser compiler, yacc, generates an executable parser that will parse your grammar. Parse::RecDescent extends this concept in a number of directions that allow the grammar writer far more freedom of expression than yacc.

Parse::RecDescent's interface is superficially object oriented—parser objects are instantiated by passing the grammar to `Parse::RecDescent->new()`. The returned parser object has methods to parse input text. However, the real interface to Parse::RecDescent is in the grammar. The syntax of Parse::RecDescent grammars is essentially an entirely new programming language designed specifically for building parsers that interact with Perl. The advantage of this approach over an entirely object-oriented interface are brevity and flexibility.

The success of Parse::RecDescent is largely the usual mix of a common problem and an efficient solution. However, like many of Damian's modules, it is also an enjoyable technical challenge for the user. Learning to use Parse::RecDescent is fun in and of itself; the fact that it helps you solve parsing problems too can seem almost secondary!

The most common complaint about Parse::RecDescent is that it's too slow and uses too much memory. My opinion is that for what Parse::RecDescent accomplishes, it's amazing that it uses as few resources as it does. However, to answer these critiques, Damian is hard at work on a completely new module, Parse::FastDescent, which may

---

25. See Dr. Damian Conway's sites at `http://www.cs.monash.edu.au/~damian` and `http://www.yetanother.org/damian/`.

be available as you read this. If it is, I heartily recommend you check it out, whether you have some parsing to do or not! It's sure to be a mind-bending experience.

Summary

This chapter has given you a quick look at some of the best the CPAN has to offer. I've also offered my opinions about why these modules in particular have been successful. Take this as a starting point and begin your own excavation of CPAN's outer reaches. The next chapter returns to solid technical ground to introduce a little known tool in your module-programming toolkit—the Perl C API.

### CHAPTER 8

Programming Perl in C

THE NEXT THREE CHAPTERS teach a black art—programming Perl modules in C. To get the most out of these chapters you'll need to have some experience with the C programming language. You don't need to be a C guru, but you do need to know your pointers and macros. If you're worried that you don't know enough C, I suggest you buy a good C reference and give it a try. When you get stuck, hit the books—I think you'll find it happening less often than you expect.

This chapter presents an introduction to Perl's C API. Next, the XS system is presented in Chapter 9. XS is the system used by the vast majority of C modules on CPAN today. Finally, in Chapter 10, I'll show you a shortcut—Inline::C. Inline::C is a brand new module that I predict will be used for the majority C modules in the future.

One thing this chapter *won't* do is explain how Perl works. This is fascinating material but largely unrelated to the task of writing Perl modules in C. For pointers to documentation on this and other related topics, see the "References" section at the end of the chapter.

Why C?

Writing Perl modules in C is a lot more work than writing them in Perl. The end result is likely to be buggier and less portable than an equivalent implementation in Perl. As such, you should be hesitant to write in C unless you have a good reason.

So, what constitutes a good reason? The best reason is simple: because you have to. There are times when Perl simply cannot do what you need done. For example, when you need to interface with a library written in C, you have no choice but to write some C code. CPAN contains numerous examples of this type of module—Tk, GD, most of the DBD drivers, and many more. When you come across a C library that provides a new service, you should consider it a great opportunity to create a new CPAN module.

A common, often misguided, reason to create Perl modules in C is to increase performance. The reasoning is misguided because the Perl interpreter itself is written in C. Thus most of what a Perl program does is already happening in highly optimized C code. You have to believe you can do better than the C gurus that created Perl to think that your module will be faster simply by being written in C.[1]

---

1. Mark-Jason Dominus's article "Why Not Translate Perl to C?" on Perl.com contains an extended proof of this assertion. You can find the article at http://www.perl.com/pub/a/2001/06/27/ctoperl.html.

That said, sometimes you can write faster code in C than in Perl. After careful profiling and tuning, sometimes it turns out that 90 percent of your module's runtime is taking place inside a small section of code. If you can replace this piece with a call to a function written in carefully crafted C, you might realize significant gains. The watchword here is *profiling*: You need to find the bottleneck and be sure you can't optimize it using more conventional techniques.

One place where C does have a notable advantage over Perl in performance is in memory usage. C requires you to be entirely responsible for every memory allocation; as a result, you gain a much higher degree of control over how your data is stored. Sometimes this can be used to allow your programs to run in a much smaller amount of memory than a Perl implementation would.[2]

The Perl C API

To write Perl modules in C, you need to have a working knowledge of the Perl C API (Perl API for short). This section will give you the basics, but you should know where to go for the details: perlapi. The perlapi documentation that comes with Perl is the Perl API bible. Nearly every C function and macro that Perl supports is listed there along with descriptions generated from comments in the Perl source.

Data Types

For every data type available to Perl programmers, there is a corresponding C type (see Table 8-1). Perl's data types are a lot like objects in that they each have a set of functions that operate on them. Note that these data types are *always* manipulated through pointers.

Table 8-1. Perl Data Types

Type	Full Name	Perl Example
SV*	Scalar value	$scalar
AV*	Array value	@array
HV*	Hash value	%hash
CV*	Code value	&sub
GV*	Glob value	*glob

---

2. But before you decide this describes your problem, make sure you check out Bit::Vector by Steffen Beyer and the many modules that use it to efficiently store data.

Perl's data types are like objects in another sense—they support a lightweight form of *polymorphism*. Polymorphism is the property of an object in a derived class to behave like an object of a parent class. In this case the inheritance tree is simple—SV behaves as the parent class, and all the other types derive from SV. The Perl internals exploit this by using function parameter and return types of SV* to actually contain any of the available data types.

Scalar Values (SV)

The SV type represents a Perl scalar (that is, $scalar). A scalar may contain a signed integer (IV), an unsigned integer (UV), a floating-point number (NV), or a string value (PV). These types are typedef aliases for fundamental C types. For example, IV may be a typedef for int or long. NV is usually a typedef for double. You can find out what the underlying types are on your system using the perl -V switch. For example, here's the output on my system:

```
$ perl -V:ivtype -V:uvtype -V:nvtype
ivtype='long';
uvtype='unsigned long';
nvtype='double';
```

Notice that PV wasn't included here—that's because PV is always char * regardless of the platform.

Perl uses aliases for C's fundamental types to improve portability; C's types can differ wildly between platforms, but Perl's aliases maintain a modicum of consistency. Perl's IV and UV types are guaranteed to be at least 32-bits wide *and* large enough to safely hold a pointer. For exact bit widths, Perl contains typedefs called I8, U8, I16, U16, I32, and U32 that are guaranteed to be at least the size specified and as small as possible.

Like all Perl data types, SV is an *opaque type*. An opaque type is one that you are not intended to interact with directly. Instead, you call functions that operate on the data type. This means that you should never dereference a pointer to a Perl data type directly—doing so exposes the underlying implementation of the data type, which may change wildly between Perl versions.

Creation

The simplest way to create a new SV is with the NEWSV macro:

```
SV *sv = NEWSV(0,0);
```

The first parameter is an "id" used to detect memory leaks; unless you're doing memory debugging, you can safely use zero. The second parameter can be used to preallocate memory inside the SV for strings. If you know you'll be using the SV to hold a large string, then you can potentially improve performance by preallocating the space.

In practice, NEWSV is rarely used. This is because the Perl API supplies convenience functions to create SVs directly from the available value types:

```
SV *sv_iv, *sv_uv, *sv_nv, *sv_pv;
sv_iv = newSViv(-10);        // sv_iv contains the signed integer value -10
sv_uv = newSVuv(10);         // sv_uv contains the unsigned integer value 10
sv_nv = newSVnv(10.5);       // sv_nv contains the floating-point value 10.5
sv_pv = newSVpv("ten", 0);   // sv_pv contains the string "ten", the second
                             // parameter tells Perl to compute the length with
                             // strlen()
```

A more efficient version of newSVpv() called newSVpvn() doesn't offer automatic strlen() calling:

```
sv_pv = newSVpvn("ten", 3);  // second parameter gives the length of "ten"
```

A version that uses sprintf()-style format strings, newSVpvf(), is also available:

```
sv_pv = newSVpvf("%d", 10);  // sv_pv contains the string "10"
```

 NOTE The comments used in the C examples are actually C++-style comments (// comment). This was done to improve readability and reduce the space required by the comments. Most modern C compilers will accept these comments, but if yours doesn't you'll need to change them to C-style comments (/* comment */) or omit them entirely.

Type Checking

You can test the type of an SV using the SV*OK macros. Specific versions exist for the specific types:

```
if (SvIOK_notUV(sv)) warn("sv contains an IV.");
if (SvIOK_UV(sv))    warn("sv contains a UV.");
if (SvNOK(sv))       warn("sv contains an NV.");
if (SvPOK(sv))       warn("sv contains a PV.");
```

There are also tests that combine one or more of the preceding tests:

```
if (SvNIOK(sv))      warn("sv contains a number of some type (IV, UV or NV)");
if (SvIOK(sv))       warn("sv contains an integer of some type (IV or UV)");
```

Getting Values

The following macros return the value stored inside the SV as the requested type. If necessary, they will convert the value to the requested type.

```
IV iv = SvIV(sv);          // get an IV from sv
UV uv = SvUV(sv);          // get a UV from sv
NV nv = SvNV(sv);          // get an NV from sv
STRLEN len;
char  *pv = SvPV(sv, len); // get a PV from sv, setting len to the
                           // length of the string
```

NOTE If an SV contains a nonnumeric string, then calling SvIV(), SvUV(), or SvNV() on it will result in the value 0. To find out if an SV contains something that will result in a valid number, use the looks_like_number() function.

These functions can have a side effect—they may change the internal representation of the SV. For example, after a call to SvPV(), the stringified form of the SV will be cached inside the SV, and both SvIOK and SvPOK will return true. As a result, future calls to SvPV on this scalar will use the cached copy instead of doing the conversion again. This has two implications: First, the type of an SV may change even if it isn't written to, and second, the memory usage of an SV may grow even if it isn't written to.

There is a version of SvPV that is guaranteed to produce an SV with only a string value, SvPV_force. The behavior is the same as SvPV, but afterward only SvPOK will return true and only the string value will be retained inside the SV. This function is necessary if you're going to be changing the string value directly with the SvPVX macro introduced later.

Setting Values

Given an initialized SV, you can load it with any of the value types using the sv_set*
family of functions:

```
sv_setiv(sv, -10);    // sv contains the signed integer (IV) -10
sv_setuv(sv, 10);     // sv contains the unsigned integer (UV) 10
sv_setnv(sv, 10.5);   // sv contains the unsigned integer (UV) -10
sv_setpv(sv, "10");   // sv contains the string value (PV) "10"
```

The PV forms also come in a few more flavors. There's one that uses an
sprintf()-style format string:

```
sv_setpvf(sv, "ten: %d", 10);  // sv contains the string value (PV) "ten: 10"
```

and one that takes a length argument to allow for strings that aren't null termi-
nated or that contain null bytes:

```
sv_setpvn(sv, "10", 2);  // sets sv to the 2-character string "10"
```

Direct Access

If you know the type of an SV, then you can directly access the underlying value
type using the an Sv*X macro. This is useful for two reasons—it is faster since it
avoids testing the type of the data, and it is *lvaluable*. In C, a macro is said to be
lvaluable if it may legally be used as an lvalue. The most common lvalue is the left-
hand side of an assignment operator. Sv*X allows you to efficiently set the value of
an SV without needing to call a function.

```
SvIVX(sv_iv) = -100;          // directly set the IV inside sv_iv to -100
SvUVX(sv_uv) = 100;           // directly set the UV inside sv_uv to 100
SvNVX(sv_nv) = 100.10;        // directly set the NV inside sv_nv to 100.5
warn("PV: %s", SvPVX(sv_pv)); // directly access the string inside sv_pv
```

Note that you *cannot* safely use the return value from SvPVX() as an lvalue—
doing so would change the string pointed to by the SV and would cause an instant
memory leak. Other bad things would happen too, because the SV structure keeps
track of more than just the pointer to the string—it also tracks the length and an
offset into the string buffer where the string begins.

CAUTION Be careful with Sv*X macros; if you use one without first checking that the SV is of the correct type, you might get a segmentation fault, or worse, silently corrupt nearby data in memory!

After using an Sv*X macro to update the value inside an SV, it's often necessary to update the type information of the SV. This is because SVs will cache conversion values when converting between types. You need to tell the SV to invalidate any other cached representations using a macro of the form Sv*OK_only(). For example:

```
SvIVX(sv_iv) = 100;     // directly set the IV inside sv_iv to 100
SvIOK_only(sv_iv);      // invalidate non-IV representations inside sv_iv
```

In general it is better to use the sv_set functions rather than Sv*X macros. However, in some cases the performance improvement can make it worth the risk.

String Functions

Just like Perl, the Perl API contains functionality to make string processing easier. There are a set of functions for string concatenation:

```
sv_catpv(sv, "foo");        // adds "foo" to the end of sv
sv_catpvn(sv, "foo", 3);    // adds "foo" to the end of sv, with a length arg
sv_catpvf(sv, "ten: %d", 10); // adds "ten: 10" to the end of sv
sv_catsv(sv_to, sv_from);   // adds the contents of sv_from to the
                            // end of sv_to
```

Getting the length of an SV is done as follows:

```
STRLEN len = sv_len(sv);
```

If you want to grow the size of the string, do the following:

```
char *new_ptr = sv_grow(sv, 1024); // grows sv to 1k and returns a pointer to
                                   // the new character buffer
```

Truncate the string in this manner:

```
SvCUR_set(sv, 10);              // the SV is now 10 bytes long
```

Inserting a string into the middle of an SV, similar to the substr built-in in Perl, is done as follows:

```
sv_insert(sv, offset, length, "string to insert", strlen("string to insert"));
```

The next example shows how to remove characters from the start of a string:

```
SV *sv = newSVpv("Just another Perl hacker.", 0);
sv_chop(sv, SvPVX(sv) + 13);  // sv contains "Perl hacker" after this
```

The second parameter to sv_chop is a pointer into the string to the new first character.

If you need to do substring searches over a large string, you can speed up the process using the Boyer-Moore search algorithm.[3] This is done by first compiling the SV to be searched for with fbm_compile()[4] and then searching with fbm_instr(). For example, here's a function that takes two SVs and returns the offset o f the second inside the first or -1 on failure. This function uses SvPVX and SvEND[5] so it's only safe to call if both SVs are SvPOK()–real code would include the necessary checks and conversions of course!

```
int fast_search (SV *source, SV *search) {
  char *found; // pointer to hold result of search

  // compile search string using Boyer-Moore algorithm
  fbm_compile(search, 0);

  // conduct the search for the search string inside source
  found = fbm_instr(SvPVX(source), SvEND(source), search, 0);

  // if the search failed, return -1
  if (found == Nullch) return -1;

  // return the offset of search within source
  return found - SvPVX(source);
}
```

In my tests (looking for a single word in a string containing all of /usr/dict/words), this version was between two and three times faster than a version that used Perl's index() function.

---

3. Boyer-Moore is a search algorithm that matches without examining every character. It has the unusual feature of actually going *faster* the longer the match string is.

4. Note that fbm_compile() modifies the SV passed to it. As a result, it can't be used on constant SVs like those produced from string constants.

5. A macro that returns a pointer to the end of the string inside an SV

Comparison Functions

The Perl API contains a set of calls to make comparing SVs easier. First, there are functions to test whether an SV is true in the Perl sense:

```
if (sv_true(sv)) warn("sv is true!");
```

Tests for equality can be expressed using these two functions:

```
if (sv_eq(sv1, sv2))      warn("The SVs are equal");
if (sv_cmp(sv1, sv2) == 0) warn("The SVs are equal");
```

The Perl API also comes with a full set of normal string comparison functions. These are useful when you have an SV and a normal C string to compare. You might be tempted to "upgrade" the string to an SV and use sv_eq(), but that's generally not an efficient solution.

```
char *string = SvPV(sv, len); // extract string from an SV
if (strEQ(string, "foo"))      warn("SV contains foo");
if (strNE(string, "foo"))      warn("SV does not contain foo");
if (strGT(string, "foo"))      warn("SV is greater than foo");
if (strGE(string, "foo"))      warn("SV is greater than or equal to foo");
if (strLT(string, "foo"))      warn("SV is less than foo");
if (strLE(string, "foo"))      warn("SV is less than or equal to foo");
if (strnEQ(string, "foo", 3))  warn("SV starts with foo");
```

You can test for undef by comparing the SV* to the globally defined PL_sv_undef:

```
if (sv == &PL_sv_undef) warn("sv is undefined!");
```

Notice that the preceding test uses the & operator to get the address of PL_sv_undef and compares it to the address of the SV since SVs are always handled using pointers. A common mistake is to leave off the & on PL_sv_undef and end up with confusing compiler errors about type mismatches.

Array Values (AV)

Perl's arrays are represented in C by the AV type. Underneath the covers an AV is simply a normal C array of SVs with some bookkeeping information to make certain operations faster. However, just like SVs, AVs are opaque types, and you must work with them through the supplied set of functions.

Creation

The simplest way to create an AV is to use the newAV() function:

```
AV *av = newAV();
```

If you have an array of SV*s, then you can create an array from them using av_make():

```
AV *av;
SV *sv_array[3];
sv_array[0] = newSVpv("foo",0);
sv_array[1] = newSVpv("bar",0);
sv_array[2] = newSVpv("baz",0);
av = av_make(3, sv_array);      // create an array from the three SVs
```

Fetching Values

AVs support access by index as well as the familiar pop and shift operations. You can fetch an SV from an array using the av_fetch() function:

```
SV **svp;
svp = av_fetch(av, 10, 0); // fetch $av[10] (the 0 indicates this isn't an
                           // lvalue)
if (!svp) croak("fetch failed: av doesn't have a tenth element!");
```

Notice that the return value from av_fetch() is a pointer to a pointer to SV (that is, an SV**) not a normal pointer to SV (that is, SV*). If you try to fetch a value that doesn't exist, then av_fetch() will return a NULL pointer. Be sure to check the return value before dereferencing or you'll end up with a segmentation fault if the element doesn't exist. The preceding code checks the return value and calls croak()—the Perl API version of die–if av_fetch() returns NULL.

However, you can skip testing the return value from av_fetch() if you know the element exists. You can get this information using av_exists(), which tests whether an index exists in an AV:

```
SV *sv;
if (av_exists(av, 9)) {          // check that the 10th element exists
    sv = *(av_fetch(av, 9, 0));  // safely trust av_fetch to return non-NULL
} else {
    croak("av doesn't have a tenth element!");
}
```

You can get the same effect using av_len() to check the length of the array:

```
SV *sv;
if (av_len(av) >= 9) {            // check that $#av >= 9
   sv = *(av_fetch(av, 9, 0));  // safely trust av_fetch to return non-NULL
} else {
   croak("av doesn't have a tenth element!");
}
```

The av_len() function works the same way as the $#array magic value—it returns the last valid index in an array.

Combining the preceding functions, you can now write a function to iterate through an array and print out each value:

```
void print_array (AV *av) {
   SV    *sv;     // SV pointer to hold return from array
   char  *string; // string pointer to hold SV string value
   STRLEN len;    // unused length value for SvPV()
   I32 i = 0;     // loop counter

   // loop over all valid indexes
   for (i = 0; i <= av_len(av); i++) {
      sv = *(av_fetch(av, i, 0));   // get the SV for this index
      string = SvPV(sv, len);       // get a stringified form of the SV
      printf("%s\n", string);       // print it out, one value per line
   }
}
```

As I mentioned earlier, AVs also support a version of Perl's pop and shift built-ins. These functions, av_pop() and av_shift(), return regular SV* pointers rather than the SV** pointers returned by av_fetch(). Using av_shift(), you could write a destructive version of the for loop just shown:

```
for (i = 0; i <= av_len(av); i++) {
  sv = av_shift(av);            // shift off the SV for this index
  string = SvPV(sv, len);       // get a stringified form of the SV
  printf("%s\n", string);       // print it out, one value per line
}
```

Or, using av_pop(), create a version that prints them out in the reverse order:

```
for (i = 0; i <= av_len(av); i++) {
  sv = av_pop(av);              // pop off the SV for this index
  string = SvPV(sv, len);       // get a stringified form of the SV
  printf("%s\n", string);       // print it out, one value per line
}
```

Storing Values

The Perl API offers two ways to store values in an AV, av_store() and av_push(). For example:

```
SV *sv = newSVpv("foo", 0);
av_store(av, 9, sv);        // $av[9] = "foo"
```

This will work fine if you know the AV has room for a tenth element. If not, you need to first grow the array with a call to av_fill():

```
av_fill(av, 9); // set av's length to 9
```

This works the same as setting the $#array magic value in Perl—it will truncate or grow the length of the array to the supplied value as required.

If you only need to add elements to the end of the array, av_push() offers a simpler solution. av_push() will automatically extend the array as it adds elements, so you don't need to call av_fill():

```
SV *sv = newSVpv("foo", 0);
av_push(av, sv);            // push(@av,"foo");
```

The Perl API does provide an av_unshift() function, but it doesn't work the same as the Perl unshift built-in. Instead of adding elements to the front of the array, it only adds empty slots. You then need to fill those slots with av_store(). For example, to unshift the string "foo" onto an AV:

```
SV *sv = newSVpv("foo", 0);
av_unshift(av, 1);          // unshift(@av, undef);
av_store(av, 0, sv);        // $av[0] = "foo";
```

It's a bit more work, but the result is identical to Perl's unshift built-in.

Deletion

An entire AV can be cleared with the av_clear() function:

```
av_clear(av); // @av = ();
```

or you can use it to clear just a single element:

```
av_delete(av, 9, 0); // delete the tenth element (the last arg is ignored)
```

Hash Values (HV)

Perl's hashes are represented in the Perl API as HVs. The HV type is the most complicated of the Perl data types, and it has many more functions and macros associated
with it than can be described here. I'll give you a subset of the available functions
that will let you do most of what you'll need to do with hashes. In particular, I've
avoided discussing the HE type that combines keys and values in one structure. For
these functions, see the perlapi documentation.

Creation

HVs have a single constructor, newHV():

```
HV *hv = newHV();
```

Fetching Values

The simplest way to fetch values from a hash is with hv_fetch():

```
SV **svp;
// fetch $hv{foo} (last arg indicates lvalue status)
svp = hv_fetch(hv, "foo", strlen("foo"), 0);
if (!svp) croak("fetch failed: hv does not contain value for key foo");
```

Notice that this call is similar to av_fetch(), and similarly returns an SV** that may be NULL if the requested key does not exist. Just like av_exists(), hv_exists() provides a simple way to avoid dealing with SV**s:

```
SV *sv;
// check that $hv{foo} exists
if (hv_exists(hv, "foo", strlen("foo"))) {
    // safely trust hv_fetch to return non-NULL
    sv = *(hv_fetch(hv, "foo", strlen("foo"), 0));
} else {
    croak("fetch failed: hv does not contain value for key foo");
}
```

Aside from reading a specific key, the other common way to read from a hash is to iterate through its keys and values. This is done using the hv_iter functions. For example, here's a function that prints out the keys and values in a hash:

```
void print_hash (HV *hv) {
    SV *sv;
    I32 i, count;
    char *key_string;
    STRLEN len;

    // initialize the iteration
    count = hv_iterinit(hv);

    // loop over key/value pairs
    for (i = 1; i <= count; i++) {
        sv = hv_iternextsv(hv, &key_string, (I32*) &len);
        printf("%s : %s\n", key_string, SvPV(sv, len));
    }
}
```

The preceding function uses two new Perl API calls, hv_iterinit() and hv_iternextsv(). The first initializes the iteration and returns the number of key-value pairs in the hash:

```
count = hv_iterinit(hv);
```

Then a loop is run for `count` iterations calling `hv_iternextsv()`. The call takes three parameters, the `HV*` for the hash, a pointer to a `char*` to store the key, and a pointer to an integer to store the length of the key. The function returns an `SV*` for the value of this key.

Storing Values

Values are stored in a hash using the `hv_store()` function. For example, the following stores the value `100` under to key `fuel_remaining` in `hv`:

```
SV *sv_value = newSViv(100);
hv_store(hv, "fuel_remaining", strlen("fuel_remaining"), sv_value, 0);
```

The last value allows you to pass in a precomputed hash value; setting it to 0 tells Perl to compute the hash value for you. Notice that this function doesn't have the restrictions that `av_store()` does—HVs grow automatically, and you don't have to extend them manually to store new values.

Deletion

An entire `HV` can be cleared with the `hv_clear()` function:

```
hv_clear(hv); // %hv = ();
```

Or you can use it to clear just a single key:

```
hv_delete(hv, "foo", strlen("foo"), 0); // delete $hv{foo}
```

Reference Values (RV)

In Perl, complex data structures are built using references. For example, if you want to create an array of hashes, you do it by assigning references to arrays as hash values:

```
%hash_of_arrays = (
    foo => [ 1, 2, 3 ],
    bar => [ 4, 5, 6 ],
);
```

In the Perl API, references are represented by SVs containing RV values. Much like SVs can contain IV or PV values, SVs can also contain RV values that reference other objects.

Creation

You can create a new RV using the newRV_inc() function:

```
SV *sv = newSVpv("foo",0); // $sv = "foo";
SV *rv = newRV_inc(sv);    // $rv = \$sv;
```

This function officially takes an SV* as a parameter, but it can actually be used with any Perl type that you can cast to an SV* (such as an AV* or an HV*). This pattern is repeated across the entire RV API—instead of having separate functions for SV, AV, and HV references, there is a single API, and you must cast everything to and from SV*. For example, the following creates the hash of arrays data structure shown earlier:

```
HV *hash_of_arrays_hv = newHV();
AV *foo_av            = newAV();
AV *bar_av            = newAV();

// fill in arrays
push_av(foo_av, newSViv(1));
push_av(foo_av, newSViv(2));
push_av(foo_av, newSViv(3));
push_av(bar_av, newSViv(4));
push_av(bar_av, newSViv(5));
push_av(bar_av, newSViv(6));

// create references and assign to hash
hv_store(hash_of_arrays_hv, "foo", 3, newRV_inc((SV*)foo_av), 0);
hv_store(hash_of_arrays_hv, "bar", 3, newRV_inc((SV*)bar_av), 0);
```

Once created, an RV can be distinguished from a normal SV using the SvROK macro. For example, this code would print "ok" twice after the preceding code:

```
if (SvROK(*(hv_fetch(hash_of_arrays_hv, "foo", 3, 0)))) printf("ok\n");
if (SvROK(*(hv_fetch(hash_of_arrays_hv, "bar", 3, 0)))) printf("ok\n");
```

Another way to create a reference is to use one of the sv_setref functions. These functions take an initialized SV and one of the value types (IV, UV, and so on) and creates a new SV. They then make the SV passed as an argument a reference to the new SV. Here are some examples:

```
SV *sv_rv = NEWSV(0,0);
sv_setref_iv(sv_rv, Nullch, -10);  // sv_rv now a ref to an SV containing -10
sv_setref_uv(sv_rv, Nullch, 10);   // sv_rv now a ref to an SV containing 10
sv_setref_nv(sv_rv, Nullch, 10.5); // sv_rv now a ref to an SV containing 10.5
sv_setref_pvn(sv_rv, Nullch, "foo", 3); // sv_rv now a ref to an SV
                                        // containing "foo"
```

The Nullch argument indicates that I'm not creating a blessed reference (that is, an object). If you pass a class name here, you'll create a blessed reference:

```
sv_setref_iv(sv_rv, "Math::BigInt", -10); // sv_rv is now a reference blessed
                                          // into the Math::BigInt class.
```

One function in the sv_setref family was left out of the preceding list: sv_setref_pv(). This function is a bit of an oddball—it doesn't copy the string passed to it. Instead it copies the pointer itself into the new SV. It's easy to misuse this function; for example:

```
sv_setref_pv(sv_rv, Nullch, "foo"); // ERROR!
```

This is an error because I just copied a pointer to an immutable string into a new SV. When the SV eventually tries to call free() on the string, it will cause the program to crash or at least misbehave. Instead the pointer passed to sv_setref_pv() must be dynamically allocated. I'll cover Perl's API for dynamically allocating memory later in the "System Wrappers" section. In general, it's best to avoid this function unless you have a good reason to want to copy a pointer into a new SV.

Type Checking

You can find out what type of object an RV points to using the SvTYPE macro on the result of dereferencing the RV with SvRV. For example:

```
if (SvTYPE(SvRV(sv_rv)) == SVt_PVAV) printf("sv_rv is a ref to an AV.\n");
if (SvTYPE(SvRV(sv_rv)) == SVt_PVHV) printf("sv_rv is a ref to an HV.\n");
if (SvTYPE(SvRV(sv_rv)) == SVt_IV ||
    SvTYPE(SvRV(sv_rv)) == SVt_NV ||
    SvTYPE(SvRV(sv_rv)) == SVt_PV)   printf("sv_rv is a ref to an SV.\n");
```

You can find the complete table of possible SvTYPE return values in perlapi.

Dereferencing

Once you know what kind of object an RV points to, you can safely cast the return value to the correct type:

```
AV *av;
if (SvTYPE(SvRV(sv_rv)) == SVt_PVAV) {
    av = (AV *) SvRV(sv_rv); // safely cast dereferenced value to an AV
} else {
    croak("sv_rv isn't a reference to an array!");
}
```

CAUTION   Always check your RVs with SvROK and SvTYPE before casting them. It's all too common for C modules to crash when passed a normal scalar where they were expecting a reference. It's much nicer to print an error message!

Memory Management

So far I've ignored memory management. As a result, most of the preceding examples will leak memory.[6] This is because, unlike Perl, C expects you to manage both allocation and deallocation. The Perl API offers some help in this area, and learning to use it correctly is the key to creating C modules that don't leak memory.

Reference Counts

Perl uses an explicit reference-counting garbage collector to manage memory. This means that every object (SV, AV, HV, and so on) created by Perl has a number associated with it called a *reference count*, or *refcount* for short. A reference count is simply a count of the number of objects that refer to the object. When the reference count of an object reaches 0, the memory used by the object is freed by the garbage collector.

---

6. A piece of code is said to leak memory when it fails to deallocate memory that is no longer being used. The classic test for memory leaks is to run a piece of code inside a loop and watch to see if the memory used by the program grows over time.

Objects start their lives with a refcount of 1. When a reference to the object is created, its refcount is incremented. When an object goes out of scope, its refcount is decremented. Finally, when a reference is removed, the refcount of the object is decremented. The object is freed when its refcount reaches 0.

Most variables don't get referenced and simply go from having a refcount of 1 to having a refcount 0 when they go out of scope:

```
{
    my $a = "foo";      # $a has a refcount of 1
}
# $a goes out of scope and has its refcount decremented.  Since its refcount is
# now 0, the memory used by $a is freed.
```

Even when references are created they are normally confined to a single scope:

```
{
    my $a = "foo";     # $a has a refcount of 1
    my $b = \$a;       # $b has a refcount of 1, $a has a refcount of 2
}
# $a and $b go out of scope and have their refcounts decremented.  Since $b
# referenced $a, $a has its refcount decremented again.  Now both $a and $b
# have refcounts of 0 and their memory is freed.
```

Things start getting complicated when an object is referenced by a variable from another scope. Here's a simple example:

```
my $a;              # $a has a refcount of 1
{
    my $b = "foo";   # $b has a refcount of 1
    $a = \$b;        # $a now references $b.  $b has a refcount of 2
}
# $b goes out of scope. $b has its refcount decremented and now has a
# refcount of 1.  $b is still live since $a has a reference to it.

$a = 10;  # $a no longer references $b.  $b now has a refcount of 0 and is
          # freed by the garbage collector.
```

Now that you understand reference counting, you can understand why circular references cause memory leaks. Consider this example:

```
{
  my $a;    # $a starts with a refcount of 1
  my $b;    # $b starts with a refcount of 1
  $a = \$b; # $b now has a refcount of 2
  $b = \$a; # $a now has a refcount of 2
}
# both $a and $b go out of scope and have their reference counts
# decremented.  Now they both have refcounts of 1.  Both are still live
# and the garbage collector cannot free them!
```

Inspecting Reference Counts

You can inspect the reference count of an object from C using the SvREFCNT macro:

```
SV *sv = newSV();
SV *rv;
printf("%d\n", SvREFCNT(sv)); // prints 1
rv = newRV_inc(sv);           // create a reference to sv
printf("%d\n", SvREFCNT(sv)); // prints 2
```

As you can see in this example, newRV_inc() increments the reference count of the target object as it creates the new RV. If this isn't what you want, then you can use newRV_noinc(), which creates a reference and doesn't increment the reference count. If you create a new SV and then attach a reference to it with newRV_noinc(), when the reference is freed the SV will be too. This is such a cozy setup that the sv_setref functions use this process to introduce earlier work. The result is that you can forget about the original SV and only worry about freeing the RV.

The same procedure works with AVs and HVs—they can even use the same macros and functions through the magic of polymorphism:

```
SV *hv = newHV();
SV *rv;
printf("%d\n", SvREFCNT((SV *) hv)); // prints 1
rv = newRV_inc(hv);                  // create a reference to hv
printf("%d\n", SvREFCNT((SV *) hv)); // prints 2
```

Explicitly Freeing Memory

A simple way to make sure you don't leak memory is to explicitly decrement the reference counts of the variables you create. This is done using the SvREFCNT_dec macro:

```
SvREFCNT_dec(sv); // decrement sv's refcount
```

Perl's garbage collector works by freeing an object the moment its reference count reaches zero. After an SvREFCNT_dec that causes an object's refcount to reach zero, the object is no longer valid—calls that attempt operate on it will usually yield crashes or other unpleasant behavior.

Using SvREFCNT and SvREFCNT_dec, you can write a function to unconditionally free any Perl object:

```
void free_it_now (SV *sv) {
   while(SvREFCNT(sv)) SvREFCNT_dec(sv);
}
```

But you shouldn't need to do something like this very often; in fact, if you do you should stop and consider what's wrong with the way you're managing the reference counts on your variables.

Implicitly Freeing Memory

The Perl API provides a way for you to hook into Perl's automatic garbage collection from C. The way this is done is by marking an SV, AV, or HV as *mortal*. Marking an object mortal is simply a way of deferring an SvREFCNT_dec until the end of the current scope. Here's an example that marks an SV as mortal using sv2_mortal():

```
SV *sv = newSVpv("foo",0); // sv contains "foo" and has a refcount of 1
sv_2mortal(sv);            // sv is now mortal.  At the next scope exit
                           // SvREFCNT_dec(sv) will be called and the sv
                           // will be freed.
```

This can be stated more succinctly, since sv_2mortal() returns the SV* passed to it:

```
SV *sv = sv_2mortal(newSVpv("foo",0)); // creates sv and mortalizes it
```

Of course, just like SvREFCNT, sv_2mortal() isn't just for SVs. You can mortalize anything you can cast to an SV*:

```
AV *av = (AV *) sv_2mortal((SV *) newAV()); // create a mortal AV
HV *hv = (HV *) sv_2mortal((SV *) newHV()); // create a mortal HV
```

There are also two constructor versions just for SVs that come in handy occasionally:

```
SV *mort_sv  = sv_newmortal();    // create an empty mortal SV
SV *mort_sv2 = sv_mortalcopy(sv); // create a mortal clone of sv
```

 CAUTION   Be careful never to mortalize an object twice accidentally. This will result in SvREFCNT_dec being called twice, with possibly disastrous results.

So, if mortalizing an SV (or AV, HV, and so on) schedules it for a SvREFCNT_dec at the end of the current scope, when does that happen? The answer is not what you might expect. In Perl, a scope ends at the next } in the code:

```
{         # scope start
  my $a;
}         # scope end
```

In C, things are a little more verbose:

```
ENTER; SAVETMPS;                        // start a new scope
SV *sv = sv_2mortal(newSVpv("foo",0)); // create a mortal variable
FREETMPS; LEAVE;                        // end a scope, freeing mortal
                                        // variables with SvREFCNT == 1
```

Using the ENTER and SAVETMPS macros, you can start a new scope roughly the same way the Perl interpreter does. Then you can close the scope with FREETMPS and LEAVE. This triggers a SvREFCNT_dec on all variables mortalized inside the scope. The exact mechanics of Perl scopes are outside the reach of this chapter; for more details, see the perlguts documentation that comes with Perl.

It is worth noting that it is rarely necessary to create new scopes in C modules just to manage memory. This is because you can usually trust the Perl code calling your module to contain a scope when calling your code. You can usually mortalize variables without worrying about when exactly the current scope will end; the answer is usually "soon enough," which is usually good enough!

The Perl Environment

Often when you're writing a C module for Perl you'll need to interact with the Perl environment. The most basic means for this interaction—providing functions written in C that can be called from Perl—will be described later in Chapters 9 and 10. This section is about going the other way—calling back into Perl from C.

Accessing Variables

The simplest way to get information from Perl is to access global and package variables. The Perl API supports this with the get_ family of calls:

```
SV *sv = get_sv("Data::Dumper::Purity", 0); // access $Data::Dumper::Purity
AV *av = get_av("main::DATA", 1);           // create/access the global @DATA
HV *av = get_hv("main::VALUES", 1);         // create/access the global %VALUES
```

Each of these calls take two parameters—the fully qualified name of the variable and a Boolean indicating whether to create the variable if it doesn't yet exist. By using a get_ function with the second argument set to true, you can create new variable in Perl space from C. If you set the second parameter to false, the calls will return NULL if the variable cannot be found.

Calling Perl Subroutines from C

The subroutine calling convention is probably the Perl API's most complicated feature. Fortunately for you, it's also its best documented one. Perl comes with an excellent manual page on the subject—perlcall. I'll demonstrate some simple examples here; you can find all the gritty details in perlcall.

Example 1: No Parameters, No Return Value

The simplest type of call is one that passes no parameters and accepts no return values. Let's say I've defined a subroutine in the package Hello called say_hello:

```
sub say_hello {
   print "Hello, world.\n";
}
```

To call this subroutine from C, I'd have to do the following:

```
dSP;                                                    // declare SP
PUSHMARK(SP);                                           // setup for call
call_pv("Hello::say_hello", G_NOARGS|G_DISCARD); // call say_hello with no args
                                                        // and no return value
```

The dSP macro is necessary to declare the SP variable used by the PUSHMARK macro. These two macros set up the correct context for a call to call_pv(). The first argument is a string giving the name of the subroutine. The second specifies options for the call. In this case, combining G_NOARGS and G_DISCARD with | specifies a call with no arguments and no return value.

Example 2: One Parameter, No Return Value

A slightly more complicated call is one that passes a parameter. For example, let's say I modified say_hello to take an argument:

```
sub say_hello {
    my $who = shift;
    print "Hello, $who.\n";
}
```

This code would be required to call it from C:

```
dSP;                                    // declare SP
ENTER; SAVETMPS;                        // start a new scope

PUSHMARK(SP) ;                          // prepare to push args
XPUSHs(sv_2mortal(newSVpv("Human",0))); // push a single parameter onto the
                                        // argument stack
PUTBACK;                                // done pushing arguments

call_pv("Hello::say_hello", G_DISCARD); // make the call

FREETMPS; LEAVE;                        // end the scope - freeing mortal
                                        // variables
```

There are a few new things to notice here. First, this code creates a new scope using the ENTER, SAVETMPS, FREETMPS, and LEAVE macros you saw back in the "Memory Management" section. This is done to provide for mortal variables created for use as parameters as well as those created by the Perl code to be called. Second, a single argument is pushed onto the argument stack using the XPUSHs macro. Next, the PUTBACK macro is used to mark that the last of the arguments has been pushed onto the stack. Finally, call_pv() is used, just as in the first example, but this time only G_DISCARD is used as an option.

Example 3: Variable Parameters, One Return Value

For a slightly more realistic example, let's call the Data::Counter::count function defined a couple of chapters back. If you remember, this subroutine takes a variable number of arguments and returns the number of arguments it received:

```
sub count { return scalar @_; }
```

To call this subroutine, I need the following code:

```
dSP;                                      // declare SP
SV *return                                // declare an SV for the return value

ENTER; SAVETMPS;                          // start a new scope

PUSHMARK(SP) ;                            // prepare to push args
XPUSHs(sv_2mortal(newSVpv("one",0)));     // push three parameters onto the stack
XPUSHs(sv_2mortal(newSVpv("two",0)));
XPUSHs(sv_2mortal(newSVpv("three",0)));
PUTBACK;                                  // done pushing arguments

call_pv("Data::Counter::count", G_SCALAR); // make the call

SPAGAIN;                                  // refresh SP - it might have changed

return = POPs;                            // get return value off the stack
printf("count: %d\n", SvIV(return));      // print out the return as an integer

FREETMPS; LEAVE;                          // end the scope - freeing mortal
                                          // variables
```

This code is similar to the last example with a couple additions. First, I passed G_SCALAR as an option to call_pv(), indicating that I expect to get a single argument back. After the call, a new macro is used: SPAGAIN. This macro refreshes SP in case it changed during the call. Finally, the return value from the subroutine is popped off the stack with POPs. The "s" in POPs refers to the fact that it pops a scalar off the stack.

NOTE   The return value from a Perl subroutine obtained by POPs is a mortal variable. This means you must handle it before you end the scope with FREETMPS and LEAVE. After that point the variable will have been freed by the garbage collector and will no longer be accessible.

Example 4: Variable Parameters, Variable Return Values

In order to demonstrate multiple value returns, let's suppose that count() were modified to take a list of array refs as a parameter and returns a list of counts for each array:

```
sub count { map { scalar @$_ } @_ }
```

Now count() would be called like this from Perl:

```
@counts = Data::Counter::count([1,2,3],[4,5,6],[7,8,9]); # returns (3,3,3)
```

Here's what the equivalent call would look like from C, assuming I already have the preceding three arrays in the variables av1, av2, and av3.

```
dSP;                                   // declare SP
int num;                               // declare an int for the return count
int i;                                 // declare a loop counter

ENTER; SAVETMPS;                       // start a new scope

PUSHMARK(SP) ;                         // prepare to push args
XPUSHs(sv_2mortal(newRV_inc((SV*)av1))); // push three arrays onto the stack
XPUSHs(sv_2mortal(newRV_inc((SV*)av2))); // by reference
XPUSHs(sv_2mortal(newRV_inc((SV*)av3)));
PUTBACK;                               // done pushing arguments

num = call_pv("Data::Counter::count", G_ARRAY); // make the call

SPAGAIN;                               // refresh SP - it might have changed
```

```
// print out the returned counts, in reverse order
for(i = num; i > 0; i++) {
  printf("count %d: %d\n", i, SvIV(POPs));
}

FREETMPS; LEAVE;                        // end the scope - freeing mortal
                                        // variables
```

There are two new pieces in this example. First, the call is made using the G_ARRAY option indicating that I expect to get a list of return values back. Also, the return value from call_pv(), the number of values returned on the stack, is saved. Then a loop is run that prints out the values in reverse order. A more elaborate loop could be written to process the return values in the "correct" order, but since POPs works in reverse, it's easiest to follow suit.

Signaling Errors

There are two ways to return from a Perl subroutine—by using return() or by generating an exception with die(). The interface to die() from the C API is croak(), which supports a printf()-style interface for generating exception strings:

```
croak("Big trouble, Indy, the %s has got the %s!", villain, bauble);
```

A warning, provided by the warn() function in Perl, can be produced using the warn() API function:

```
warn("Ouch, don't touch that, %s!", SvPVX(name_sv));
```

This is an unconditional warning—it will always generate output no matter what the state of the warnings pragma. If you want to check whether warnings are on or not, you can use the isLEXWARN_on macro:[7]

```
if (isLEXWARN_on) warn("You use warnings; good for you!");
```

You can also test if a particular category of warnings is on using the ckWARN macro:[8]

```
if (ckWARN(WARN_DEPRECATED)) warn("Use of this function is deprecated.");
```

The constants used by this macro are lists in the warnings.h file in the Perl source.

---

7. Which isn't listed in perlapi and as such may change without notice

8. Also not listed in perlapi—beware!

System Wrappers

The Perl API provides a number of wrappers around common system functions. These allow you to do things like dynamically allocate memory and perform IO operations without needing to worry about the underlying platform details. Using these wrappers instead of calling the functions directly will improve the portability of your code.

Memory Allocation

Perl provides a wrapper around `malloc()` called `New()`. For example, the following allocates a buffer of 1024 bytes:

```
char *buffer = NULL;
New(0, buffer, 1024, char);
if (buffer == NULL) croak("Memory allocation failed!");
```

The first argument to all of these functions is an ID used to track memory allocations during debugging; for most purposes it can be left at 0. The second parameter is a pointer variable to receive the newly allocated pointer. The third is the number of items to be allocated. Finally, the last argument is the type of object to be allocated, in this case a `char`.

New() allocates memory without initializing it. Use `Newz()` to allocate a zero-filled buffer:

```
char *zbuffer = NULL;
Newz(0, zbuffer, 1024, char);
if (zbuffer == NULL) croak("Memory allocation failed!");
```

To access `realloc()`, use `Renew`:

```
Renew(buffer, 2048, char); // increase buffer to 2048 bytes
```

The Perl API interface to `free()` is called `Safefree()`:

```
Safefree(buffer); // free buffer
```

You must call `Safefree()` on every pointer allocated with `New()` or `Newz()` to avoid leaking memory. No garbage collection is performed on buffers allocated with these functions.

Also provided are wrappers around `memcpy()` (`Copy()`) and `memmove()` (`Move()`) that can be used to efficiently copy sections of memory. For example:

```
Copy(src, dst, 1024, char);      // copy 1024 bytes from src to dst
Move(buf, buf + 10, 1024, char); // copy 1024 bytes down 10 bytes in buf
```

IO Operations

The Perl API defines wrappers around most of the `stdio` functions you know and love. These wrappers all begin with `PerlIO_` and are usually followed by the name of the `stdio` function they wrap. The `perlapio` documentation included with Perl contains a complete listing the available functions and their signatures. Be aware that in some cases the Perl developers have "fixed" parameter ordering and function names while wrapping `stdio` functions.

The principal difference between `stdio`'s functions and the `PerlIO` set is that `stdio` uses the `FILE*` type to represent file handles, whereas the Perl API uses `PerlIO*`. For example, to open a log file and print a line to it, you might use code like this:

```
PerlIO *fh = PerlIO_open("/tmp/my.log", "a"); // open logfile in append mode
if (!fh) croak("Unable to open /tmp/my.log"); // check that open succeeded
PerlIO_printf(fh, "Log test...\n");            // print a test line
PerlIO_close(fh);                              // close the file
```

Notice that the `PerlIO_printf()` is actually a wrapper around `fprintf()`. For `printf()` functionality, use `PerlIO_stdoutf()`:

```
PerlIO_stdoutf("Hello world!\n");
```

The Perl API also provides functions for interfacing the `PerlIO` model with existing `stdio` systems. For example, you can translate between `PerlIO*` and `FILE*` file handles with the `PerlIO_import` and `PerlIO_export` functions:

```
PerlIO *pfh;
FILE   *fh;
pfh = PerlIO_open("some.file", "r");  // open a PerlIO handle
fh  = PerlIO_export(pfh, 0);          // export to a FILE *
// ... do some stdio work with fh
PerlIO_releaseFILE(pfh, fh);          // release fh mapping to pfh
PerlIO_close(pfh);
```

The Perl IO API is currently under development, and it is expected that in the near future Perl will cut its ties to `stdio` entirely. At that point, only C modules that use the `PerlIO` interface will work correctly. As such, it is important to get used to using `PerlIO` now.

References

To work comfortably in the Perl API, you'll need to keep the documentation that comes with Perl close at hand. Nearly every function and macro in the Perl API is documented in the `perlapi` perldoc. The IO functions are described in depth in `perlapio`. Finally, the Perl calling conventions are detailed in `perlcall`.

Although this chapter has covered a great deal of material, you still have miles to go if you wish to become a true Perl internals guru. Continue your education by reading the `perlguts` manual. Also of interest is Simon Cozen's excellent Perl internals tutorial available at `http://www.netthink.co.uk`.

Summary

This chapter has introduced you to the Perl C API. With this knowledge in hand, proceed to the next chapter and learn to program Perl modules in C with XS.

CHAPTER 9

Writing C Modules
with XS

Now that you're a Perl API yellow belt, it's time to learn to write Perl modules in C. XS is the name for the toolkit used to create most of the existing C modules on CPAN. It consists of two pieces: the XS language for expressing interfaces and the xsubpp compiler that generates C code from XS.

A Real-World Example

This section will use a real-world module as an example—Gnome::MIME. Gnome::MIME will provide an interface to the Gnome system's MIME-handling routines. The Gnome system is a desktop and component system for UNIX-like operating systems produced by the Free Software Foundation.[1] You can find more information at the Gnome Web site: http://gnome.org.

CPAN already has a Perl module that provides a binding to some of Gnome, although not to the MIME functions at present; you can find the Gnome module, written by Kenneth Albanowski and Paolo Molaro, on CPAN.

The Gnome MIME functions come from the packages gnome-mime and gnome-mime-info. They provide functions to guess *MIME types* given a file and functions to retrieve information about a MIME type. A MIME type is a standardized system for describing the type of a file. Example MIME types that you might be familiar with are text/html, image/gif, and application/pdf. MIME types are used in many applications, from Web browsers to e-mail programs to operating systems. You can find more information on the MIME types in RFC 2046, which is available here (among many other locations): http://www.rfc-editor.org/rfc/rfc2046.txt.

This example module is, by nature, platform specific and will only work on UNIX systems with Gnome installed. However, the basic techniques demonstrated can be used to create cross-platform XS modules.

---

1. See http://www.fsf.org.

Getting Started with XS

The same tool used in Chapter 4, h2xs, is used to generate the module skeleton for an XS module. As you can probably guess from the name, this was its original purpose. The difference between the use of h2xs in Chapter 4 and here is in the options employed. In Chapter 4, I created a Perl-only module using the following h2xs line:

```
h2xs -XA -n Data::Counter
```

To create an XS module, I just need to drop the –X option. I'll still keep the –A option to remove support for the Autoloader. The –n option naming the module is always required. To create the skeleton for Gnome::MIME, you use the following:

```
h2xs -A -n Gnome::MIME
```

This creates all of the same files examined in Chapter 4 with one addition, MIME.xs (see Table 9-1 for a listing of files created). For the most part, the files are the same as those created for a Perl-only module, with the exception of the module file, MIME.pm, and Makefile.PL.

Table 9-1. Files Generated by h2xs -X -n Gnome::MIME

File	Description
MIME.pm	The module file itself, which contains Perl code and POD documentation
MIME.xs	The XS file itself, which contains XS and C code
Makefile.PL	A script that uses ExtUtils::MakeMaker to generate a Makefile
test.pl	A test script run when a user types "make test" or installs your module with the CPAN module
README	A quick description of your module and how to install it
Changes	A change log in which you can describe differences between versions of your module
MANIFEST	A list of all the files in your distribution

MIME.pm—The Module File

The module file generated for an XS module is mostly the same as that for a
Perl-only module with a few additions. First, a new require is specified:

```
require DynaLoader;
```

This line pulls in the DynaLoader module that allows Perl modules to load shared
libraries. Next, DynaLoader is added to the @ISA inheritance array:

```
our @ISA = qw(Exporter DynaLoader);
```

Inheriting from DynaLoader is the standard way to allow your module to be
partially implemented in XS. Later in the file, the bootstrap() subroutine from
DynaLoader is called:

```
bootstrap Gnome::MIME $VERSION;
```

This call to DynaLoader::bootstrap() finds and loads a shared library corresponding to
Gnome::MIME. By passing $VERSION as the second argument, DynaLoader will
check that the loaded shared library matches this version of the Perl half of the
module. This is not a required parameter, but h2xs defaults to including it since it
helps prevent a very common class of errors.

Listing 9-1 shows a module file generated for an XS module.

Listing 9-1. MIME.pm *Generated by* h2xs -A -n Gnome::MIME

```
package Gnome::MIME;

use 5.006;
use strict;
use warnings;

require Exporter;
require DynaLoader;

our @ISA = qw(Exporter DynaLoader);

# Items to export into callers namespace by default. Note: do not export
# names by default without a very good reason. Use EXPORT_OK instead.
# Do not simply export all your public functions/methods/constants.
```

```
# This allows declaration        use Gnome::MIME ':all';
# If you do not need this, moving things directly into @EXPORT or @EXPORT_OK
# will save memory.
our %EXPORT_TAGS = ( 'all' => [ qw(

) ] );

our @EXPORT_OK = ( @{ $EXPORT_TAGS{'all'} } );

our @EXPORT = qw(

);
our $VERSION = '0.01';

bootstrap Gnome::MIME $VERSION;

# Preloaded methods go here.

1;
__END__
# Below is stub documentation for your module. You better edit it!

=head1 NAME

Gnome::MIME - Perl extension for blah blah blah

=head1 SYNOPSIS

  use Gnome::MIME;
  blah blah blah

=head1 DESCRIPTION

Stub documentation for Gnome::MIME, created by h2xs. It looks like the
author of the extension was negligent enough to leave the stub
unedited.

Blah blah blah.

=head2 EXPORT

None by default.
```

```
=head1 AUTHOR

A. U. Thor, E<lt>a.u.thor@a.galaxy.far.far.awayE<gt>

=head1 SEE ALSO

L<perl>.

=cut
```

Aside from the preceding changes, the module file is identical to the normal Perl-only module file generated by h2xs -X. This similarity is more than skin-deep—XS modules often contain a significant portion of their code in Perl, resorting to C only when necessary. I'll demonstrate this style later in this chapter.

Makefile.PL—The Makefile Generator

Like the module file, the Makefile.PL generated for XS modules (see Listing 9-2) is the same as the Makefile.PL in Chapter 4, with a few additional lines.

Listing 9-2. Makefile.PL *Generated by* h2xs -A -n Gnome::MIME

```
use ExtUtils::MakeMaker;
# See lib/ExtUtils/MakeMaker.pm for details of how to influence
# the contents of the Makefile that is written.
WriteMakefile(
    'NAME'            => 'Gnome::MIME',
    'VERSION_FROM'    => 'MIME.pm', # finds $VERSION
    'PREREQ_PM'       => {}, # e.g., Module::Name => 1.1
    ($] >= 5.005 ?    ## Add these new keywords supported since 5.005
      (ABSTRACT_FROM  => 'MIME.pm', # retrieve abstract from module
       AUTHOR         => 'A. U. Thor <a.u.thor@a.galaxy.far.far.away>') : ()),
    'LIBS'            => [''], # e.g., '-lm'
    'DEFINE'          => '', # e.g., '-DHAVE_SOMETHING'
    # Insert -I. if you add *.h files later:
    'INC'             => '', # e.g., '-I/usr/include/other'
    # Un-comment this if you add C files to link with later:
    # 'OBJECT'        => '$(O_FILES)', # link all the C files too
);
```

The added section starts with a new key to include additional libraries to link to:

```
'LIBS'             => [''], # e.g., '-lm'
```

This configuration variable is actually a little more complicated than it seems. You might be tempted to fill it with a list of libraries to link to:

```
'LIBS'             => ["-lm", "-lfoo", "-lbar"],  # ERROR: only links to -lm
```

However, the list assigned to LIBS is actually a list of complete library sets. The first one that "works" on the target platform will be used. This allows you to specify sets that work on different operating systems without having to actually write code to do the testing. If you need to link to three libraries, then all three must be in a single string:

```
'LIBS'             => ["-lm -lfoo -lbar"],  # link to 3 libraries
```

The next new line allows you to add a –D command-line option to the compilation of your module's C code:

```
'DEFINE'           => '', # e.g., '-DHAVE_SOMETHING'
```

Next is a line to add –I include directories:

```
'INC'              => '', # e.g., '-I/usr/include/other'
```

and a line to include object files in the build explicitly:

```
# Un-comment this if you add C files to link with later:
# 'OBJECT'         => '$(O_FILES)', # link all the C files too
```

This line is commented out because using it requires you to explicitly list all the object files to be compiled. For example, the functional equivalent of not specifying an OBJECT key is

```
'OBJECT'           => 'MIME.o'
```

or, using the Makefile variables:

```
'OBJECT'           => '$(O_FILES)'
```

MIME.xs—The XS Source File

The new file generated by h2xs is MIME.xs (see Listing 9-3). This is the source file for the XS half of the module.

Listing 9-3. MIME.xs *Generated by* h2xs -A -n Gnome::MIME

```
#include "EXTERN.h"
#include "perl.h"
#include "XSUB.h"



MODULE = Gnome::MIME          PACKAGE = Gnome::MIME
```

The MIME.xs file consists of two parts. The first part is a series of #include directives:

```
#include "EXTERN.h"
#include "perl.h"
#include "XSUB.h"
```

These are passed straight through to the generated C source by xsubpp. In fact, xsubpp passes through all text until it hits a line that starts with a MODULE directive:

```
MODULE = Gnome::MIME          PACKAGE = Gnome::MIME
```

After this line, everything must be valid XS code, none of which is generated by h2xs.[2]

Modifying Makefile.PL

The Makefile.PL generated by h2xs works right away. You can see the XS build process without writing any XS code:

```
$ perl Makefile.PL && make
Checking if your kit is complete...
Looks good
Writing Makefile for Gnome::MIME
```

---

2. Actually, there is a way to get h2xs to generate some XS code for you. If you install the C::Scan module from CPAN, then you can use the -x option to attempt to auto-generate XS from a C header file. At present this process only succeeds with very simple header files. See the h2xs documentation for more details.

As you can see, the `Makefile` gets built as it normally would. Then the `MIME.pm` file is copied into `blib` as usual:

```
cp MIME.pm blib/lib/Gnome/MIME.pm
```

The first XS-specific step happens next when `xsubpp` is run on `MIME.xs` to produce `MIME.xs`, which is renamed `MIME.c`:

```
/usr/local/bin/perl -I/usr/local/lib/perl5/5.6.1/i686-linux              \
  -I/usr/local/lib/perl5/5.6.1 /usr/local/lib/perl5/5.6.1/ExtUtils/xsubpp \
  -typemap /usr/local/lib/perl5/5.6.1/ExtUtils/typemap MIME.xs > MIME.xsc \
  && mv MIME.xsc MIME.c
```

Next `MIME.c` is compiled into `MIME.o` by the `cc` compiler (actually `gcc` in this case):

```
cc -c  -fno-strict-aliasing -I/usr/local/include -D_LARGEFILE_SOURCE       \
  -D_FILE_OFFSET_BITS=64 -O2   -DVERSION=\"0.01\" -DXS_VERSION=\"0.01\"    \
  -fpic -I/usr/local/lib/perl5/5.6.1/i686-linux/CORE   MIME.c
```

After that a bootstrap file is created—`MIME.bs`. Depending on your platform, the bootstrap file might contain some Perl code used by DynaLoader to load the shared library. You can mostly ignore this as it is not something you should modify.

```
Running Mkbootstrap for Gnome::MIME ()
chmod 644 MIME.bs
```

Finally the shared library, `MIME.so`, is linked using `cc` again and copied into `blib`:

```
rm -f blib/arch/auto/Gnome/MIME/MIME.so
LD_RUN_PATH="" cc  -shared -L/usr/local/lib MIME.o -o                      \
  blib/arch/auto/Gnome/MIME/MIME.so
chmod 755 blib/arch/auto/Gnome/MIME/MIME.so
cp MIME.bs blib/arch/auto/Gnome/MIME/MIME.bs
chmod 644 blib/arch/auto/Gnome/MIME/MIME.bs
```

Like most XS modules, Gnome::MIME needs to make an addition to `Makefile.PL` to allow the module to link with extra libraries and find its header files. In this case this information is provided by Gnome itself, via the `gnome-config` program. First, I'll add a block to check for `gnome-config` and make sure the Gnome version falls within the supported range:

```
# check to make sure we have Gnome 1.2, 1.3 or 1.4 and can use gnome-config
my $version = `gnome-config --version gnome`;
unless ($version and $version =~ /1.[234]/) {
  print <<END;
#####################################################################
Gnome 1.[234].x not found.  Please make sure you have Gnome installed
and that gnome-config is in your path.  Then re-run "perl Makefile.PL".
You can find more information about Gnome at http://gnome.org
#####################################################################
END
  exit 1;
}
```

Next I'll modify the call to WriteMakefile() to use gnome-config to get the correct LIBS and INC settings:

```
WriteMakefile(
              NAME          => "Gnome::MIME",
              VERSION_FROM  => "MIME.pm",
              PREREQ_PM     => {},
              ABSTRACT_FROM => "MIME.pm",
              AUTHOR        => 'Sam Tregar <sam@tregar.com>',
              LIBS          => [`gnome-config --libs   gnome`],
              INC           => `gnome-config --cflags gnome`,
             );
```

A rebuild shows the effect in the compilation line:

```
cc -c -I/usr/include -DNEED_GNOMESUPPORT_H -I/usr/lib/gnome-libs/include   \
  -I/usr/include/gtk-1.2 -I/usr/include/glib-1.2 -I/usr/lib/glib/include   \
  -I/usr/X11R6/include -fno-strict-aliasing -I/usr/local/include           \
  -D_LARGEFILE_SOURCE -D_FILE_OFFSET_BITS=64 -O2   -DVERSION=\"0.01\"       \
  -DXS_VERSION=\"0.01\" -fpic -I/usr/local/lib/perl5/5.6.1/i686-linux/CORE \
  MIME.c
```

and the link line:

```
LD_RU_PATH="/usr/lib" cc  -shared -L/usr/local/lib MIME.o                  \
  -o blib/arch/auto/Gnome/MIME/MIME.so   -L/usr/lib -lgnome -lgnomesupport \
  -lesd -laudiofile -lm -ldb1 -lglib -ldl
```

Although the preceding code is specific to the needs of Gnome::MIME, it demonstrates a general technique for XS modules that link to external libraries. You'll typically need to add some custom Perl code to your Makefile.PL to check that the library you need exists and has the right version. Then you'll need to figure out what to set LIBS and INC to so that your module will compile and link successfully. Sometimes this will be a static string, but it's becoming more and more common for large projects to provide a binary like gnome-config that makes determining these variables easier.

A First XSUB

The fundamental unit of an XS module is an *XSUB*. An XSUB is simply a definition of a single C function for which the xsubpp compiler will produce a Perl subroutine. The first XSUB I'll provide for Gnome::MIME is a wrapper for the gnome_mime_type() function. This function takes a single parameter, a filename, and returns its MIME type based on an examination of the filename alone. The C signature for gnome_mime_type() is as follows:

```
const char * gnome_mime_type(const gchar *filename);
```

Here is an XSUB that provides an interface to this function:

```
char *
gnome_mime_type(filename)
    char *filename
```

See Listing 9-4 for the new MIME.xs.

Listing 9-4. MIME.xs *with First XSUB Added*

```
#include "EXTERN.h"
#include "perl.h"
#include "XSUB.h"

MODULE = Gnome::MIME    PACKAGE = Gnome::MIME

char *
gnome_mime_type(filename)
    char * filename
```

After adding this XSUB to the end of `MIME.xs`, I'll edit my `test.pl` to read as follows:

```
use Test::More 'no_plan';
BEGIN { use_ok('Gnome::MIME'); }

# test some simple mime-type recognitions
is(Gnome::MIME::gnome_mime_type("foo.gif"),  'image/gif',  "recognizes .gif");
is(Gnome::MIME::gnome_mime_type("foo.jpg"),  'image/jpeg', "recognizes .jpg");
is(Gnome::MIME::gnome_mime_type("foo.html"), 'text/html',  "recognizes .html");
```

Now a normal `perl Makefile.PL`, `make`, and `make test` run will build and test the new module.

XSUB Anatomy

As you can see in the preceding section, an XSUB resembles a C function signature in K&R format. The first line contains the return type of the function. Then comes a line containing the function name and a list of parameters. Finally, a line per parameter specifies the type of each parameter. Here's an annotated version of the previous example (note that XS doesn't actually allow comments inline with XSUBs, so this won't compile):

```
char *                     # returns a string
gnome_mime_type(filename)  # takes a single parameter named filename
    char *filename         # filename is a string
```

This is the simplest possible type of XSUB—it maps a C function directly to a Perl function with the same parameters and return type. The `xsubpp` compiler takes this definition and produces C code in the generated `MIME.c` (see Listing 9-5). This C code makes use of functions in the Perl API introduced in the previous chapter. For example, to translate the incoming `SV` into a `char *`, `MIME.c` contains this line:

```
char *   filename = (char *)SvPV(ST(0),PL_na);
```

The `ST` macro provides access to the argument array of an XSUB, but the rest of the call should be familiar.

Listing 9-5. C Function Generated by xsubpp *for* gnome_mime_type() *XSUB*

```
XS(XS_Gnome__MIME_gnome_mime_type)
{
    dXSARGS;
    if (items != 1)
            Perl_croak(aTHX_ "Usage: Gnome::MIME::gnome_mime_type(filename)");
    {
            char *         filename = (char *)SvPV(ST(0),PL_na);
            char *         RETVAL;
            dXSTARG;

            RETVAL = gnome_mime_type(filename);
        sv_setpv(TARG, RETVAL); XSprePUSH; PUSHTARG;
    }
    XSRETURN(1);
}
```

XSUB Techniques

The XSUB shown earlier is about as simple as an XSUB can be. However, there are many useful changes that can be made to enhance the usability and functionality of XSUBs.

Types and Typemaps

You might have noticed that the types used in the gnome_mime_type() XSUB are subtly different from those used in the actual function signature. In the gnome_mime_type() function, the return type is a const char * and the filename argument type is const gchar *, whereas the XSUB used char * for both. This was done because XS comes with a *typemap* for char *, but doesn't know anything about const char * and const gchar *. A typemap is a description of how to map Perl types to and from C types.

  If you try to use the real types in an XSUB as follows:

```
const char *
gnome_mime_type(filename)
    const gchar *filename
```

you'll receive this compilation error:

```
Error: 'const gchar *' not in typemap in MIME.xs, line 10
Error: 'const char *' not in typemap in MIME.xs, line 10
```

To use types that XS doesn't natively support, you need to create a new file called typemap in your module directory that contains code to translate to and from the new types. In this case, only two lines are required:

```
const char  *    T_PV
const gchar *    T_PV
```

This tells XS that const char * and const gchar * are both to be treated as T_PV, which is the supplied typemap for char *. The T_PV typemap is defined in the system-wide typemap file installed with Perl. You can find it in under the module directory for the ExtUtils modules in your Perl library. I'll explore typemaps in more detail later in this chapter.

The preceding code still doesn't work, though; it produces a syntax error because it doesn't recognize Gnome's gchar type. To fix this problem, I need to add an #include line below the three #includes already in the file:

```
#include "EXTERN.h"
#include "perl.h"
#include "XSUB.h"
#include <gnome.h>
```

This is part of the section before the MODULE command that is passed through to the generated MIME.c file verbatim.

Modifying the XSUB Name with PREFIX

Calling gnome_mime_type() from Perl with the XSUB shown earlier is done using a line that looks like this one:

```
my $type = Gnome::MIME::gnome_mime_type($filename);
```

This works just fine, but it's awfully verbose; the user is forced to type the words "Gnome" and "MIME" twice. One solution would be to export the function as-is, but XS offers a simpler solution. By modifying the MODULE line, shown here:

```
MODULE = Gnome::MIME    PACKAGE = Gnome::MIME
```

to include a new directive, PREFIX:

```
MODULE = Gnome::MIME    PACKAGE = Gnome::MIME    PREFIX = gnome_mime_
```

XS will automatically remove the specified prefix, gnome_mime_, from the front of the Perl interface. After this change, test.pl needs changes to use the new interface:

```
# test some simple mime-type recognitions
is(Gnome::MIME::type("foo.gif"),  'image/gif',  "recognizes .gif");
is(Gnome::MIME::type("foo.jpg"),  'image/jpeg', "recognizes .jpg");
is(Gnome::MIME::type("foo.html"), 'text/html',  "recognizes .html");
```

Writing Your Own CODE

Changing the XSUB name from gnome_mime_type() to type() with PREFIX is certainly an improvement, but it isn't very flexible. Modifying the XSUB name beyond removing a fixed prefix will require a new technique—writing the actual code to call the underlying C function with the CODE keyword. For example, to rename the XSUB to file_type(), I could use this XS code:

```
const char *
file_type(filename)
      const gchar * filename
CODE:
      RETVAL = gnome_mime_type(filename);
OUTPUT:
      RETVAL
```

This example shows a new wrinkle in the XS syntax: keywords that come after the function definition and declare blocks of C code. This is a pattern that you'll see repeated by most of XS. In this case, two keywords are used, CODE and OUTPUT. The CODE keyword allows you to override the default XSUB call with your own custom call.

The CODE block shown previously makes use of the automatic RETVAL variable. RETVAL is an automatic variable with the same type as the return type in the XSUB definition. In this case, RETVAL is a const char * variable. The CODE block simply calls gnome_mime_type() and places the return value in RETVAL.

The OUTPUT block tells xsubpp which variable (or variables) should be returned back to Perl. In most cases, your CODE blocks will be immediately followed by an OUTPUT block exactly like the one shown earlier.

After this change, the tests would need to be updated to reflect the new function name, but underneath the call is still going to gnome_mime_type():

```
# test some simple mime-type recognitions
is(Gnome::MIME::file_type("foo.gif"),  'image/gif',  "recognizes .gif");
is(Gnome::MIME::file_type("foo.jpg"),  'image/jpeg', "recognizes .jpg");
is(Gnome::MIME::file_type("foo.html"), 'text/html',  "recognizes .html");
```

Managing Memory Usage

As it turns out, the preceding XSUB *does not* leak memory. This came as a surprise to me—I assumed that the gnome_mime_type() function returned a dynamically allocated string that I would need to clean up. If you look at the generated code in MIME.c (Listing 9-5), you'll see this line at the end of the function:

```
sv_setpv(TARG, RETVAL); XSprePUSH; PUSHTARG;
```

This line copies the string pointed to by RETVAL into TARG. TARG is the SV that will actually be returned by the subroutine. After that, TARG is pushed onto the stack and the function returns. My expectation was that this would result in a leak since the pointer stored in RETVAL wouldn't be freed before going out of scope. As it turns out, this pointer doesn't need to be freed because it comes from an internal pool managed by the Gnome API.

But, for the sake of the example, what would I need to do if the return value from gnome_mime_type() did need to be freed? My first draft might have been as follows:

```
const char *
file_type(filename)
    const gchar * filename
CODE:
    RETVAL = gnome_mime_type(filename);
OUTPUT:
    RETVAL
CLEANUP:
    Safefree(RETVAL);
```

The CLEANUP block specifies code to be run at the end of the generated function. This might work fine, but it's incorrect. The problem is that Gnome and Perl might be using different memory allocators. Thus, calling Perl's Safefree() function on memory allocated by Gnome is not guaranteed to yield the expected results. Instead, I would need to use the same call that Gnome uses, g_free():

```
CLEANUP:
    g_free(RETVAL);
```

The moral of this story is that managing memory usage in C modules is rarely simple. It requires you to think carefully about the way the underlying library allocates memory. Often the only way to get some of the information you need is to test. For example, the only way I could find out that gnome_mime_type() doesn't dynamically allocate its return value was to run my wrapped version in a loop and watch the system with top in another window:

```
$ perl -Mblib -MGnome::MIME -e 'while(1) { Gnome::MIME::file_type("foo.gif"); }'
```

It's a good idea to do this sort of testing on all your XS functions—at least until someone finds a way to write ExtUtils::LeakDetector!

XS Interface Design and Construction

Being able to easily produce one-to-one mappings between a set of C functions and subroutines in a Perl module is undeniably very useful. XS is designed to allow you to accomplish this task with a minimum amount of coding required; simply describe the C functions, and out pops a new module, fully baked and ready to consume. Unfortunately, much like a microwave dinner, the ease of preparation comes at a price in palatability.

Consider the interface that Gnome::MIME would provide if this recipe were followed for each function in the API. The Gnome MIME type functions follow a common pattern in C APIs—they provide a variety of functions that all perform the same task with different parameters:

```
$type = Gnome::MIME::type($filename);
$type = Gnome::MIME::type_or_default($filename, $default);
$type = Gnome::MIME::type_of_file($filename);
$type = Gnome::MIME::type_or_default_of_file($filename, $default);
```

The or_default versions allow the user to specify a default to be returned if the MIME-type cannot be determined. The of_file versions actually read from the file to guess its MIME type rather than relying on the filename alone. However, every one of these functions provides the same core functionality—determining the MIME type of a file. Clearly this would be a difficult module for a Perl programmer to use if he or she had to pick from the preceding function list. To make matters worse, module authors who allow XS to write their interfaces often abdicate on the documentation as well, saying something along the lines of "I've wrapped every C function in the library, see the docs for the C library for details."

Every module needs to have a sensible interface. Whether it's implemented in Perl or in C shouldn't determine the interface used. This section will give you some ideas about how to design and code better XS interfaces.

Supporting Named Parameters

In Perl, a better interface to the preceding MIME type functions might be this one:

```
$type = Gnome::MIME::file_type(filename      => $filename,
                               default_type => "text/html",
                               read_file     => 1);
```

This follows the named-parameter function style introduced in Chapter 2.

Using XS

Unfortunately XS doesn't have native support for this highly Perl-ish function style, but it's not hard to support it with a little code (see Listing 9-6 for the full XSUB).

Listing 9-6. Named-Parameter XSUB

```
const char *
file_type(...)
PREINIT:
  char *filename = NULL;      // variables for named params
  char *default_type = NULL;
  IV read_file = 0;
  IV x;                       // loop counter
CODE:
  // check that there are an even number of args
  if (items % 2) croak("Usage: Gnome::MIME::file_type(k => v, ...)");

  // loop over args by pairs and fill in parameters
  for(x = 0; x < items; x+=2) {
    char *key = SvPV(ST(x), PL_na);
    if (strEQ(key, "filename")) {
      filename = SvPV(ST(x+1), PL_na);
    } else if (strEQ(key, "default_type")) {
      default_type = SvPV(ST(x+1), PL_na);
    } else if (strEQ(key, "read_file")) {
      read_file = SvIV(ST(x+1));
    } else {
      croak("Unknown key found in Gnome::MIME::file_type parameter list: %s",
                SvPV(ST(x), PL_na));
    }
  }
```

```
  // make sure we have a filename parameter
  if (filename == NULL) croak("Missing required parameter filename.");

  // call the appropriate function based on arguments
  if (read_file && default_type != NULL) {
    RETVAL = gnome_mime_type_or_default_of_file(filename, default_type);
  } else if (read_file) {
    RETVAL = gnome_mime_type_of_file(filename);
  } else if (default_type != NULL) {
    RETVAL = gnome_mime_type_or_default(filename, default_type);
  } else {
    RETVAL = gnome_mime_type(filename);
  }
OUTPUT:
  RETVAL
```

The XSUB starts with syntax for a variable argument function that mimics C's syntax:

```
const char *
file_type(...)
```

Note that unlike C's . . . , you don't need to have at least one fixed parameter.

Next, I set up a number of local variables in a PREINIT block. The contents of PREINIT are placed first in the output XSUB. In some cases this is essential, but in this case it's merely a convenient place for local declarations:

```
PREINIT:
  char *filename    = NULL; // variables for named params
  char *default_type = NULL;
  IV read_file      = 0;
  IV x;                     // loop counter
```

Next comes the CODE block proper, where the automatic XS variable items is used to check the number of parameters:

```
  // check that there are an even number of args
  if (items % 2) croak("Usage: Gnome::MIME::file_type(k => v, ...)");
```

and then iterate through the key/value pairs:

```
// loop over args by pairs and fill in parameters
for(x = 0; x < items; x+=2) {
  char *key = SvPV(ST(x), PL_na);
  if (strEQ(key, "filename")) {
  filename = SvPV(ST(x+1), PL_na);
} else if (strEQ(key, "default_type")) {
  // ...
```

The preceding block uses the ST macro to access the SVs passed in as arguments. The strEQ() function is used to compare the keys to the available parameter names. When a match is found, the value is assigned to one of the variables initialized in the PREINIT section. After that, a series of conditionals determines which gnome_mime_type function to call:

```
// call the appropriate function based on arguments
if (read_file && default_type != NULL) {
  RETVAL = gnome_mime_type_or_default_of_file(filename, default_type);
} else if (read_file) {
  // ...
```

With the new named-parameter style, the test cases will need adjusting:

```
# test some simple mime-file_type recognitions
is(Gnome::MIME::file_type(filename => "foo.gif"), 'image/gif',  "test .gif");
is(Gnome::MIME::file_type(filename => "foo.jpg"), 'image/jpeg', "test .jpg");
is(Gnome::MIME::file_type(filename => "foo.html"), 'text/html', "test .html");

# test defaulting
is(Gnome::MIME::file_type(filename => "", default_type => "text/html"),
   "text/html", "test default");
# ...
```

Using Perl

The XSUB shown previously gets the job done, but at the cost of some long and relatively complicated C code. An easier way to get the same functionality is to divide the module into an XS back end and a Perl front end. The XS layer will provide a thin wrapper around the existing API, and the Perl front end will add the code necessary to support a friendly interface.

To start with, I'll define the back-end XSUBs in a separate package using the PACKAGE command on the MODULE line:

```
MODULE = Gnome::MIME    PACKAGE = Gnome::MIME::Backend    PREFIX = gnome_mime_
```

After this line every XSUB defined will have its Perl interface defined in the Gnome::MIME::Backend package. An XS file can contain any number of such lines and PACKAGEs, although only one MODULE may be used.

Then each of the functions is wrapped in the plain style shown earlier:

```
const char *
gnome_mime_type(filename)
  char * filename

const char *
gnome_mime_type_or_default(filename, default)
  char * filename
  char * default

const char *
gnome_mime_type_of_file(filename)
  char * filename

const char *
gnome_mime_type_of_file_or_default(filename, default)
  char * filename
  char * default
```

The Perl code to implement the named-parameter interface is then added to MIME.pm:

```perl
use Carp qw(croak);

sub file_type {
  croak("Usage: Gnome::MIME::file_type(k => v, ...)") if @_ % 2;
  my %args = @_;

  # check for bad parameter names
  my %allowed = map { $_, 1 } qw(filename default_type read_file);
  for (keys %args) {
    croak("Unknown key found in Gnome::MIME::file_type parameter list: $_")
      unless exists $allowed{$_};
  }
```

```
# make sure filename is specified
croak("Missing required parameter filename.") unless exists $args{filename};

# call appropriate back-end function
if ($args{read_file} and $args{default_type}) {
  return Gnome::MIME::Backend::type_or_default_of_file($args{filename},
                                      $args{default_type});
} elsif ($args{read_file}) {
  return Gnome::MIME::Backend::type_of_file($args{filename});
} elsif ($args{default_type}) {
  return Gnome::MIME::Backend::type_or_default($args{filename},
                                      $args{default_type});
} else {
  return Gnome::MIME::Backend::type($args{filename});
}
}
```

This code essentially does the same things as the XS code in the previous section, but instead of being in C, it's in good-old maintainable, forgiving Perl. As an added bonus, instead of translating the calls to croak() in the XS version into die() calls, I added a use Carp and used Carp's version of croak(), which will yield much better error messages than die() or its C equivalent.

This pattern, a thin layer of XS with a Perl front end, is worthy of emulation. It provides a way to write Perl-ish interfaces in Perl and get the most out of XS at the same time.

Providing Access to Complex Data Structures

Many C interfaces are more complicated than the gnome_mime_type functions—they manipulate complex data structures, often using C structs and arrays. Providing a convenient interface to Perl programmers is often a matter of translating data from C structs into Perl arrays and hashes, and back again.

It just so happens that the Gnome::MIME module has need of this functionality. The Gnome MIME API supplies two functions that access a set of key/value pairs associated with each MIME type, gnome_mime_get_keys() and gnome_mime_get_value(). There are keys for the program the user has chosen to open the MIME type (that is, an image viewer for image/gif, a text editor for text/plain, and so on) as well as other types of metadata.

It would, of course, be possible to provide a Perl interface directly to these calls. For example, to print out the available key/value pairs for image/gif, you could do the following:

```
@keys = Gnome::MIME::get_keys("image/gif");
foreach $key (@keys) {
   $value = Gnome::MIME::get_value("image/gif", $key);
   print "$key => $value\n";
}
```

If your Perl-sense isn't screaming *hash* by now, you might want to see a doctor! A much better interface would be this one:

```
my $type_data = Gnome::MIME::type_data("image/gif");
while (($key, $value) = each %$type_data) {
   print "$key => $value\n";
}
```

To provide this interface, you need to build a hash dynamically from the results of calling gnome_mime_get_keys() and gnome_mime_get_value(). The full XSUB used to support this interface is shown in Listing 9-7.

Listing 9-7. XSUB Implementing Gnome::MIME::type_data()

```
SV *
type_data(type)
  const gchar * type
PREINIT:
  GList *keys, *iter;
  HV *hv;
  SV *value;
  char *key;
CODE:
  // initialize hash
  hv = newHV();

  // get GList of keys for this type
  keys = gnome_mime_get_keys(type);

  // iterate through keys
  for (iter = keys; iter; iter = iter->next) {
    // get the key from the iterator
    key = iter->data;

    // create a new SV and load it with the value for this key
    value = newSVpv(gnome_mime_get_value(type, key), 0);
```

```
    // store the key/value pair in
    hv_store(hv, key, strlen(key), value, 0);
  }

  // return a reference to the new hash
  RETVAL = newRV_noinc((SV *)hv);
OUTPUT:
  RETVAL
CLEANUP:
  g_list_free(keys);
```

The XSUB starts with a return type of SV:

```
SV *
type_data(type)
  const gchar * type
```

Since the subroutine will return a reference to a hash, the return type must be
SV*. Next, several local variables are declared in a PREINIT block, including two
GLists. The GList type is the Gnome API's linked-list type. The CODE body starts by
initializing the HV that will be returned to the user:

```
  // initialize hash
  hv = newHV();
```

Next, I call gnome_mime_get_keys() and begin iterating over the GList:

```
  // get GList of keys for this type
  keys = gnome_mime_get_keys(type);

  // iterate through keys
  for (iter = keys; iter; iter = iter->next) {
    // get the key from the iterator
    key = iter->data;
```

If keys returns a NULL pointer, then this loop won't be executed, and an empty hash
will be returned to the user. Next, the key-value pairs are stored in the HV:

```
    // create a new SV and load it with the value for this key
    value = newSVpv(gnome_mime_get_value(type, key), 0);

    // store the key/value pair in
    hv_store(hv, key, strlen(key), value, 0);
```

Finally, RETVAL is assigned a reference to the hash to be returned:

```
// return a reference to the new hash
RETVAL = newRV_noinc((SV *)hv);
```

You might have expected to see a call to sv_2mortal() at the end, but XSUB return values of SV* are automatically mortalized by xsubpp. As proof, here's the relevant slice of the generated MIME.c:

```
 // return a reference to the new hash
 RETVAL = newRV_noinc((SV *)hv);
#line 52 "MIME.c"
            ST(0) = RETVAL;
       sv_2mortal(ST(0));
```

The generated code places RETVAL into the return stack and is then mortalized. Since the reference to hv was created with newRV_noinc(), the hv has a refcount of 1 and will live as long RETVAL does. The same is true of the SVs stored in hv—they have a refcount of 1 and will be freed when hv is freed. The end result is a chain of Perl objects with refcounts of 1 anchored by a single mortal reference. When building up complex data structures in XS, this is the end result you should be working toward.

Returning Multiple Values in List Context

The new interface for Gnome::MIME::type_data() is a big improvement. Now a user who wants to open a file can do something like the following:

```
$type_data = Gnome::MIME::type_data("text/html");
$program = $type_data->{open};
```

However, inevitably a less-experienced user is going to mix up the hash reference with a hash and try something like this:

```
%type_data = Gnome::MIME::type_data("text/html");
$program = $type_data{open};
```

This will only work if Gnome::MIME::type_data() is smart enough to return a list of key/value pairs in list context. Supporting this usage provides a chance to demonstrate a new technique for building XSUBs: using PPCODE to access the return stack directly. The complete listing for the new XSUB is in Listing 9-8.

Listing 9-8. XSUB for Gnome::MIME::type_data() *with Multiple-Value Return*

```
void
type_data(type)
  const gchar * type
PREINIT:
  GList *keys, *iter;
  HV *hv;
  SV *value;
  char *key;
PPCODE:
  // initialize hash
  hv = newHV();

  // get GList of keys for this type
  keys = gnome_mime_get_keys(type);

  // iterate through keys
  for (iter = keys; iter; iter = iter->next) {
    // get the key from the iterator
    key = iter->data;

    // create a new SV and load it with the value for this key
    value = newSVpv(gnome_mime_get_value(type, key), 0);

    // store the key/value pair in
    hv_store(hv, key, strlen(key), value, 0);
  }

  // free keys GList
  g_list_free(keys);

  // test context with GIMME_V
  if (GIMME_V == G_ARRAY) {
    // list context - return a list of key/value pairs
    IV count = hv_iterinit(hv);
    IV i;
    I32 len;

    // loop over key/value pairs
    for (i = 1; i <= count; i++) {
      value = hv_iternextsv(hv, &key, &len);
```

```
        // push key and value
        XPUSHs(sv_2mortal(newSVpvn(key, len)));
        XPUSHs(sv_mortalcopy(value));
    }

    // free hv explicitly
    SvREFCNT_dec((SV *)hv);

    // return two SVs for each key in the hash
    XSRETURN(count * 2);
    }


    // G_SCALAR or G_VOID context - return a reference to the new hash
    XPUSHs(sv_2mortal(newRV_noinc((SV *)hv)));
```

The first change in the XSUB is in the return value. By using PPCODE instead of
CODE, the XSUB is responsible for managing the return stack. As a result, the return
type is set to void so that xsubpp knows not to provide RETVAL:

```
void
type_data(type)
    const gchar * type
```

After that, aside from using PPCODE instead of CODE, the function begins much like
the XSUB in Listing 9-7. The first new statement is as follows:

```
    // free keys GList
    g_list_free(keys);
```

This line used to live in the CLEANUP block, but PPCODE blocks cannot have CLEANUP
blocks, so the call to g_list_free() is moved into the main code body.

The next section uses a new macro, GIMME_V, to examine the context of the
current call. GIMME_V is the XS author's version of Perl's wantarray built-in. It can
return three possible values—G_ARRAY,[3] G_SCALAR, and G_VOID. In this case, I test for
list context:

```
    // test context with GIMME_V
    if (GIMME_V == G_ARRAY) {
```

If you're in list context, the code iterates through the hash and pushes key/value
pairs onto the return stack. The hash iteration code should look familiar from the

---

3. Which probably should be G_LIST since there's no such thing as "array context!"

"Hash Values (HV)" section in Chapter 8, but instead of printing out keys and values, I'm pushing them onto the return stack with XPUSHs:

```
// loop over key/value pairs
for (i = 1; i <= count; i++) {
  value = hv_iternextsv(hv, &key, &len);

  // push key and value
  XPUSHs(sv_2mortal(newSVpvn(key, len)));
  XPUSHs(sv_mortalcopy(value));
}
```

Notice that each value pushed onto the stack is made mortal. If this weren't done, then this subroutine would leak memory on every call.

After pushing the key/value pairs onto the return stack, the code explicitly frees the HV used by the XSUB:

```
// free hv explicitly
SvREFCNT_dec((SV *)hv);
```

At this point the HV and all SVs contained in it as values are freed. This is the reason that when pushing the values onto the stack I used sv_mortalcopy(). Actually, a slightly more efficient implementation would be as follows:

```
SvREFCNT_inc(value);       // value will now survive the destruction of hv
XPUSHs(sv_2mortal(value)); // and is mortal on the return stack
```

This avoids the copy of the value at the expense of some dangerous refcount manipulation. Now when the HV is freed, the value SVs will still be live with a ref-count of 1 and mortal. This is dangerous since this kind of manipulation is easy to get wrong, resulting in memory leaks or crashes. Using sv_mortalcopy() offers a simpler solution at a the expense of a small amount of time and memory.

Once the list of return values is pushed onto the stack, the code returns early with the XSRETURN macro:

```
// return two SVs for each key in the hash
XSRETURN(count * 2);
```

This macro takes as an argument the number of items pushed on the stack, in this case twice the number of keys in the hash.

In scalar or void context, the code behaves the same as before, returning a reference to the hash:

```
// G_SCALAR or G_VOID context - return a reference to the new hash
XPUSHs(sv_2mortal(newRV_noinc((SV *)hv)));
```

The only difference here is that since I'm in a PPCODE block, I have to manually call XPUSHs and mortalize the return value. Note that an XSRETURN(1) isn't required since xsubpp will automatically provide a return at the end of the function.

With this new XSUB, the test cases can now be written to work with both scalar and list context calls:

```
# test type_data in scalar context
my $type_data = Gnome::MIME::type_data("image/gif");
ok($type_data->{open}, "image/gif has an open key");

# test type_data in list context
my %type_data = Gnome::MIME::type_data("image/gif");
ok($type_data{open}, "image/gif has an open key");
```

Now, if that's not quality service I don't know what is!

Writing a Typemap

In terms of Gnome::MIME, wrapping gnome_mime_get_keys() and gnome_mime_get_value() as a single function returning a hash was a good choice. However, exploring an alternate implementation will provide a look at an important aspect of XS development: typemap creation. In particular, imagine that you wanted to provide an interface similar to one passed over earlier:

```
$keys = Gnome::MIME::get_keys("image/gif");
foreach $key (@$keys) {
    $value = Gnome::MIME::get_value("image/gif", $key);
    print "$key => $value\n";
}
```

In the preceding code, get_keys() returns a reference to an array of keys that are then used to call get_value().

To get started, I would create two literal XSUBs:

```
MODULE = Gnome::MIME   PACKAGE = Gnome::MIME   PREFIX = gnome_mime_

GList *
gnome_mime_get_keys(type)
  const char * type

const char *
gnome_mime_get_value(type, key)
  const char * type
  const char * key
```

But this generates a compilation error:

```
Error: 'GList *' not in typemap in MIME.xs, line 10
```

The last time you saw this error, it was for const char * and const gchar *, and the solution was to simply alias those types to the type used for char *. In this case, the solution won't be so easy—there's no existing typemap with the behavior I'm looking for. In particular, I want a typemap that will take a GList* and return a reference to an AV*. You can find the completed typemap file in Listing 9-9.

Listing 9-9. typemap *File with* GList* *Typemap*

```
const char   *    T_PV
const gchar  *    T_PV
GList *           T_GLIST

INPUT
T_GLIST
        croak("GList * input typemap unimplemented!");

OUTPUT
T_GLIST
        $arg = GList_to_AVref($var);
```

A typemap file has three sections. The first is a list of C type names and corresponding typemap names. This allows a group of C types to share a single typemap. This section already has two lines in my typemap file:

```
const char   *    T_PV
const gchar  *    T_PV
```

I'll add a line for the GList* type:

```
GList *          T_GLIST
```

The next section in a typemap is the INPUT section. An INPUT typemap describes how to translate from an SV* to the specified type. It is used when an XSUB takes the type as a parameter. Since gnome_mime_get_keys() returns GList* and nothing I'm wrapping uses a GList* as a parameter, I'll leave this one unimplemented:

```
INPUT
T_GLIST
        croak("GList * input typemap unimplemented!");
```

Next comes the OUTPUT section, which specifies how to turn the type into an SV*:

```
OUTPUT
T_GLIST
        $arg = GList_to_AVref($var);
```

Typemap code uses two placeholder variables: $arg and $var. In an OUTPUT typemap, $var is a variable of the type being output and $arg is the SV* to be returned. As you can see, my OUTPUT typemap calls the GList_to_AVref() function. This function doesn't exist in either Perl or Gnome, so I'll have to write it!

Where to place external functions like GList_to_AVref() is a matter of preference. Some XS coders prefer to put them in a separate .c file compiled and linked separately. I prefer to place them in the C section above the XSUB declarations, and that's the way I'll do it here (see Listing 9-10).

Listing 9-10. GList_to_AVref() *Function Included in* MIME.xs

```
#include "EXTERN.h"
#include "perl.h"
#include "XSUB.h"
#include <gnome.h>

SV * GList_to_AVref(GList *list) {
  GList *iter;       // list iterator
  AV *av = newAV(); // initialize new array

  // iterate through GList
  for (iter = list; iter; iter = iter->next) {
    // push data onto array
    av_push(av, newSVpv(iter->data,0));
  }
```

```
// free glist passed into function
g_list_free(list);

// return a reference to the new array
return sv_2mortal(newRV_noinc((SV *)av));
}
```

The code for the function should be easy enough to understand. It simply takes a GList* and adds each data item contained inside to an array, returning a new mortal reference to the array constructed. Notice that the function also frees the GList*:

```
// free glist passed into function
g_list_free(list);
```

This could just as well have been done in a CLEANUP block, but putting it in the typemap function provides the cleanest access for the XSUB.

With this XSUB in place, the test code is updated to use the new interface:

```
# test get_keys and get_value
$keys = Gnome::MIME::get_keys("image/gif");
isa_ok($keys, 'ARRAY', "get_keys return");
foreach $key (@$keys) {
  ok(Gnome::MIME::get_value("image/gif", $key), "got value for \"$key\"");
}
```

The best way to learn to program typemaps is to examine the typemaps that come with Perl. You'll find them in a file called typemap in the library directory where the ExtUtils modules are installed. On my system, the path to typemap is /usr/lib/perl5/5.6.1/ExtUtils/typemap, but different platforms will place the file in different locations.

Learning More about XS

The examples in this chapter have explored many useful XS programming techniques. However, there are many useful commands and options that I didn't have space to cover. Included with Perl is perlxstut, a tutorial that covers much the same ground as this chapter. Also included with Perl is perlxs, an exhaustive reference to all of XS.

Summary

This chapter has explored the most popular way to create Perl modules in C—XS. The next chapter introduces a new technology, Inline::C, that can be provide an easier way to achieve the same results.

CHAPTER 10

Writing C Modules
with Inline::C

INLINE::C[1] PROVIDES a new way to write Perl modules with C. Instead of separating out the Perl and C parts of your module into different files, you can include them both in the same file. Instead of learning a new programming language (XS), you can create C functions in pure C. If this sounds pretty great, it is! My prediction is that the majority of new C modules will be written using Inline::C. It's easy, it works, and what more could you ask for?

Inline::C is essentially a compiler for XS. You give Inline::C some C code. Inline::C takes that code, parses it, and produces an XS wrapper to make that code callable from Perl. This XS code is written out to disk in a special temporary directory. Then Inline::C compiles the code using the normal XS tools: ExtUtils::MakeMaker, xsubpp, and your system's C compiler This compiled code is saved to disk and then loaded into memory.

Since the compiled code is saved to disk, it can be reused as long as the C code hasn't changed. This magic is accomplished by using Digest::MD5 to produce a fingerprint of your code. When that fingerprint is changed, the code is automatically recompiled the next time it's passed to Inline::C.

Inline::C Walkthrough

Here's a simple example script that uses Inline::C to print out "Just Another Perl Hacker":

```
#!/usr/bin/perl -w
use Inline C => <<END_OF_C;
  void japh() {
    PerlIO_stdoutf("Just Another Perl Hacker.\n");
  }
END_OF_C

japh();
```

---

1. Written by Brian Ingerson and available on a CPAN mirror near you

This script uses the Perl C API function `PerlIO_stdoutf()` to print a string. When you run this script, it works as expected, after a sizable pause for compilation:

```
$ ./inline.pl
Just Another Perl Hacker.
```

The second time you run it there's no pause. So, what's happening here? Inline::C follows these steps:

1. Inline::C receives the C source code passed as an argument to `use Inline C`. This happens at compile time.

2. Next, Inline::C checks to see if it already has a compiled version of this code available. If so, it loads the compiled code with DynaLoader and returns. More on how this works in Step 5.

3. A directory is created in which to build the code if one doesn't already exist. Since I didn't provide any configuration options to control this selection, Inline::C will create a directory called `_Inline` in the current directory.

4. The C code is then parsed with Parse::RecDescent, which looks for a C function to wrap with XS.

5. Inline::C creates all the files and directories necessary to build an XS module containing the C code. This includes `Makefile.PL`, a `.pm` file, and an `.xs` file. The name for the directory used to build the code is derived from an MD5 signature of the code to be compiled. This is how Inline::C is able to know in Step 2 if the code needs to be recompiled or not.

6. The code is built using the normal `perl Makefile.PL && make` procedure employed by XS modules.

7. The compiled code is loaded with the DynaLoader module.

All of this is transparent to the Inline::C programmer, unlike with XS. Better yet, it works in scripts just as well as it works in modules. This makes testing new C functions easy: Just create a script that uses the function and run it—no compile step required!

Getting Up Close and Personal

Inline::C supports a powerful tracing mechanism that can give you information about what it's doing while it's doing it. For example, if I call the preceding script with the command-line parameter –MInline=INFO,FORCE,NOCLEAN, the following output is produced:

```
$ perl -MInline=INFO,FORCE,NOCLEAN ./inline.pl
<---------------------Information Section--------------------------->

Information about the processing of your Inline C code:

Your source code needs to be compiled. I'll use this build directory:
./_Inline/build/inline_pl_927a

and I'll install the executable as:
./_Inline/lib/auto/inline_pl_927a/inline_pl_927a.so

The following Inline C function(s) have been successfully bound to Perl:
            void japh()

<---------------------End of Information Section-------------------->
Just Another Perl Hacker.
```

The FORCE option tells Inline::C to compile the code even if it hasn't changed. The INFO option produces the output included earlier. As you can see, Inline::C is building in ./_Inline/build/inline_pl_927a. The compiled module (referred to as an *executable*) is created in this directory. Finally, Inline::C helpfully reports that a single function was successfully bound to Perl: void japh().

By specifying NOCLEAN, Inline::C leaves all its temporary files around for you to inspect. Entering the build directory, I find the following files:

```
$ cd _Inline/build/inline_pl_927a
$ ls
blib                 inline_pl_927a.c   Makefile      out.Makefile_PL
INLINE.h             inline_pl_927a.o   Makefile.PL   out.make_install
inline_pl_927a.bs    inline_pl_927a.xs  out.make      pm_to_blib
```

All of these files are useful to understanding how Inline::C works, but the file out.make is of particular importance. It records the output of the compilation phase of your code. If you have a compilation error, Inline::C will output a message like this one:

```
A problem was encountered while attempting to compile and install your Inline
C code. The command that failed was:
  make > out.make 2>&1

The build directory was:
/home/sam/book/_Inline/build/inline_pl_8143

To debug the problem, cd to the build directory, and inspect the output files.

 at ./inline.pl line 2
```

By examining the out.make file in the build directory you can determine the exact cause of the compilation error.

Getting Started with Inline::C

Writing a module with Inline::C is a lot like writing an XS module with no XS. As such, you can get started with h2xs the same was as you would with a pure Perl module. To generate a skeleton for Gnome::MIME, I use the following command:

```
h2xs -XA -n Gnome::MIME
```

This creates the same files as you examined in Chapter 4 (for a quick refresher, see Table 10-1). Since I'm using Inline::C, all the C code for the module will go in MIME.pm alongside the Perl code.

Table 10-1. Files Generated by h2xs -XA -n Gnome::MIME

File	Description
MIME.pm	The module file itself, which contains Perl code, C code, and POD documentation
Makefile.PL	A script that uses ExtUtils::MakeMaker to generate a Makefile
test.pl	A test script run when a user types "make test" or installs your module with the CPAN module
README	A quick description of your module and how to install it
Changes	A change log in which you can describe differences between versions of your module
MANIFEST	A list of all the files in your distribution

Modifying Makefile.PL

However, before I can get started, the generated Makefile.PL requires some modification to build an Inline::C module (see Listing 10-1).

Listing 10-1. Makefile.PL *for Inline::C Version of Gnome::MIME*

```
use Inline::MakeMaker;
WriteInlineMakefile(
                NAME          => "Gnome::MIME",
                VERSION_FROM  => "MIME.pm",
                PREREQ_PM     => { Inline::C => 0.43 },
                AUTHOR        => 'Sam Tregar <sam@tregar.com>',
               );
```

This file is considerably different from the version created for XS. First, it starts by using a different MakeMaker module:

```
use Inline::MakeMaker;
```

Also, it calls WriteInlineMakefile() rather than WriteMakefile(). Inline::C modules use a different MakeMaker to allow them to be compiled and installed just like XS modules rather than being compiled the first time they're used. Also, notice that Inline::C is listed as a requirement in PREREQ_PM:

```
PREREQ_PM     => { Inline::C => 0.43 },
```

A future version of Inline::C will make it possible to build modules that do not depend on Inline::C, but at least for version 0.43 users of Inline::C-based modules must also install Inline::C.

What's new isn't as notable as what's missing—the calls to gnome-config to set up LIBS and INC. This logic will still be needed by the module, but it will go in the module itself rather than living in the Makefile.PL.

Modifying MIME.pm

The configuration that was part of Makefile.PL in the XS version is now part of MIME.pm (Listing 10-2).

Listing 10-2. MIME.pm *with a Single C-Function Wrapper*

```
package Gnome::MIME;
our $VERSION = "0.01";

use Inline C       => 'DATA',
           NAME    => "Gnome::MIME",
           VERSION => "0.01",
           LIBS    => 'gnome-config gnome --libs',
           INC     => 'gnome-config gnome --cflags';


1;


__DATA__
__C__
#include <gnome.h>

char * file_type (char *filename) {
  return gnome_mime_type(filename);
}
```

This module uses Inline::C differently from the inline.pl script shown at the beginning of the chapter. Instead of passing the C code in a string, this code points Inline::C at the __DATA__ section where the code will follow a __C__ identifier:

```
use Inline C       => 'DATA',
```

The next lines specify the name and version of the module. This information is slightly redundant, but Inline::C uses these options as a cue that it's building C code for a module and not a script:

```
           NAME    => "Gnome::MIME",
           VERSION => "0.01",
```

Next comes the configuration data that the XS version set up in Makefile.PL, LIBS, and INC:

```
           LIBS    => 'gnome-config gnome --libs',
           INC     => 'gnome-config gnome --cflags';
```

The C code is placed after the __DATA__ symbol. Below __DATA__, __C__ marks the start of the C code:

```
__DATA__
__C__
#include <gnome.h>

char * file_type (char *filename) {
  return gnome_mime_type(filename);
}
```

I'll discuss the actual C code in the next section.

A First Inlined Function

Just as in the first XS example in the last chapter, I'll start with the gnome_mime_type() function. This function takes a filename as an argument and returns a string containing the MIME type of the filename. It has the following signature:

```
const char * gnome_mime_type(const gchar *filename);
```

One way to wrap this function is shown in Listing 10-2, with the function file_type():

```
char * file_type (char *filename) {
  return gnome_mime_type(filename);
}
```

With this function in place, test.pl can be written:

```
use Test::More 'no_plan';
BEGIN { use_ok('Gnome::MIME'); }

# test some simple mime-file_type recognitions
is(Gnome::MIME::file_type("foo.gif"),  'image/gif',  "recognizes .gif");
is(Gnome::MIME::file_type("foo.jpg"),  'image/jpeg', "recognizes .jpg");
is(Gnome::MIME::file_type("foo.html"), 'text/html',  "recognizes .html");
```

The module can then be built and tested:

```
$ perl Makefile.PL && make && make test
Checking if your kit is complete...
Looks good
Writing Makefile for Gnome::MIME
cp MIME.pm blib/lib/Gnome/MIME.pm
/usr/local/bin/perl -Mblib -MInline=_INSTALL_ -MGnome::MIME -e1 0.01 blib/arch
Using /home/sam/Gnome/MIME/blib
PERL_DL_NONLAZY=1 /usr/local/bin/perl -Iblib/arch -Iblib/lib \
    -I/usr/local/lib/perl5/5.6.1/i686-linux -I/usr/local/lib/perl5/5.6.1 test.pl
ok 1 - use Gnome::MIME;
ok 2 - recognizes .gif
ok 3 - recognizes .jpg
ok 4 - recognizes .html
1..4
```

That's all there is to it! No extra files; just a pure C function in the body of the module.

Notice that this case is different from the starting point with XS, where the simplest XSUB was one without any code at all. XS and Inline::C are tuned for different uses. XS is tuned to produce direct mappings from C function signatures to Perl functions. Inline::C prefers full C functions. However, just as XS has CODE and PPCODE to support full C functions, Inline::C has facilities for generating wrappers from function signatures. The difference is more one of emphasis than of capability.

Inline::C Techniques

This section will explore ways that Inline::C can be used to enhance the basic inlined function shown earlier. Many of these techniques will be very similar to those shown in the "XS Techniques" section in Chapter 9. This is natural; Inline::C is just a layer on top of XS, so many of the things that can be done with XS can be done the same way in Inline::C.

Using Typemaps

Typemaps work mostly the same way in Inline::C as they do in XS. The biggest difference is that to use a typemap with Inline::C, you have to include the TYPEMAPS option:

```
use Inline C        => 'DATA',
        NAME    => "Gnome::MIME",
        VERSION => "0.01",
        LIBS    => 'gnome-config gnome --libs',
        INC     => 'gnome-config gnome --cflags',
        TYPEMAPS => 'typemap';
```

The TYPEMAPS option is set to the path of the typemap file. For example, to use the gchar type in the file_type(), I would create a file called typemap and put a single line in it:

```
gchar *    T_PV
```

Now the file_type() function can written as follows:

```
char * file_type (gchar * filename) {
  return gnome_mime_type(filename);
}
```

Inline::C uses typemap files in two ways. They're used by the generated XS to bind function parameters and return values in the same way as in the XS section. However, they're also used by the Inline::C parser to determine which functions can be wrapped for use by Perl. Inline::C will silently ignore functions with signatures that don't have matching typemaps. The result is that if Inline::C doesn't accept your typemap for one reason or another, it will simply ignore functions that are trying to use that typemap. You can find out if this is happening by setting the PRINT_INFO option:

```
use Inline C        => 'DATA',
        NAME    => "Gnome::MIME",
        VERSION => "0.01",
        LIBS    => 'gnome-config gnome --libs',
        INC     => 'gnome-config gnome --cflags',
        TYPEMAPS => 'typemap',
        PRINT_INFO => 1;
```

This will cause Inline::C to produce the same information block shown earlier with the –MInline=INFO invocation. Included is a list of functions bound by Inline::C; if functions are missing, then you may have a problem with your typemaps.

Supporting Named Parameters

One way in which XS modules and Inline::C modules are essentially the same is that they both benefit from careful interface design. In terms of Gnome::MIME, this means supporting a named-parameter style interface to file_type():

```
$type = Gnome::MIME::file_type(filename     => $filename,
                               default_type => "text/html",
                               read_file    => 1);
```

The full inlined function implementing this interface is shown in Listing 10-3.

Listing 10-3. Inline Function with Named-Parameter Support

```
char * file_type (SV *dummy, ...) {
  Inline_Stack_Vars;          // get access to the Inline stack macros

  char *filename     = NULL; // variables for named params values
  char *default_type = NULL;
  IV    read_file    = 0;
  int x;                      // loop counter

  // loop over args by pairs and fill in parameters
  for (x = 0; x < Inline_Stack_Items; x+=2) {
    char *key = SvPV(Inline_Stack_Item(x), PL_na);
    if (strEQ(key, "filename")) {
      filename = SvPV(Inline_Stack_Item(x+1), PL_na);
    } else if (strEQ(key, "default_type")) {
      default_type = SvPV(Inline_Stack_Item(x+1), PL_na);
    } else if (strEQ(key, "read_file")) {
      read_file = SvIV(Inline_Stack_Item(x+1));
    } else {
      croak("Unknown key found in Gnome::MIME::file_type parameter list: %s",
          key);
    }
  }

  // make sure we have a filename parameter
  if (filename == NULL) croak("Missing required parameter filename.");
```

```
  // call the appropriate function based on arguments
  if (read_file && default_type != NULL)
    return gnome_mime_type_or_default_of_file(filename, default_type);
  if (read_file)
    return gnome_mime_type_of_file(filename);
  if (default_type != NULL)
    return gnome_mime_type_or_default(filename, default_type);

  return gnome_mime_type(filename);
}
```

This function is very similar to the XS implementation introduced earlier, but there are some significant differences. First, the function's signature is different:

```
char * file_type (SV *dummy, ...) {
```

The dummy argument is required by Inline::C; due to the way it compiles C code to XS, it won't allow an argument list of (. . .) like the XS implementation uses. This makes it impossible to create an Inline::C function that can take zero or more parameters. I expect this limitation to be removed in a future version of Inline::C.

Next, a special Inline::C macro is used to initialize some temporary variables employed by the other Inline::C stack macros:

```
  Inline_Stack_Vars;          // get access to the Inline stack macros
```

These macros are included in the block of code following the variable declarations:

```
  // loop over args by pairs and fill in parameters
  for (x = 0; x < Inline_Stack_Items; x+=2) {
    char *key = SvPV(Inline_Stack_Item(x), PL_na);
    if (strEQ(key, "filename")) {
      filename = SvPV(Inline_Stack_Item(x+1), PL_na);
    } else if (strEQ(key, "default_type")) {
```

This block of code uses Inline_Stack_Items where the XS code used items, and Inline_Stack_Item where the XS code used ST. Their meaning is the same though, and they can be used interchangeably in Inline::C code.

The final change is that with the absence of the RETVAL special variable the control flow in the final section is simplified. The function simply returns when it has found the correct function to call:

```
  // call the appropriate function based on arguments
  if (read_file && default_type != NULL)
    return gnome_mime_type_or_default_of_file(filename, default_type);
```

Returning Multiple Values Using Inline::C

Rounding out the set of XSUBs redone as inlined functions, Listing 10-4 contains an Inline::C version of the type_data() function from Chapter 9.

Listing 10-4. Inline Function Using Multivalue Return

```
void type_data(gchar *type) {
  Inline_Stack_Vars;
  GList *keys, *iter;
  HV *hv;
  SV *value;
  char *key;

  // initialize hash
  hv = newHV();

  // get GList of keys for this type
  keys = gnome_mime_get_keys(type);

  // iterate through keys
  for (iter = keys; iter; iter = iter->next) {
    // get the key from the iterator
    key = iter->data;

    // create a new SV and load it with the value for this key
    value = newSVpv(gnome_mime_get_value(type, key), 0);

    // store the key/value pair in
    hv_store(hv, key, strlen(key), value, 0);
  }

  // free keys GList
  g_list_free(keys);

  // test context with GIMME_V
  if (GIMME_V == G_ARRAY) {
    // list context - return a list of key/value pairs
    int count = hv_iterinit(hv);
    int i;
    I32 len;

    // get ready for Inline_Stack_Push
    Inline_Stack_Reset;
```

```
  // loop over key/value pairs
  for (i = 1; i <= count; i++) {
    value = hv_iternextsv(hv, &key, &len);

    // push key and value
    Inline_Stack_Push(sv_2mortal(newSVpvn(key, len)));
    Inline_Stack_Push(sv_mortalcopy(value));
  }

  // done pusing on the stack
  Inline_Stack_Done;

  // free hv explicitly
  SvREFCNT_dec((SV *)hv);

  // return two SVs for each key in the hash
  Inline_Stack_Return(count * 2);
}

// G_SCALAR or G_VOID context - return a reference to the new hash
Inline_Stack_Reset;
Inline_Stack_Push(sv_2mortal(newRV_noinc((SV *)hv)));
Inline_Stack_Done;
Inline_Stack_Return(1);
}
```

This function returns a hash reference in scalar context and a list of key-value pairs in list context:

```
# scalar context
$type_data = Gnome::MIME::type_data("text/html");
$program = $type_data->{open};

# list context
%type_data = Gnome::MIME::type_data("text/html");
$program = $type_data{open};
```

The code used is substantially similar to the XS version, and again the difference is largely a matter of the Inline::C macros used.

To start, the function begins with a void return type, which works similarly to a PPCODE block in XS in that it allows you to handle the return stack explicitly:

```
void type_data(gchar *type) {
```

Next, the `Inline_Stack_Vars` macro is used to initialize temporaries for the Inline::C stack macros:

```
Inline_Stack_Vars;
```

The next new macro usage is the pair `Inline_Stack_Reset` and `Inline_Stack_Done`. These are required around any usage of `Inline_Stack_Push`. These macros push the list of key/value pairs onto the return stack:

```
// get ready for Inline_Stack_Push
Inline_Stack_Reset;

// loop over key/value pairs
for (i = 1; i <= count; i++) {
  value = hv_iternextsv(hv, &key, &len);

  // push key and value
  Inline_Stack_Push(sv_2mortal(newSVpvn(key, len)));
  Inline_Stack_Push(sv_mortalcopy(value));
}

// done pushing on the stack
Inline_Stack_Done;
```

Then Inline::C's version of XSRETURN, `Inline_Stack_Return`, is used to return from the function:

```
// return two SVs for each key in the hash
Inline_Stack_Return(count * 2);
```

A similar sequence is used in scalar context to return a single value:

```
// G_SCALAR or G_VOID context - return a reference to the new hash
Inline_Stack_Reset;
Inline_Stack_Push(sv_2mortal(newRV_noinc((SV *)hv)));
Inline_Stack_Done;
Inline_Stack_Return(1);
```

This marks a difference from the XS code where the final XSRETURN(1) wasn't required; in Inline::C `Inline_Stack_Return` is a required call regardless of the number of return values.

Learning More about Inline::C

Inline::C provides many options and capabilities that I didn't have room to explore. There are options that provide automatic wrapper generation as well as functions for binding C code at runtime. You can find information about these abilities in the Inline::C documentation. Inline::C also comes with a documentation-only module called Inline::C-Cookbook, which contains solutions to a wide variety of C module programming problems.

Inline::C is actually just the most prominent member of the Inline family. To learn about the Inline parent module, see the Inline documentation. This is where you'll find "big picture" documentation that lays out the basic usage of Inline. Also, there are many other Inline modules worthy of investigation: Inline::CPP (for C++), Inline::Java, Inline::Guile, Inline::Asm (for assembly!), to name a few.

Summary

This chapter completed the picture of Perl module development in C by introducing a cutting-edge tool, Inline::C. The next chapter explores another corner of CPAN development, building CGI modules using CGI::Application.

CHAPTER 11
CGI Application Modules for CPAN

COMMON GATEWAY INTERFACE (CGI) programming is probably the most common use for the Perl language. CGI provides the interactivity in nearly every popular site on the Web today. Although CGI is an old technology by Internet standards, what it lacks in sex appeal it more than makes up for in utility and portability. Unlike the many CGI-replacement technologies available, it is supported on virtually every platform and Web server. If you can use Perl on your platform of choice, the chances are excellent that you can use CGI too.

CGI::Application[1] provides a new and better way to build CGI programs as reusable modules. Since CGI::Application modules are normal Perl modules, they can be released on CPAN and reused by the Perl community. This chapter will introduce you to CGI::Application and explore the ways in which it encourages software reuse.

One thing this chapter won't do is teach you CGI programming or explain how to use CGI.pm. To get the most out of this chapter, you'll need some prior experience with CGI. If you're new to the technology, then you should consider reading a good book on the topic first.[2]

Introduction to CGI::Application

The CGI::Application module represents an evolution in the way CGI programs (known as *CGIs*) are developed. CGIs provide services to users through their Web browsers, usually by displaying a series of screens containing forms for the user to interact with. CGIs are commonly coded in Perl by creating a script that generates HTML forms and processes the results of those forms. There are many drawbacks to this approach, as I'll explain in the upcoming text.

CGI::Application offers a different model. Instead of writing your CGI code in scripts specific to the task at hand, CGI::Application allows you to create flexible

---

1. Written by Jesse Erlbaum, the technical editor for this book. You can find it on CPAN, of course!

2. There are many books written about this subject. A favorite of mine is *CGI Programming with Perl, 2nd Edition* by Guelich, Gundavaram, and Birznieks (O'Reilly & Associates).

modules that can be used on multiple projects. Furthermore, CGI::Application provides a solution for some of the more common problems plaguing CGI development today.

A Typical CGI

Imagine, if you will, a typical CGI program—a simple bulletin board system. The program allows users to list all messages on the board, read a particular message, search for messages, enter new messages, and reply to existing messages. Of course a real bulletin board system would offer more features, but for this example I'll keep it simple. Figures 11-1, 11-2, 11-3, and 11-4 show the four screens of the application as they would appear in a Web browser.

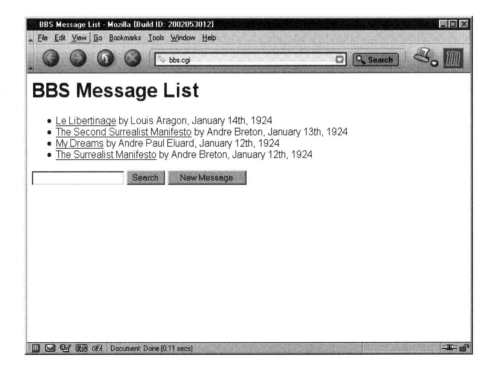

Figure 11-1. Bulletin board message list screen

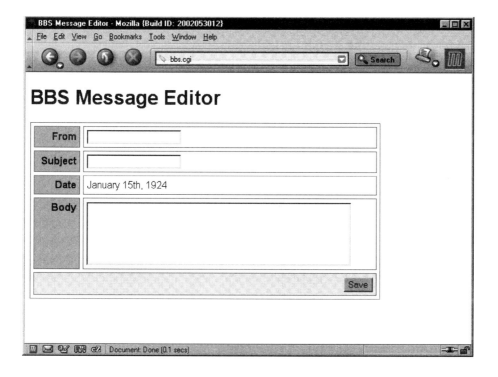

Figure 11-2. Bulletin board message viewer screen

Figure 11-3. Bulletin board message entry screen

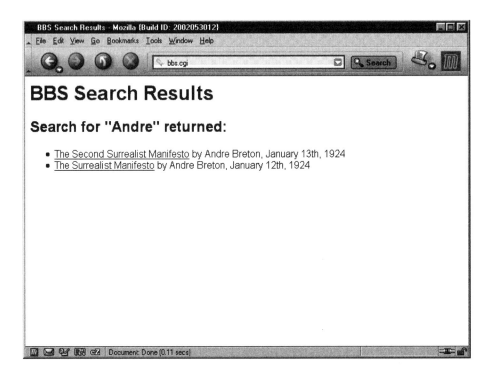

Figure 11-4. Bulletin board message search screen

A typical implementation might start with a structure like this, implementing just the listing, reading, and saving of new messages:

```perl
#!/usr/bin/perl
use CGI;
$query = CGI->new();  # instantiate CGI object

# determine what to do
if ($query->param("msg_id")) {       # user is reading to a message?
   do_read();
} elsif ($query->param("subject")) { # user is saving a message
   do_save();
} else {                             # list messages by default
   do_list();
}

# code for do_read(), do_save() and do_list() ...
```

The preceding code uses CGI.pm's param() method to examine incoming CGI parameters to determine what the user wants to do. Each subroutine called in the if-else block performs the required action using more CGI.pm calls, and ends by printing out the HTML for the page. Since I'm not trying to teach CGI programming, I've left out the implementation of these functions.

This code employs a set of heuristics to determine which action to perform for the user. For example, it knows the user is saving a message by the presence of a CGI parameter called `subject`. If a user wants to read a message, then the `msg_id` parameter will be included in the request and the script will know to act accordingly. This approach has a major flaw—it makes adding new features much harder than it should be.

For example, imagine adding support for replying to a message. This action will need only one parameter—the message ID for the message being replied to. Thus, the elsif block might look like the following:

```
} elsif ($query->param("msg_id")) { # is the user replying to a message?
  do_reply();
}
```

But this won't work; the `do_read()` functionality is already using `msg_id`, and `do_reply()` will never be called! Instead you'd have to distort your parameter names to avoid clashing by adding a new parameter:

```
} elsif ($query->param("reply_msg_id")) { # is the user replying to a message?
  do_reply();
}
```

The problem here is that the CGI script has no way to know what the user is really doing—it just looks at the incoming request and makes an educated guess. A small error on one form can lead your program down the wrong path with disastrous results. Also, understanding how the program works is unnecessarily difficult.

CGIs as State Machines

Many CGI programs, including the example shown earlier, can be viewed as *finite state machines* (or just *state machines*). A state machine is a system characterized by a series of discreet *states* and *events* that provide transitions between states. In a CGI like the BBS, the events are actions performed by the user, usually by clicking a button or following a link. In response, the application enters a particular state. In the preceding example, the `do_save()` subroutine is a state entered in response to the user saving a message. The output of this subroutine is displayed to the user. Thus, from a user's perspective, events are mouse-clicks and states are screens of the application.

State machines can be pictured visually using symbols from the Unified Modeling Language (UML), which was introduced briefly at the end of Chapter 3. Figure 11-5 shows a state machine for the BBS application. The four boxes represent the four screens of the application. The arrows pointing from one state to the next are the events. From any given state, there are a fixed number of available events, or *transitions*. The diagram begins with an initial state, shown as a filled circle. The default event—list—leads from the initial state to the first real state. This means that when users first arrive at the application, they should be shown a list of messages.

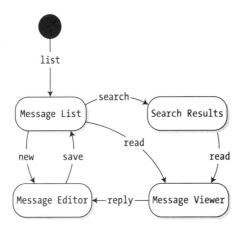

Figure 11-5. State machine for BBS application

By using a state machine to design your CGIs, you are able to view the application as a whole. Each event that is accessible from a particular state will generally show up in the final application as a button or link. With this knowledge, you can use state-transition diagrams to assist you in designing both your user interface and your program code. Also, the state-transition diagram can notify you if you're missing a button on a particular screen.

The CGI::Application module recognizes that Web applications are best understood as state machines. As you are about to see, this module provides a reusable alternative to rolling your own ad hoc flow control from if-elsif blocks.

CGI::Application to the Rescue

CGI::Application offers a cleaner solution to this CGI project. Listings 11-1 and 11-2 show the full CGI::Application version—browse through it and then I'll walk you through the code.

Listing 11-1. BBS.pm, *the CGI::Application BBS*

```perl
package BBS;
use CGI::Application;
@ISA = qw(CGI::Application);

sub setup {
  my $self = shift;
  $self->mode_param("rm");
  $self->start_mode("list");
  $self->run_modes(list  => "list",
                   save  => "save",
                   new   => "new_message",
                   read  => "read",
                   reply => "reply",
                   search => "search");
}

# show list of messages
sub list {
  my $self = shift;
  my $query = $self->query();
  my $output;
  # ...
  return $output;
}

# save the message, then switch to list mode
sub save {
  my $self = shift;
  my $query = $self->query();
  # ...
  return $self->list();
}

# run a search and show the results
sub search {
  my $self = shift;
  my $query = $self->query();
  my $output;
  # ...
  return $output;
}
```

```perl
# view a message
sub read {
  my $self = shift;
  my $query = $self->query();
  my $output;
  # ...
  return $output;
}


# show edit screen with blank entry
sub new_message {
    my $self = shift;
    return $self->_edit();
}

# show edit screen with message quoted
sub reply {
  my $self = shift;
  my $query = $self->query;
  my $reply_id = $query->param('reply_id');
  return $self->_edit(reply_to => $reply_id);
}

# private method to show edit screen for new_message and reply
sub _edit {
  my $self = shift;
  my $query = $self->query();
  my $output;
  # ...  return $output;
}

1;
```

Listing 11-2. bbs.cgi, *the BBS Stub Script*

```perl
#!/usr/bin/perl
use lib '.';  # load BBS.pm from the current directory
use BBS;

# instantiate the BBS application object and run it
my $bbs = BBS->new();
$bbs->run();
```

CGI::Application is an *abstract base class* in object-oriented terminology. This means it provides all its functionality by serving as a parent class. You can't use CGI::Application directly, you have to create a subclass. The start of Listing 11-1, placed in a file called BBS.pm, does just that:

```
package BBS;
use CGI::Application;
@ISA = qw(CGI::Application);
```

This creates a new module called BBS that inherits from CGI::Application.

Next, the class implements the one required method, setup(). The setup() method is called from CGI::Application->new(). It is responsible for setting up the *run modes* for the class. Run-modes provide a direct implementation of the events shown in the state machine for this application. They replace the if-elsif structure of the earlier example.

The setup() method works by calling methods inherited from CGI::Application, specifically mode_param(), start_mode(), and run_modes():

```
sub setup {
  my $self = shift;
  $self->mode_param("rm");
  $self->start_mode("list");
  $self->run_modes(list   => "list",
                   save   => "save",
                   new    => "new_message",
                   read   => "read",
                   reply  => "reply",
                   search => "search");
}
```

The mode_param() method tells CGI::Application that the CGI parameter with the name rm will control the run mode of the program. This means that each HTML form sent to this CGI will have a parameter called rm set to a run mode. For example, this might take the form of a hidden input field:

```
<input type="hidden" name="rm" value="save">
```

When the form containing this tag is submitted, the application will enter the "save" run mode. By tracking the run mode in a single parameter, CGI::Application always knows which event is being called. In contrast to the heuristic if-elsif structure seen earlier, this system is durable and simple to understand. CGI::Application simply looks up the value of the rm parameter in the table passed to run_modes() and finds a method to call in the application class.

The next call, to start_mode(), sets "list" as the default run mode. When the CGI is called without an rm parameter set, the run mode will be "list." This is generally what happens when the user first hits the application—which is why it's called start_mode() and not default_mode().

Finally, run_modes() sets up the run-mode table. The keys are names of run modes and the values are method names. Notice that the application defines a run mode named "new" but uses the method name new_message(). Using new() would have caused problems since CGI::Application defines a new() method already and the BBS class is derived from CGI::Application.

After that, the class implements each of its run modes as a separate method. For example, the list() method looks like this:

```
# show list of messages
sub list {
    my $self = shift;
    my $query = $self->query;
    my $output;
    # ...
    return $output;
}
```

Since run modes are methods, they receive their object as the first parameter ($self). The inherited query() method is used to create and return a CGI.pm object. As a result, the internals of the function may be very similar to the pure CGI.pm implementation shown earlier. However, there is one major difference— CGI::Application run-mode methods must never print directly to STDOUT. Instead, they return their output.

CAUTION   Never print to STDOUT from a CGI::Application run mode. All output must be returned as a string.

Since all run modes are methods, transferring control from one to another is easy. For example, the save() method is intended to show the list of messages when it finishes saving the message. To do this it just calls list() at the end of the method and returns the result:

```
# save the message, then switch to list mode
sub save {
   my $self = shift;
   my $query = $self->query();
   # ...
   return $self->list();
}
```

Just as in the earlier example, the "new" and "reply" run modes share the same underlying functionality. With CGI::Application this is easily done by having them both call the same private method, _edit():

```
# show edit screen with blank entry
sub new_message {
   my $self = shift;
   return $self->_edit();
}
```

```
# show edit screen with message quoted
sub reply {
  my $self = shift;
  my $query = $self->query;
  my $reply_id = $query->param('reply_id');
  return $self->_edit(reply_to => $reply_id);
}
```

The _edit() method isn't listed as a run mode, so it can't be called directly by users. This is an important feature—if users could access arbitrary methods, then CGI::Application would be a security breach waiting to happen!

The end result is a system that allows you to directly express the flow control of your CGI system in code. Instead of using an ad hoc flow-control mechanism to guess which action to perform, CGI::Application modules use a table of run modes that map the contents of the run-mode parameter to methods in the class. And as I'll explore later, by building your applications as modules rather than scripts, you'll be able to reuse them in multiple projects and even release them on CPAN.

Advanced CGI::Application

The use of CGI::Application shown previously is enough to accomplish a great improvement in CGI development. By abstracting your application logic into a series of run modes, you'll immediately get a cleaner and more comprehensible structure. This section will show how CGI::Application can be used to add further improvements.

Using Templates

In the state machine shown for the BBS application in Figure 11-5, the run modes are depicted as events connecting one state to the next. For each state there may be any number of run modes leading to and from the state. As you've seen already, run modes are implemented by individual methods in the CGI::Application subclass. How do you implement the states?

The common answer would be to use a series of calls to the CGI.pm's HTML-generation functions.[3] Listing 11-3 shows a simple version of how the message entry screen entered through the "new" and "reply" run modes might be implemented. Figure 11-6 shows the CGI in action. As you can probably see, this code has a serious flaw—the output is unbearably ugly. Fixing this would mean complicating the code with table setup, CSS attributes, images, and more. I've found that on a typical CGI project at least half the time is devoted to tweaking the HTML output to look just right. Worse, using this approach, the display code can only be modified by a Perl programmer (you!).

Listing 11-3. Message Entry Screen Implemented with CGI.pm

```perl
use CGI ':standard';

# the _edit method is called from the "new" and "reply" run-modes.
sub _edit {
  my $self = shift;
  my %options = @_;
  my $output;

  # output message entry page body
  $output .= start_html("Message Editor") .
             h1("Enter Your Message Below") .
             start_form .
             "Name: " . textfield("name") . p .
             "Subject: " . textfield("subject") . p .
             "Message Body" . p .
             textarea(-name => "body", -rows => 4, -cols => 40) . p .
             submit("Save Message").
             hidden(-name => "rm", -default => "save", -override => 1);
```

---

3. Or possibly just a series of print() statements containing raw HTML. That's so ugly, I can't even bring myself to type up an example!

```perl
  # include reply_id in hidden field if replying
  if (exists $options{reply_id}) {
    $output .= hidden(-name => "reply_id", -default => $options{reply_id});
  }

  # end form and html page
  $output .= end_form . end_html;

  # return output, as all run-modes must!
  return $output;
}
```

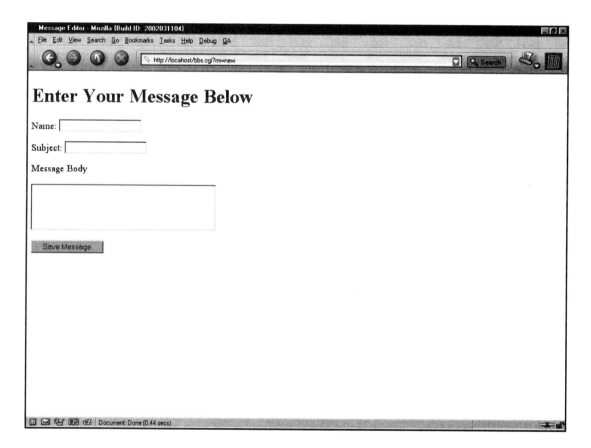

Figure 11-6. Message entry screen in action

A better solution is to use a templating system. There are many templating systems available, most of which would meet this challenge with ease. However, CGI::Application includes support for HTML::Template,[4] and the two have been specially designed to work well together.[5] Listings 11-4 and 11-5 show how the exact same output could be generated using HTML::Template.

Listing 11-4. Message Entry Screen Implemented with HTML::Template

```
sub _edit {
  my $self = shift;
  my %options = @_;

  # load template for edit screen
  my $template = $self->load_tmpl('edit.tmpl');

  # include reply_id in hidden field if replying
  $template->param(reply_id => $reply_id) if exists $options{reply_id};

  # return template output
  return $template->output;
}
```

Listing 11-5. Message Entry Screen Template File edit.tmpl

```
<html>
<head>
  <title>Message Editor</title>
</head>
<body>
  <h1>Enter Your Message Below</h1>
  <form method="post">
    Name: <input type="text" name="name"><p>
    Subject: <input type="text" name="subject"><p>
    Message Body<p>
    <textarea name="body" rows=4 cols=40></textarea><p>
    <input type="submit" value="Save Message">
    <input type="hidden" name="rm" value="save">
```

---

4. I wrote HTML::Template while working for Jesse Erlbaum, the author of CGI::Application, at Vanguard Media (http://www.vm.com). It is, of course, available on CPAN!

5. However, if HTML::Template isn't your tool of choice, using an alternative templating system is as easy as implementing a replacement for the load_tmpl() method in your subclass.

```
  <tmpl_if reply_id>
    <input type="hidden" name="reply_id" value="<tmpl_var reply_id>">
  </tmpl_if>
 </form>
</body>
</html>
```

Listing 11-4 shows the new_edit() method. Now all the code does is load the template using CGI::Application's load_tmpl() method. This method takes the name of an HTML::Template template file and calls HTML::Template->new() to load it, returning the new HTML::Template object. Next, if the user is replying to a message, the reply_id template parameter is set using HTML::Template's param() method. This method works similarly to the CGI.pm param() method, but instead of accessing CGI parameters it sets variables declared in the template with <tmpl_var>.

Finally, the template output is generated using the output() method and returned. Yes, it really is that simple!

Listing 11-5, the template file (edit.tmpl) used in Listing 11-4, is a bit more complicated, but you can blame HTML for that. It's unfortunate that no one thought to ask Larry Wall to design the markup language for the Web! However, since this is mostly plain HTML, there are many skilled designers available to take this stuff off your hands. The only part of this template that's not plain HTML is the section that optionally sets up the reply_id parameter:

```
<tmpl_if reply_id>
  <input type="hidden" name="reply_id" value="<tmpl_var reply_id>">
</tmpl_if>
```

This section uses two of HTML::Template's special tags, <tmpl_if> and <tmpl_var>, to conditionally include the reply_id hidden field in the form. I don't have time to explore HTML::Template fully here—for that see the HTML::Template documentation.

The benefits of this approach are numerous. By separating the HTML from the code that drives the application, both can be made simpler. Furthermore, people with different skills can work more efficiently on the part of the application they know best. In this example, I could spend my time working on adding features to the BBS.pm file while an HTML designer works on making the form easier to look at and use. In addition, as I'll demonstrate later, a proper use of templating is critical to allowing your CGI applications to be reused by others.

Instance Parameters

Every CGI::Application needs at least two pieces—a module containing a subclass of CGI::Application and an instance script that uses that module. The example instance script in Listing 11-2 does nothing more than call new() on the BBS class and then run() on the returned object:

```
my $bbs = BBS->new();
$bbs->run();
```

For simple applications this is all you'll need. However, it is possible to use the instance script to modify the behavior of the application.

One way CGI::Application provides configurability is through the TMPL_PATH option. When your application calls the load_tmpl() method to instantiate an HTML::Template object, the filename must be either an absolute path or relative to the current directory. But if you specify the TMPL_PATH option to new(), you can tell CGI::Application to look elsewhere for your templates. For example, if I wanted to keep the templates for the BBS application in /usr/local/templates, I could adjust the call to new() to look as follows:

```
my $bbs = BBS->new(TMPL_PATH => "/usr/local/templates/");
```

This option could be used to deploy multiple instances of the BBS module with different designs coming from different template sets. Each instance script uses the same module, but the constructed objects will use different templates, and as a result the user will see a different design in his or her browser.

Aside from configuring CGI::Application, new() also includes support for application-specific parameters. Using the PARAMS option, you can specify a set of key-value pairs that can be accessed later by the application. For example, imagine that the BBS module was written to store its messages in a Berkley DB file accessed using the DB_File module. Each instance of the BBS will need its own file to store messages. This could be provided using the PARAMS option to new():

```
my $bbs = BBS->new(PARAMS => { message_db => "/tmp/bbs1.db" });
```

Now in the BBS code this value can be accessed using the param() method on the CGI::Application object:

```
use DB_File;
sub list {
  my $self = shift;
  my $filename = $self->param('message_db'); # get the configured db filename
  tie %db, "DB_File", $filename;              # access it with DB_File
  # ...
}
```

Note that the param() method offered by CGI::Application is different from the param() method offered by CGI.pm objects. CGI::Application's param() accesses configuration data from the instance script, whereas CGI.pm's param() accesses incoming CGI parameters. Be careful not to confuse the two—you don't want to start opening arbitrary files on your file system based on CGI input!

By making your applications configurable through their instance scripts, you'll increase your opportunities for application reuse. As I'll show you next, building a CGI::Application module for CPAN requires you to focus on configurability as a primary goal.

CGI::Application and CPAN

Now that you know how to build reusable applications using CGI::Application, you're ready to learn to release your creations on CPAN. But first, I should address a burning question that's likely on your mind—why release CGI applications on CPAN? To me the answer is simple: because it will help reduce the needless work that Perl CGI programmers do every day. The Web is filled with endless incarnations of the same applications done and redone—bulletin boards, Web counters, shopping carts, and so on. Each one needs to be done again and again primarily because they need to *look* or function slightly differently.

Since most CGIs include their HTML inline with their code, either by including it in the source or including the source in the HTML (that is, HTML::Mason or EmbPerl), it is unusual to be able to reuse applications across projects. Furthermore, since most CGIs are built as scripts, the only way to reuse them is to copy them from project to project. With CGI::Application comes the opportunity for the Perl community to pool its collective strength and create powerful, configurable, *reusable* Web applications. And after all, isn't reusability what CPAN is all about?

Okay, enough manifesto, let's get down to the mechanics.

Size and Shape

A good CGI::Application module has to be the right size and shape; otherwise, it won't fit into the large variety of Web sites on the Internet. What I mean is that an ideal module should be sized to serve a clear and defined purpose within the larger scheme of a site. And it should be shaped to fill several screens without requiring a great deal of overlap with the rest of the site. For example, the BBS application discussed earlier would make a good CPAN module (if it actually worked and had a better name like, say, CGI::Application::BBS). It is clearly a separate application within a larger site that can safely control its own screens.

An example of a CGI project that wouldn't make an ideal module might be a search application. Typically search functionality is tightly integrated into the underlying data and user interface of a Web site. It may still be possible to solve this problem with CGI::Application, but the results are unlikely to be usable on other sites.

Configurability

The primary goal of a successful CGI::Application module on CPAN has to be configurability. These applications will live in a varied environment, and their mode of operation has to be flexible. For example, the CGI::Application::MailPage module,[6] which provides a "mail this page to a friend" application for static HTML documents, is configurable in how it sends mail, what options it offers to its users, and how it accesses the underlying documents. For example, here's a typical instance script used with CGI::Application::MailPage:

```perl
#!/usr/bin/perl
use CGI::Application::MailPage;
my $mailpage = CGI::Application::MailPage->new(
                PARAMS => { document_root  => '/home/httpd',
                            smtp_server    => 'smtp.foo.org',
                            use_page_param => 1,
                          });
$mailpage->run();
```

Template Usage

All CGI::Application modules on CPAN will have to use templating of some sort to be widely reusable. Otherwise it would be impossible for the output of the module to be reconfigured to match the look of the site where it is being used. However, this doesn't mean that CGI::Application modules should *require* users to provide their own templates. The modules should come with a default set with simple HTML formatting. This serves two purposes. First, it provides an example for users to build off of. Second, it allows users to more easily evaluate the module and test its functionality.

One issue does arise in packaging default templates—how will the module find them after installation? Perl doesn't (yet!) support a default template path, so you'll have to do something about it yourself. The technique I used in building

---

6. I wrote CGI::Application::MailPage as a proof-of concept in building a CGI::Application for CPAN.

CGI::Application::MailPage was to install them in a Perl module path by specifying them as modules using the `PM` option to `WriteMakeFile()` in my `Makefile.PL`:

```
WriteMakefile(
            'NAME' => 'CGI::Application::MailPage',
            'VERSION_FROM' => 'MailPage.pm',
            'PM' => {
                    'MailPage.pm' => '$(INST_LIBDIR)/MailPage.pm',
                    'email.tmpl'  => '$(INST_LIBDIR)/MailPage/email.tmpl',
                    'form.tmpl'   => '$(INST_LIBDIR)/MailPage/form.tmpl',
                    'thanks.tmpl' => '$(INST_LIBDIR)/MailPage/thanks.tmpl',
                 },
            );
```

Then when loading them, I simply added the contents of `@INC` to HTML::Template's search path for template files (via the `path` option):

```
$template = $self->load_tmpl('CGI/Application/MailPage/form.tmpl',
                           path => [@INC]);
```

Another possibility would have been to include the template text directly inside the module file or interactively prompt the user for a template location during module installation.

Summary

This chapter has introduced you to a new module, CGI::Application, that can greatly improve the way you build CGI programs. CGI::Application also provides an opportunity, for the first time, to distribute fully functional Web applications through CPAN. This could be an area of tremendous growth in the utility of CPAN and you now have the tools you need to make a major contribution. See you on PAUSE!

Index

Symbols

\ (backslash) operator, using with references, 36

-> (arrow operator), using, 38–39

. (dot), using in filenames, 124

:: (double colon)

    meaning of, 12

    using with symbol tables, 25

& operator, using with SVs in C, 183

() (parentheses), using with File::Find, 23

$ (dollar) symbol, using with references, 36

$self, usage of, 41

+ (plus sign), meaning in unified diff format, 146

++, overloading, 51–52

- (minus) sign, meaning in unified diff format, 146

--, overloading, 51–52

< (left angle bracket), using with single-file patches, 145

= (equal sign)

    appearance before POD commands, 67

    overloading, 55–56

> (right angle bracket), using with single-file patches, 145

@ (at sign), using with references, 36–37

@ATTRIBUTES package variable, using with accessor-mutators, 86

@INC, modifying for usage with modules, 29

@ISA

    explained, 45

    using with DynaLoader, 207

[] (square brackets), using with references, 37

{} (curly braces), using with references, 37

00whois.html file, contents of, 11

A

-A option, using with cvs update command, 158

accessors, using, 42–43, 85–92

ActivePerl PPM utility, usage of, 19

anonymous access, using with CVS repositories, 151

anonymous arrays, using with references, 37

$arg placeholder variables, using with typemaps, 234

arithmetic operations, symbols for, 49

array variables. *See* AV* (array value) data type.

arrays, using references with, 36–37. *See also* AV* (array value) data type

arrow notation, using with references, 37

arrow operator (->), using, 38–39

Artistic License, choosing, 127

[ask] default answer in CPAN modules, selecting, 14–15

at sign (@), using with references, 36–37

attributes, explanation of, 41

author, browsing CPAN by, 11

AUTHOR section of modules

    in Makefile.PL, 108

    purpose of, 67

auto-generation, using with overload methods, 54–55

AUTOLOAD() method, using with accessor-mutators, 86–87

AV* (array value) C data type. *See also* arrays

    clearing, 187

    creation of, 184

    features of, 184

    fetching values from, 184–186

    full name and example in Perl, 176

    inspecting reference counts with, 194

    storing values in, 186–187

av_clear() function, using, 187

av_exists(), testing AV indexes with, 184–185

av_len(), checking array lengths with, 185

av_make() function, using, 184

av_pop(), usage of, 186

av_push(), adding elements to ends of arrays with, 186

av_shift(), writing destructive version of for loop with, 185–186

av_unshift(), using, 186–187

P

Apress Titles

ISBN	PRICE	AUTHOR	TITLE
1-893115-73-9	$34.95	Abbott	Voice Enabling Web Applications: VoiceXML and Beyond
1-893115-01-1	$39.95	Appleman	Dan Appleman's Win32 API Puzzle Book and Tutorial for Visual Basic Programmers
1-893115-23-2	$29.95	Appleman	How Computer Programming Works
1-893115-97-6	$39.95	Appleman	Moving to VB .NET: Strategies, Concepts, and Code
1-59059-023-6	$39.95	Baker	Adobe Acrobat 5: The Professional User's Guide
1-59059-039-2	$49.95	Barnaby	Distributed .NET Programming
1-893115-09-7	$29.95	Baum	Dave Baum's Definitive Guide to LEGO MINDSTORMS
1-893115-84-4	$29.95	Baum, Gasperi, Hempel, and Villa	Extreme MINDSTORMS: An Advanced Guide to LEGO MINDSTORMS
1-893115-82-8	$59.95	Ben-Gan/Moreau	Advanced Transact-SQL for SQL Server 2000
1-893115-91-7	$39.95	Birmingham/Perry	Software Development on a Leash
1-893115-48-8	$29.95	Bischof	The .NET Languages: A Quick Translation Guide
1-59059-053-8	$44.95	Bock/Stromquist/ Fischer/Smith	.NET Security
1-893115-67-4	$49.95	Borge	Managing Enterprise Systems with the Windows Script Host
1-59059-019-8	$49.95	Cagle	SVG Programming: The Graphical Web
1-893115-28-3	$44.95	Challa/Laksberg	Essential Guide to Managed Extensions for C++
1-893115-39-9	$44.95	Chand	A Programmer's Guide to ADO.NET in C#
1-59059-015-5	$39.95	Clark	An Introduction to Object Oriented Programming with Visual Basic .NET
1-893115-44-5	$29.95	Cook	Robot Building for Beginners
1-893115-99-2	$39.95	Cornell/Morrison	Programming VB .NET: A Guide for Experienced Programmers
1-893115-72-0	$39.95	Curtin	Developing Trust: Online Privacy and Security
1-59059-014-7	$44.95	Drol	Object-Oriented Macromedia Flash MX
1-59059-008-2	$29.95	Duncan	The Career Programmer: Guerilla Tactics for an Imperfect World
1-893115-71-2	$39.95	Ferguson	Mobile .NET
1-893115-90-9	$49.95	Finsel	The Handbook for Reluctant Database Administrators
1-59059-024-4	$49.95	Fraser	Real World ASP.NET: Building a Content Management System
1-893115-42-9	$44.95	Foo/Lee	XML Programming Using the Microsoft XML Parser
1-893115-55-0	$34.95	Frenz	Visual Basic and Visual Basic .NET for Scientists and Engineers
1-893115-85-2	$34.95	Gilmore	A Programmer's Introduction to PHP 4.0
1-893115-36-4	$34.95	Goodwill	Apache Jakarta-Tomcat
1-893115-17-8	$59.95	Gross	A Programmer's Introduction to Windows DNA
1-893115-62-3	$39.95	Gunnerson	A Programmer's Introduction to C#, Second Edition
1-59059-030-9	$49.95	Habibi/Patterson/ Camerlengo	The Sun Certified Java Developer Exam with J2SE 1.4
1-59059-009-0	$49.95	Harris/Macdonald	Moving to ASP.NET: Web Development with VB .NET

ISBN	PRICE	AUTHOR	TITLE
1-893115-30-5	$49.95	Harkins/Reid	SQL: Access to SQL Server
1-59059-006-6	$39.95	Hetland	Practical Python
1-893115-10-0	$34.95	Holub	Taming Java Threads
1-893115-04-6	$34.95	Hyman/Vaddadi	Mike and Phani's Essential C++ Techniques
1-893115-96-8	$59.95	Jorelid	J2EE FrontEnd Technologies: A Programmer's Guide to Servlets, JavaServer Pages, and Enterprise JavaBeans
1-893115-49-6	$39.95	Kilburn	Palm Programming in Basic
1-893115-50-X	$34.95	Knudsen	Wireless Java: Developing with Java 2, Micro Edition
1-893115-79-8	$49.95	Kofler	Definitive Guide to Excel VBA
1-893115-57-7	$39.95	Kofler	MySQL
1-893115-87-9	$39.95	Kurata	Doing Web Development: Client-Side Techniques
1-893115-75-5	$44.95	Kurniawan	Internet Programming with VB
1-893115-38-0	$24.95	Lafler	Power AOL: A Survival Guide
1-893115-46-1	$36.95	Lathrop	Linux in Small Business: A Practical User's Guide
1-893115-19-4	$49.95	Macdonald	Serious ADO: Universal Data Access with Visual Basic
1-893115-06-2	$39.95	Marquis/Smith	A Visual Basic 6.0 Programmer's Toolkit
1-893115-22-4	$27.95	McCarter	David McCarter's VB Tips and Techniques
1-59059-021-X	$34.95	Moore	Karl Moore's Visual Basic .NET: The Tutorials
1-893115-76-3	$49.95	Morrison	C++ For VB Programmers
1-59059-003-1	$39.95	Nakhimovsky/Meyers	XML Programming: Web Applications and Web Services with JSP and ASP
1-893115-80-1	$39.95	Newmarch	A Programmer's Guide to Jini Technology
1-893115-58-5	$49.95	Oellermann	Architecting Web Services
1 59059-020-1	$44.95	Patzer	JSP Examples and Best Practices
1-893115-81-X	$39.95	Pike	SQL Server: Common Problems, Tested Solutions
1-59059-017-1	$34.95	Rainwater	Herding Cats: A Primer for Programmers Who Lead Programmers
1-59059-025-2	$49.95	Rammer	Advanced .NET Remoting (C# Edition)
1-59059-062-7	$49.95	Rammer	Advanced .NET Remoting in VB .NET
1-893115-20-8	$34.95	Rischpater	Wireless Web Development
1-893115-93-3	$34.95	Rischpater	Wireless Web Development with PHP and WAP
1-893115-89-5	$59.95	Shemitz	Kylix: The Professional Developer's Guide and Reference
1-893115-40-2	$39.95	Sill	The qmail Handbook
1-893115-24-0	$49.95	Sinclair	From Access to SQL Server
1-59059-026-0	$49.95	Smith	Writing Add-ins for Visual Studio .NET
1-893115-94-1	$29.95	Spolsky	User Interface Design for Programmers
1-893115-53-4	$44.95	Sweeney	Visual Basic for Testers
1-59059-002-3	$44.95	Symmonds	Internationalization and Localization Using Microsoft .NET
1-59059-010-4	$54.95	Thomsen	Database Programming with C#
1-893115-29-1	$44.95	Thomsen	Database Programming with Visual Basic .NET
1-893115-65-8	$39.95	Tiffany	Pocket PC Database Development with eMbedded Visual Basic

ISBN	PRICE	AUTHOR	TITLE
1-59059-027-9	$59.95	Torkelson/Petersen/Torkelson	Programming the Web with Visual Basic .NET
1-59059-018-X	$34.95	Tregar	Writing Perl Modules for CPAN
1-893115-59-3	$59.95	Troelsen	C# and the .NET Platform
1-59059-011-2	$59.95	Troelsen	COM and .NET Interoperability
1-893115-26-7	$59.95	Troelsen	Visual Basic .NET and the .NET Platform
1-893115-54-2	$49.95	Trueblood/Lovett	Data Mining and Statistical Analysis Using SQL
1-893115-68-2	$54.95	Vaughn	ADO.NET and ADO Examples and Best Practices for VB Programmers, Second Edition
1-59059-012-0	$49.95	Vaughn/Blackburn	ADO.NET Examples and Best Practices for C# Programmers
1-893115-83-6	$44.95	Wells	Code Centric: T-SQL Programming with Stored Procedures and Triggers
1-893115-95-X	$49.95	Welschenbach	Cryptography in C and C++
1-893115-05-4	$39.95	Williamson	Writing Cross-Browser Dynamic HTML
1-893115-78-X	$49.95	Zukowski	Definitive Guide to Swing for Java 2, Second Edition
1-893115-92-5	$49.95	Zukowski	Java Collections
1-893115-98-4	$54.95	Zukowski	Learn Java with JBuilder 6

Available at bookstores nationwide or from Springer Verlag New York, Inc. at 1-800-777-4643; fax 1-212-533-3503. Contact us for more information at sales@apress.com.

Apress Titles Publishing **SOON!**

ISBN	AUTHOR	TITLE
1-59059-022-8	Alapati	Expert Oracle 9i Database Administration
1-59059-041-4	Bock	CIL Programming: Under the Hood of .NET
1-59059-000-7	Cornell	Programming C#
1-59059-033-3	Fraser	Managed C++ and .NET Development
1-59059-038-4	Gibbons	Java Development to .NET Development
1-59059-044-9	MacDonald	.NET User Interfaces with VB .NET: Windows Forms and Custom Controls
1-59059-001-5	McMahon	A Programmer's Introduction to ASP.NET WebForms in Visual Basic .NET
1-893115-74-7	Millar	Enterprise Development: A Programmer's Handbook
1-893115-27-5	Morrill	Tuning and Customizing a Linux System
1-59059-028-7	Rischpater	Wireless Web Development, Second Edition
1-893115-43-7	Stephenson	Standard VB: An Enterprise Developer's Reference for VB 6 and VB .NET
1-59059-035-X	Symmonds	GDI+ Programming in C# and VB .NET
1-59059-032-5	Thomsen	Database Programming with Visual Basic .NET, Second Edition
1-59059-007-4	Thomsen	Building Web Services with VB .NET
1-59059-004-X	Valiaveedu	SQL Server 2000 and Business Intelligence in an XML/.NET World

Available at bookstores nationwide or from Springer Verlag New York, Inc. at 1-800-777-4643; fax 1-212-533-3503. Contact us for more information at sales@apress.com.

books for professionals by professionals™

apress™

About Apress

Apress, located in Berkeley, CA, is a fast-growing, innovative publishing company devoted to meeting the needs of existing and potential programming professionals. Simply put, the "A" in Apress stands for *"The Author's Press™"* and its books have *"The Expert's Voice™"*. Apress' unique approach to publishing grew out of conversations between its founders Gary Cornell and Dan Appleman, authors of numerous best-selling, highly regarded books for programming professionals. In 1998 they set out to create a publishing company that emphasized quality above all else. Gary and Dan's vision has resulted in the publication of over 50 titles by leading software professionals, all of which have *The Expert's Voice™*.

Do You Have What It Takes to Write for Apress?

Apress is rapidly expanding its publishing program. If you can write and refuse to compromise on the quality of your work, if you believe in doing more than rehashing existing documentation, and if you're looking for opportunities and rewards that go far beyond those offered by traditional publishing houses, we want to hear from you!

Consider these innovations that we offer all of our authors:

- **Top royalties with *no* hidden switch statements**
  Authors typically only receive half of their normal royalty rate on foreign sales. In contrast, Apress' royalty rate remains the same for both foreign and domestic sales.

- **A mechanism for authors to obtain equity in Apress**
  Unlike the software industry, where stock options are essential to motivate and retain software professionals, the publishing industry has adhered to an outdated compensation model based on royalties alone. In the spirit of most software companies, Apress reserves a significant portion of its equity for authors.

- **Serious treatment of the technical review process**
  Each Apress book has a technical reviewing team whose remuneration depends in part on the success of the book since they too receive royalties.

Moreover, through a partnership with Springer-Verlag, New York, Inc., one of the world's major publishing houses, Apress has significant venture capital behind it. Thus, we have the resources to produce the highest quality books *and* market them aggressively.

If you fit the model of the Apress author who can write a book that gives the "professional what he or she needs to know™," then please contact one of our Editorial Directors, Dan Appleman (dan_appleman@apress.com), Gary Cornell (gary_cornell@apress.com), Jason Gilmore (jason_gilmore@apress.com), Simon Hayes (simon_hayes@apress.com), Karen Watterson (karen_watterson@apress.com), or John Zukowski (john_zukowski@apress.com) for more information.